NATIVE ART OF THE PACIFIC NORTHWEST

A Bill Holm Center Series

The mission of this publication series is to foster appreciation and understanding of Pacific Northwest Native art and culture.

In the Spirit of the Ancestors: Contemporary Northwest Coast Art at the Burke Museum
edited by Robin K. Wright and Kathryn Bunn-Marcuse

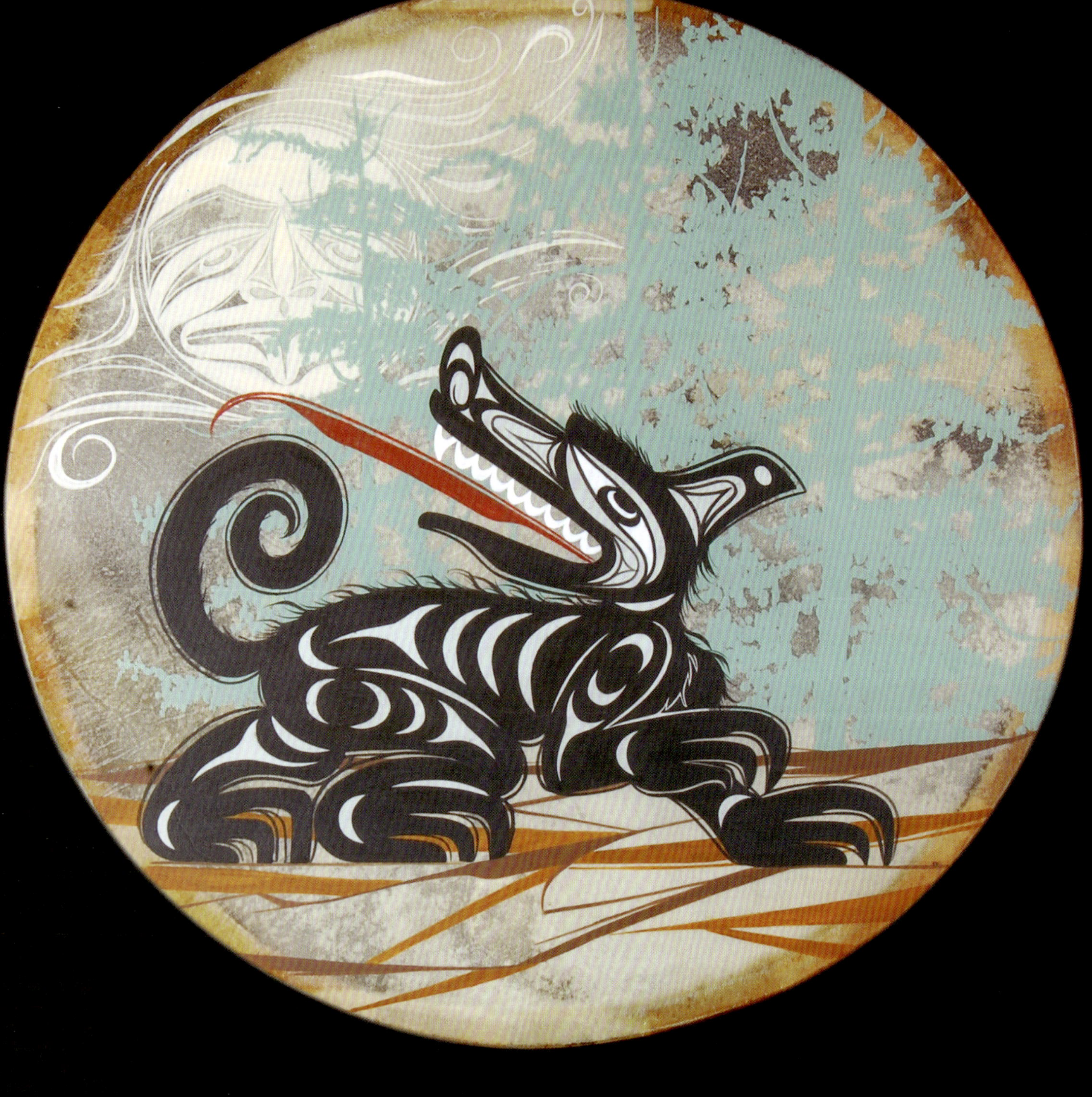

IN THE SPIRIT OF THE ANCESTORS

Contemporary Northwest Coast Art at the Burke Museum

Edited by
ROBIN K. WRIGHT and
KATHRYN BUNN-MARCUSE

BILL HOLM CENTER FOR THE STUDY OF NORTHWEST COAST ART
Burke Museum, Seattle

in association with

UNIVERSITY OF WASHINGTON PRESS
Seattle and London

Bill Holm Center
for the Study of Northwest Coast Art
BURKE MUSEUM

This book was published with the assistance of the Quest for Truth Foundation.

First paperback edition, 2015
Printed and bound in China
Design by Thomas Eykemans
Composed in Minion, typeface designed by Robert Slimbach
20 19 18 17 16 15 5 4 3 2 1

BILL HOLM CENTER FOR THE STUDY OF NORTHWEST COAST ART
Burke Museum of Natural History and Culture
www.burkemuseum.org/bhc

UNIVERSITY OF WASHINGTON PRESS
www.washington.edu/uwpress

All dimensions are expressed in tenths of an inch. Detail illustrations used in chapter openings are reproduced in full within the book.

FRONTISPIECE: Manuel Salazar, *Staki-yah—Wolf Drum*, 2006. See fig. 1.4.
P. IV: Beau Dick, Mussels, 1987. See fig. 2.2.

LIBRARY OF CONGRESS CATALOGING-IN-PUBLICATION DATA
Burke Museum of Natural History and Culture.
In the spirit of the ancestors : contemporary Northwest coast art at the Burke Museum / edited by Robin K. Wright and Kathryn Bunn-Marcuse.
pages cm. — (Native art of the Pacific Northwest: a Bill Holm Center series)
ISBN 978-0-295-99260-0 (hardback);
ISBN 978-0-295-99521-2 (paperback)
1. Indian art—Northwest Coast of North America—20th century. 2. Indian art—Northwest Coast of North America—21st century. 3. Art—Washington (State)—Seattle. 4. Burke Museum of Natural History and Culture. I. Wright, Robin Kathleen. II. Bunn-Marcuse, Kathryn B. III. Title. IV. Title: Contemporary Northwest coast art at the Burke Museum.
N6538.A4B87 2013
704.03'970795074797772—dc23
2012046997

The paper used in this publication meets the minimum requirements of American National Standard for Information Sciences—Permanence of Paper for Printed Library Materials, ANSI Z39.48–1984.∞

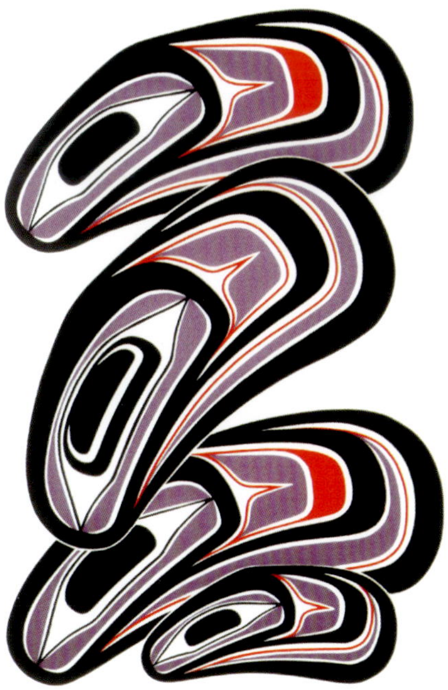

Contents

Foreword

MUSEUM. The very word conjures an image of dusty shelves of old things, relics of ancient civilizations or times past. And, in fact, the idea of collecting the old, *original* relics of a culture, rather than what was characteristic of a given society of the time, was once a guiding rule of Franz Boas, one of the great scholars of American anthropology. He was not alone. Somehow there was a pervasive belief that human societies (at least those thought of as "primitive," or non-European) had fixed cultures that, once influenced by contact with more "advanced" societies, lost their integrity. The idea that there had been ongoing changes and outside influences on those cultures for generations was seldom considered.

Many museum collections and exhibits of human cultures still reflect that concept, but attitudes are changing. The Northwest Coast art material in the collections of the Burke Museum were largely antiquarian in nature until, through a series of fortuitous circumstances, there came a new appreciation of the role of art in contemporary Northwest Coast societies. Little by little, contemporary examples of the arts of the region had been infiltrating the collections, but the acquisition of the Blackman Hall Collection of prints and the Arthur Steinman Collection of mostly sculptural objects, as well as other smaller collections and individual objects, changed the character if not the focus of the museum's Northwest Coast art image.

As Robin Wright explains in her introduction, there was some discussion, if not disagreement, as to what "contemporary" means in relation to Northwest Coast art. The *In the Spirit of the Ancestors* curatorial team never really solved the time dilemma but settled on a reasonable date for the exhibit to include pieces made since 1985 (see Wright's "Introduction"). But it is clear that "contemporary" means different things as far as the character of art expression goes. Many of today's artists are striving to understand the characteristics and subtleties of the art of their ancestral predecessors, while others strive for an innovative or individually expressive twist to their work. Although new materials have sometimes been seen by observers as jarring, it's easy to forget that many of the accepted masterpieces of the past also incorporate exotic materials, pigments, and subject matter of the time.

One of the most interesting aspects of the "new" Northwest Coast art scene is the dual character of the uses of art. In traditional Northwest Coast societies art functioned largely as a visual or tangible record of identity and rank, and as a manifestation of supernatural power. But there was also in those days a commercial aspect that is sometimes forgotten today. Artists were often professionals, and the work of skilled artisans and visionary craftsmen was sought by nobles and ceremonial and religious leaders. The best artists, those whose work was admired and desired, were often hired by patrons in distant locations, just as today's carvers, painters, and weavers sell their productions to customers sometimes continents away. It's not uncommon for a master artist to be whisked across an ocean to complete a commission. But at the same time, this contemporary Northwest Coast artist is just as likely to spend long hours applying his or her practiced skills to produce regalia for a family potlatch. Or to design and print an image to be distributed to the hundreds of guests at a memorial potlatch, a wedding, or a pole raising. These are all traditional uses of the art. The fact that the artists may use contemporary printmaking methods, or travel by jetliner rather than by canoe, doesn't detract from the central significance of the art.

The assembled contributions by curators, collectors, and artists in this edited volume tell the story of this ongoing activity in Native Northwest Coast art and its manifestation in the collections of the Burke Museum.

BILL HOLM
Curator Emeritus, Northwest Coast Indian Art
Burke Museum
Seattle

Acknowledgments

The Burke Museum could not have assembled its strong contemporary Northwest Coast Native art collection without the generosity of many collectors and donors. We would like to thank in particular Margaret B. Blackman and Edwin Hall, the late Lawrence Christian, Bill and Marty Holm, Mark Kernaghan, Doug and Thelma McTavish, Simon Ottenberg, and Arthur B. Steinman.

We are also indebted to many artists who have donated their work to us, including John Beard and the Damascus Weavers Group, David Boxley, Marvin Oliver, Susan Point, Nicholas Galanin, and Evelyn Vanderhoop. Thanks as well to the contributors to this volume for their thoughtful essays and to Steve Brown for his comments and additions to the portfolio captions. We would not have been able to launch the Bill Holm Center's Native Art of the Pacific Northwest series without the support of the many donors to the Bill Holm Center, including the many artists who donated their work to the Bill Holm Center auction in 2004. We would especially like to thank the late Delancey B. Lewis Jr. and the Quest for Truth Foundation for their generous support of the Bill Holm Center and this publication.

A special thanks goes to Bill Holm, for doing what he does and being who he is: a teacher, a scholar, an artist, a mentor, a donor, and a friend.

ROBIN K. WRIGHT

KATHRYN BUNN-MARCUSE

In the Spirit of the Ancestors

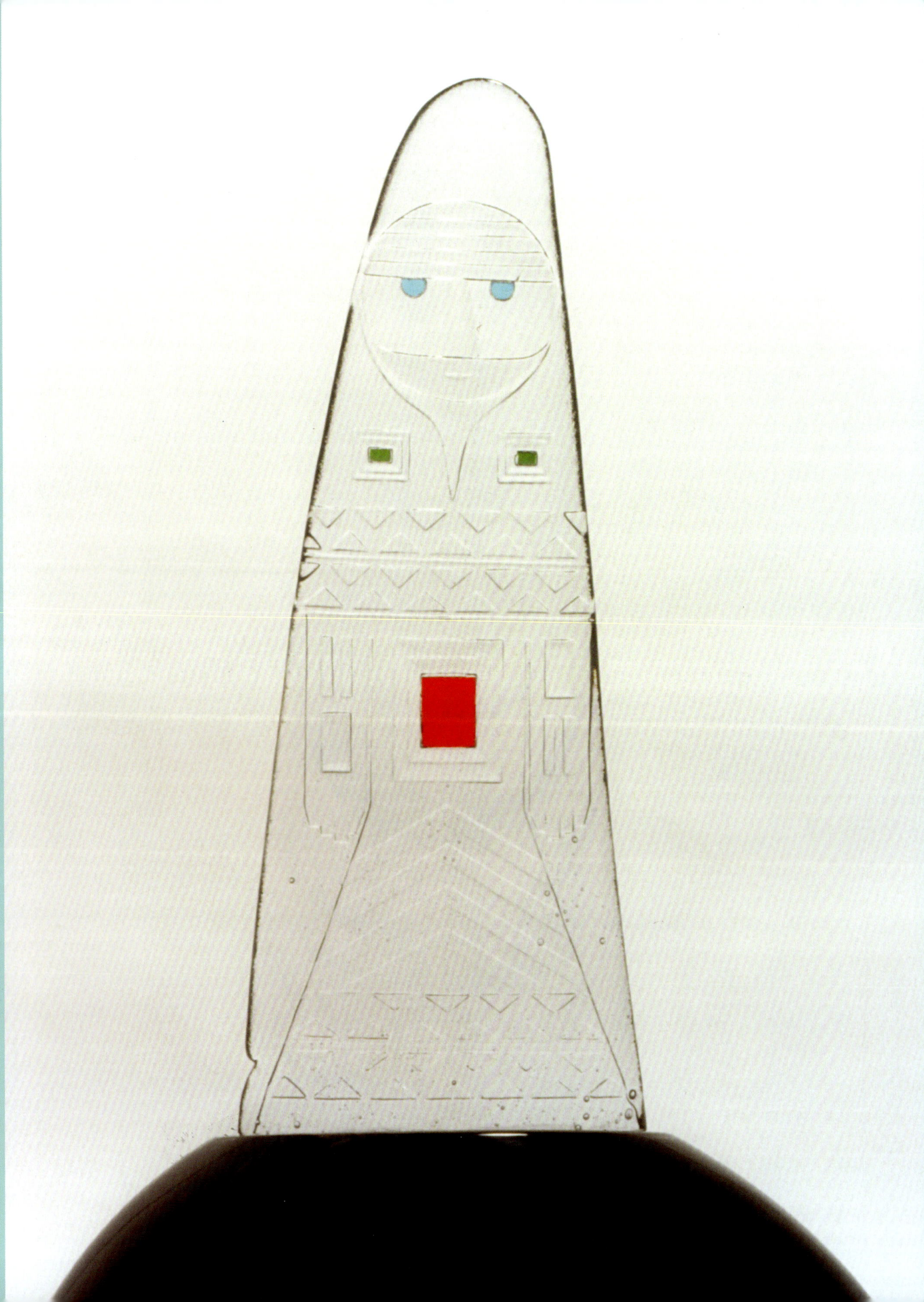

INTRODUCTION

ROBIN K. WRIGHT

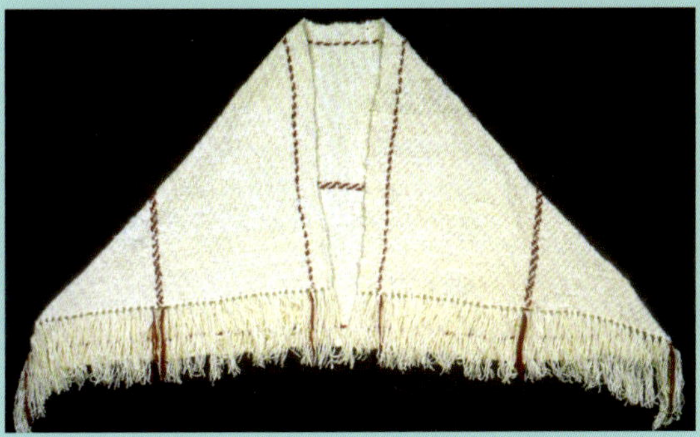

FIGURE I.2 Bill and Fran James (Coast Salish—Lummi). *Robe*, 1988. Mountain goat wool, sheep wool. 9.1 × 38.2 in. Burke Museum, A Time of Gathering Commission, Burke Museum #1988–84/1.

FIGURE I.1 Marvin Oliver (Coast Salish—Quinault/Isleta Pueblo). *Journey*, 1988. Cast glass, inlaid cut waterglass, cast marble base. 33.5 × 22.4 in. A Time of Gathering commission, Burke Museum #1989–21/1.

This book celebrates the vitality of contemporary Pacific Northwest Coast Native art and the role the Burke Museum has played in encouraging the study and appreciation of the art.[1] In 1985 the Burke Museum celebrated its centennial—one hundred years of preserving and understanding the cultural legacy of Pacific Rim peoples and their natural environments. In honor of that milestone, Bill Holm, curator of Northwest Coast Indian art, wrote *Spirit and Ancestor: A Century of Northwest Coast Indian Art at the Burke Museum* (Holm 1987). That book featured one hundred objects selected by Holm to represent the strengths of the Burke's Pacific Northwest Coast collection at that time.

Holm retired from the University of Washington in 1985, and I was hired into his position. The first major exhibit I curated was the 1989 state centennial exhibit, *A Time of Gathering: Native Heritage in Washington State*, which featured ten contemporary works commissioned for the exhibit after a juried selection process (Wright 1991: 134–49). Included in this group were Marvin Oliver's *Journey* (fig. 1.1), perhaps the first glass art produced by a Northwest Coast Native artist, and Bill and Fran James's woven robe, the first mountain goat wool robe made in the modern era (fig. 1.2). Since that time, the contemporary collection has grown significantly. In 2006 the Burke Museum celebrated its growing collection of contemporary Northwest Coast Native art by featuring the work of seventy-one artists who had worked "in the spirit of the ancestors" since Holm's *Spirit and Ancestor* was written. That exhibit provided an opportunity to draw attention to the newest portions of our collection. In 2009 we acquired Preston Singletary's glass *Killer Whale*, which allows us to represent Seattle's growing contemporary glass art phenomenon of which Singletary is a leader (fig. 1.3). The Burke Museum has now passed its one hundred and twenty-fifth year and continues to build its Pacific Northwest Coast Native art collection and share knowledge about it.

THE 2007 EXHIBITION: *IN THE SPIRIT OF THE ANCESTORS*

The 2007 exhibition (fig. 1.4) was curated by a team

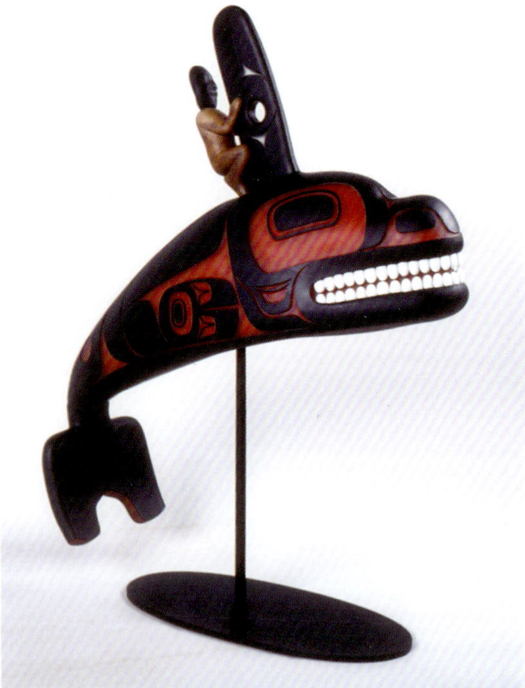

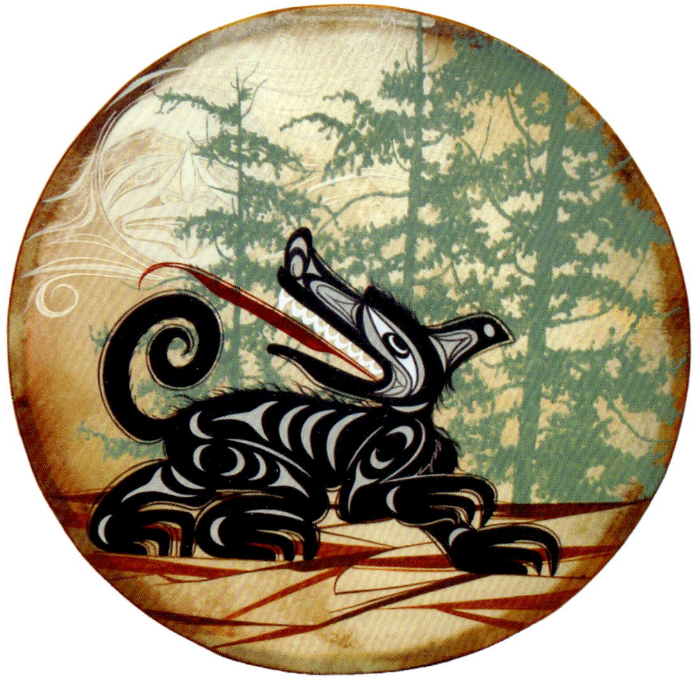

of four: curator emeritus Bill Holm, Coast Salish artists Susan Point (Musqueam) and Shaun Peterson (Puyallup/Tulalip), and myself. When we selected the objects in this exhibit, the first question we confronted was, "What is contemporary?" Coming from a range of ages and perspectives, the curators' understanding of when the contemporary era began ranged from the 1930s (Holm) to the 1990s (Peterson). Certainly a major turning point in the history of Northwest Coast art was the dropping of the anti-potlatch law in Canada in 1951. This led to the building of Mungo Martin's big house at the Royal British Columbia Museum in Victoria in 1953, and, ten years later in 1963, the Alert Bay big house. The building of these two houses was coupled with the first legal potlatching in Canada since its ban in the 1880s. The renewal of potlatching traditions over the past sixty years has injected a vitality into the visual as well as the performance arts that had been suppressed for nearly seven decades.

Shortly after the anti-potlatch law was dropped, renewed knowledge as well as new media affected Northwest Coast art. By the late 1960s the analysis, description, and revival of the northern Northwest Coast two-dimensional "formline design" system had occurred (Holm 1965). At the same time, the new medium of printmaking was introduced (Hall, Blackman, and Rickard 1981). Ceremonial wear on the Northwest Coast has been transformed by the resurgence in the weaving of both *naaxiin* (Chilkat) and Coast Salish twined robes in the 1970s and 1980s (kept alive by Tlingit weaver Jenny Thlunaut and a few Coast Salish weavers, respectively). More recently we have seen the spectacular reappearance of northern geometric Ravenstail weaving, sparked by Cheryl Samuel, as well as Northwest Coast–

FIGURE I.3 Preston Singletary (Tlingit). *Killer Whale*, 2009. Blown and sandblasted glass. 25 × 20 × 6 in. Gift of Doug and Thelma McTavish, Burke Museum #2009–35/1.

FIGURE I.4 Manuel Salazar (Coast Salish—Cowichan). *Staki-yah—Wolf Drum*, 2006. Deerskin, wood, paint. D. 24 × 2.8 in. Purchased with funds donated by Lawrence Christian, Burke Museum #2006–152/1.

inspired fashion design, exemplified by Dorothy Grant's Feastwear. The resurgence of canoe carving and the associated cultural events—Paddle-To-Seattle in 1989, Paddle to Bella Bella in 1993, Paddle to La Push in 1997, the Paddle to Puyallup in August 1998, and yearly canoe journeys thereafter—are energizing intertribal contact and cultural exchange (Blackman 1992; Henrikson 1992; Neel 1995; Samuel 1982, 1987).

Many of these developments involved the collaboration of artists, scholars, and the museums that house Northwest Coast Native art. The study of previously undocumented works of art has led to the attribution of large bodies of work to such artists as Willie Seaweed, Charles Edenshaw, Kadjisdu.axch' II, B. A. Haldane, Simeon Stilthda, and Zacherias Nicholas, among others, whose art had been unidentified or misattributed in the past (Askren 2007; Brown 1987; Holm 1981, 1983b; Wright 1998, 2009). Projects to preserve, restore, and replicate old works of Northwest Coast art have led to new knowledge of the old masters and the revelation of pieces that had literally become invisible (McLennan and Duffek 2000).

When the curatorial team for *In the Spirit of the Ancestors* began discussing the content of the Burke Museum's contemporary collection, this history was considered. Given the constraints of the space, we were not able to include the broad range of objects that would document this history going back to the 1950s. Working to narrow our lists was a painful process for us, and many fine pieces could not be included. In the end we included only works dating since 1985 and the publication of Holm's *Spirit and Ancestor*. The exhibit of seventy-four pieces represented only about 3 percent of the Burke's contemporary Northwest Coast collection, which numbered over twenty-four hundred twentieth- and twenty-first-century pieces.

The difficulty of our selection was testimony to the strength of contemporary Northwest Coast Native art, and we saluted the artists who were not included along with those who were. The process of curating this exhibition also revealed certain gaps in the collection, particularly in the areas of contemporary silver jewelry, glass art, and "avant garde" art. Thanks to very generous donors, we are beginning to fill those gaps (see figs. 1.3, 1.5, 1.7, and 8.6). Since 2006, we have added more than four hundred contemporary Northwest Coast pieces to the collection. With the publication of this book, we have the luxury of including some of the objects acquired since 2006 as well as some that were left out of the exhibition.

THE ESSAYS

To mark this quasquicentennial, Katie Bunn-Marcuse and I invited six people who have studied and created the art to join us and share their reflections. We invited the essayists to write on contemporary art without specifying what approach to take, and all chose to focus on how artists have drawn on the historical work of the ancestors for inspiration, whether they are working in traditional or new media, for ceremonial use or for sale in the art market. These essays are not intended to provide comprehensive coverage of any of the topics discussed but rather provide selected examples and in some cases personal approaches to issues.

The Burke Museum's silkscreen print collection forms the foundation of its contemporary holdings. The Blackman Hall Collection of 1,168 prints, acquired in 1998, was featured in the exhibition *Graphic Culture: Northwest Coast Prints from the Blackman-Hall Collection*, in 1998–99. This collection was made by Dr. Margaret B. Blackman and Dr. Edwin S. Hall Jr., both professors of anthropology at the State University of New York–Brockport.

First drawn to the Northwest by their fieldwork as anthropologists, they developed an avid interest in the then new art form of silkscreened prints. Over twenty years, from the early 1970s through the late 1980s, Hall and Blackman assembled the largest private collection of Northwest Coast prints in the world, 1,166 prints by 134 artists.[2] They published extensively on Northwest Coast prints, beginning with a book coauthored with Vincent Rickard, *Northwest Coast Indian Graphics: An Introduction to Silk Screen Prints*, (Hall, Blackman, and Rickard 1981; Blackman 1982a and 1982b; Blackman and Hall 1986a and 1986b; Blackman 1985; Blackman and Hall 1988). Blackman's chapter in this book provides her reflections on the collection and the collectors. She looks back from the perspective of one who has experienced the transformation of what began as personal passion and has now become a foundational institutional resource.

From 1986 through 2012, University of Washington professor emeritus Dr. Simon Ottenberg donated to the Burke Museum an extensive collection of 686 Coast Salish art, including 147 by Musqueam artist Susan Point. This expanded the print collection in this important Southern Northwest Coast area, which had blossomed dramatically after 1988, when Blackman and Hall stopped collecting.

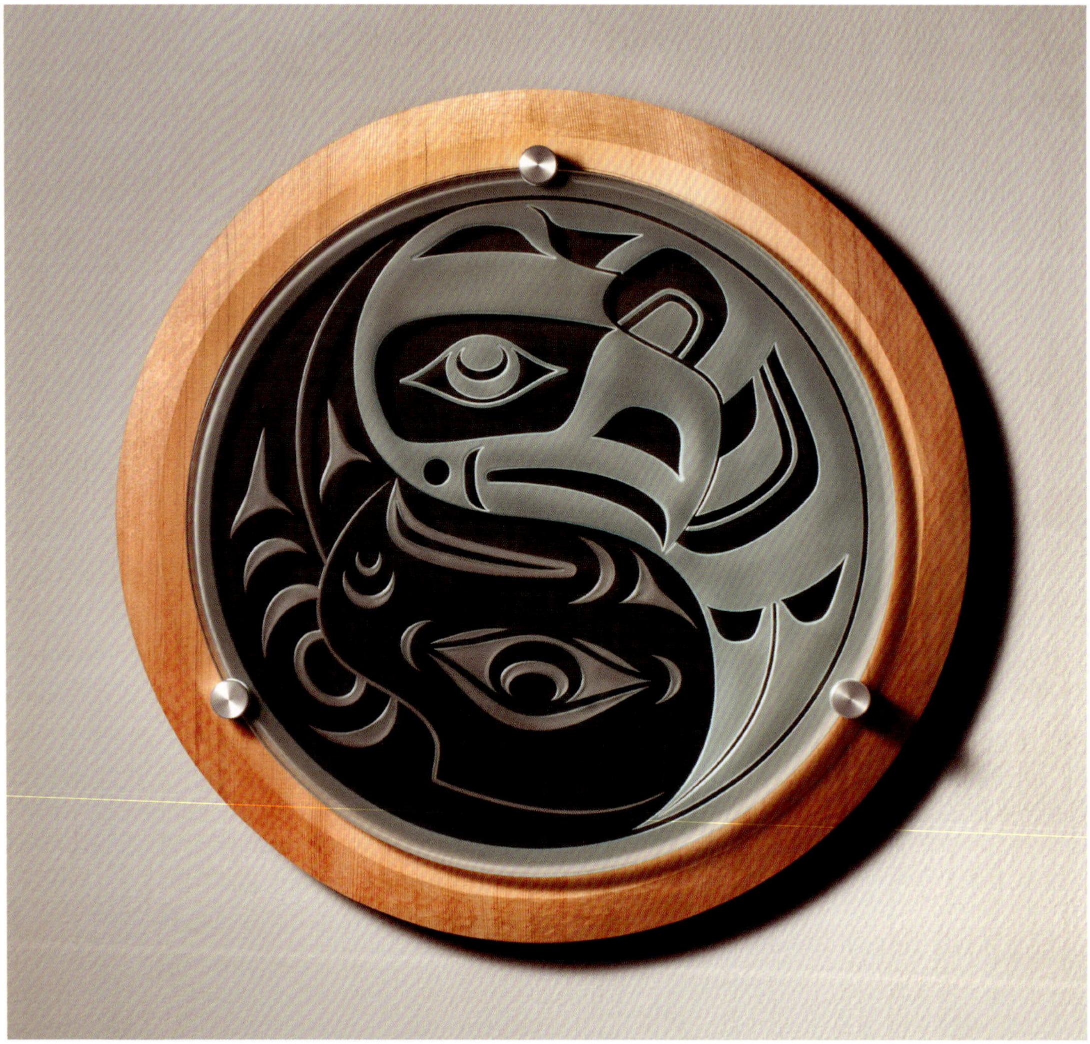

FIGURE I.5 Shaun Peterson (Coast Salish—Tulalip, Puyallup). *North and South*, 2011. Glass, cedar. 21.8 in. Burke Museum #2011–184/1. Photograph by Russell Johnson.

The latest glass piece acquired, *North and South* (fig. I.5), is also by Peterson. It pairs a Northern formline-style eagle with a Salish-style eagle, illustrating some of the issues he discusses in his essay, "Coast Salish Design: An Anticipated Southern Analysis." Peterson looks at Coast Salish design from the viewpoint of an artist who has become a teacher, inspired to explain the style in its own terms, much as Bill Holm did for the Northern style some thirty-five years earlier (Holm 1965).

The important work of Bill Holm, curator emeritus for the Burke, has affected both the development of contemporary Native art and the general public's understanding of it, beginning with the publication of his *Northwest Coast Indian Art: An Analysis of Form*, now in its eighteenth printing (Holm 1965). In this book he provided the vocabulary and grammar for the visual language of the northern Northwest Coast "formline" design system that continues to be used and expanded by artists and scholars alike (Bunn-Marcuse in press). The book's impact has been so significant that many forget it was never intended to be an analysis of Northwest Coast Native art as a whole. It focused only on the two-dimensional art conventions used on the northern Northwest Coast (Tlingit, Haida, and Tsimshian art) in the nineteenth century.[3]

Holm's subsequent work on form in three-dimensional tribal styles across the entire Coast, and artist attributions from the Haida to the Kwakwaka'wakw (Duff, Holm, and Reid 1967; Holm 1972, 1974, 1981, 1983a, 1983b, 1988, 1990), has provided a foundation for a new generation of art historians. Holm has challenged his students and others to describe the visual language of the Central and Southern Northwest Coast in a way that might balance his work on the Northern design system (Brown 1998; Brown 2005; Calkins 1977). Peterson has taken up that challenge with his essay in this volume, explaining why Coast Salish design should not be described with the terms "formline" or "U-form." He proposes instead of U-form the term "extended crescent," focusing on the negative rather than the positive elements. Peterson describes his own realization that rather than simply substituting Southern shapes for formlines, his most successful designs grew not from substitution, but from an organic understanding of the rippling energy of traditional Coast Salish design. Peterson's chapter provides an eloquent justification for why many contemporary Coast Salish artists have used and continue to use Northern formline designs in their work. He explains how many external styles have been incorporated in Coast Salish work, and he provides the tools for artists and consumers to create and see Coast Salish art on its own terms.

While Holm's descriptive writing and teaching on the Northern Northwest Coast formline design system influenced the development of contemporary Northwest Coast painting, printmaking, and sculpture, his research on and teaching about textile arts has also had an impact on contemporary Northwest Coast weavers (Holm 1982). During the period of social and economic disruption in the late nineteenth and early twentieth centuries, when the ritual display of status at potlatches was discouraged by government and missionary agents in both Canada and the United States, ceremonial robes ceased to be made in many places. However, Kwakwa̲ka̲'wakw button blankets and *naaxiin* ("Chilkat") robes continued to be made by a few important women. Today the weaving of Ravenstail and Coast Salish twined robes has been revived and revitalized by a handful of weavers.

Ravenstail weaving is an ancient weaving style that fell from use in the early nineteenth century after the more complex *naaxiin* technique was invented. The revival of Ravenstail weaving in the 1980s was led by the weaver Cheryl Samuel, who studied with Bill Holm at the Burke. She began by talking with Holm and studying his research slides of *naaxiin* and what we then called "proto-Chilkat" or "northern geometric" (Ravenstail) robes. She went on to conduct research at museums holding *naaxiin* and the few fragments of the old robes. Her research resulted in two books (Samuel 1987; Samuel 1982), and her weaving workshops have influenced many contemporary weavers, including Delores Churchill. Churchill's daughter, Evelyn Vanderhoop, has become one of the very few expert weavers of both *naaxiin* and Ravenstail robes. In her essay "The *Naaxiin*: Robe of Sacred Honor," she shares her reflections on her research on the earliest Haida *naaxiin* weaving. Vanderhoop's use of the term "naaxiin" for formline weavings, rather than the tribally specific "Chilkat" robe, emphasizes the importance of our understanding the much more widespread ancient and contemporary use of this unique technique. Inspired by Vanderhoop's research for this essay, her unique *Spirit Belt* (see fig. 3.2) is the newest Northwest Coast weaving in the Burke's collection.

The weaving of spruce root and cedar bark basketry has been carried on by Northwest Coast weavers continuously. Churchill and her family learned basketry from Churchill's mother, the Haida weaver Selina Peratrovich. Lisa Telford is also a member of the Haida weaving family descended from Selina Peratrovich. In her essay "Intertwining: Learning for the Future from Our Past," Telford shares her reflections of growing up in this family, learning to weave, and how she tackled the difficult problem of weaving shoes. Acquired for *In the Spirit of the Ancestors*, two pairs of her cedar bark shoes in the Burke collection (see figs. 5.6 and 5.7) were not woven to be worn but rather as a display of weaving virtuosity, much like the basketry shoes, tea pots, cups, and saucers woven a hundred years earlier. Telford has also woven wearable bustiers and dresses (Bunn-Marcuse 2010; McFadden and Taubman 2005; Reid 2010).

"Worn art," woven and appliquéd robes and other clothing items, are more than garments on the Pacific Northwest Coast. They can be emblems of status used in ceremony or everyday reminders of cultural identity. Kathryn Bunn-Marcuse's essay, "Wearing Identity: The Strength of Identity through Personal Adornment," discusses the continuing importance of ceremonial regalia and other worn art—from tattoo and jewelry to everyday fashion such as T-shirts. Bunn-Marcuse's contribution brings scholarly attention to these subjects, which too often are relegated to the category of "decorative arts," despite their cultural importance. The Burke Museum collection includes a small but growing collection of Northwest Coast T-shirts and looks forward to building that collection, along with other worn, wearable, and unwearable garments. The Burke's most recent T-shirt acquisition is a set of twelve shirts with designs by a distinguished group of indigenous artists to protest the proposed Pebble Mine in Alaska (fig. 1.6). These designs were donated by the artists for the touring exhibit *fashion STATEMENT: Native Artists Against Pebble Mine*, curated by Anna Hoover.[4] One of the T-shirt artists in this set was designed by Joe David, who was a leader in the successful protest against the clear-cutting of Meares Island in the 1980s. David's work was inspirational to Hoover's work on this environmental campaign.

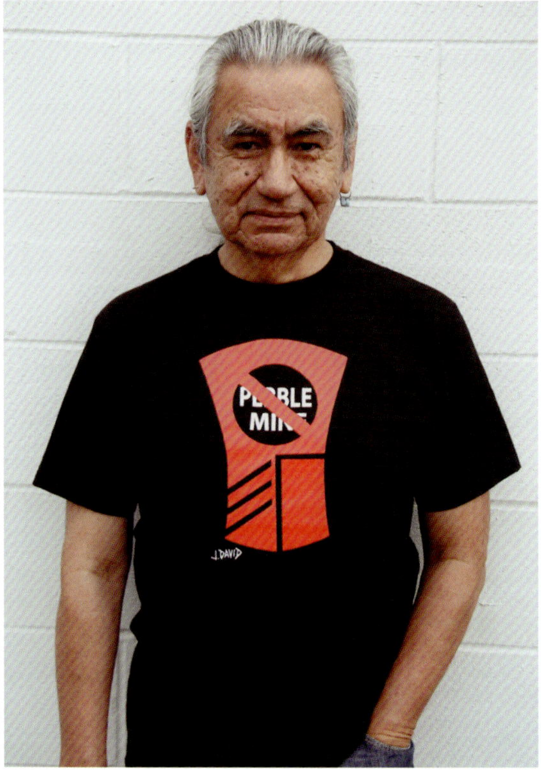

FIGURE I.6 Joe David (Nuu-chah-nulth—Tla-o-qui-aht). *Broken Copper Anti-Pebble Mine T*, 2011. 29.9 × 21.9 in. Burke Museum #2011–133/3.

Several masks made by members of the David family were added to the Burke's collection with Arthur Steinman's gift in 2004. Masks made by contemporary Northwest Coast Native artists are sometimes worn, sometimes not, and often it is impossible to determine which may be which. This distinction may not matter, although for some collectors, those masks that have been worn or "danced" take on an added value. The Burke Museum's collection of masks grew by 132 with the donation of the Steinman collection in 2004, including 7 masks by members of the David family. The Tla-o-qui-aht artist Joe David is one of the premier contemporary Northwest Coast artists. His essay "Notes on Masks" provides insight into his life's passion. Masks made for sale have been a mainstay of the output of many contemporary Northwest Coast artists. This is not the case for box drums. Made today primarily for ceremonial use by Native dance groups, box drums provide another example of the revival of an art form that was dormant for many years and has become an important part of contemporary ceremony, similar to Ravenstail weaving. As with all of the other contributions in this volume, my essay on Northwest Coast box drums draws attention to the importance of historical art to contemporary artists.

The history of contemporary Northwest Coast Native art revolves around themes of revival and respect for the works of the ancestors. Since the

1980s, resistance to colonial histories and narratives has become very important in the motivations of many contemporary artists. Likewise, respect for the resistance of First Nations peoples has become an important focus in the research of contemporary art historians. Emily Moore's essay on the Kaats' house posts, "Acts of Propatriation," highlights the new post-NAGPRA (the 1990 Native American Graves Protection and Repatriation Act) era in the history of the relationships between museums and Native communities. The Burke Museum's curators have prided themselves in establishing and maintaining close relationships with indigenous communities, and have welcomed First Nations artists who have researched the museum's collections. We had known of the infamous theft by the Harriman Expedition of poles and other objects from the Cape Fox village of Gaash long before the NAPGRA law was passed in 1990. We welcomed the opportunity to right a wrong in 2001, by returning two stolen house posts to the Cape Fox Corporation.

An unexpected bonus of this return was the opportunity to acquire two new posts, one by Nathan Jackson and one by Stephen Jackson. Nathan Jackson was among the small and important group of contemporary Native artists working in the 1960s and 1970s, whose work is the foundation of contemporary Tlingit art. He credits his early friendship with Bill Holm, and through him access to the Burke Museum's collections, as a positive early influence on his art. His visit to one of Holm's classes at the University of Washington in the 1970s led to meeting his wife, Dorica, then a student in Holm's class. She has gone on to become one of the few expert *naaxiin* weavers, and their son, Stephen, is one of a small group of "avant garde" artists on the Northwest Coast. Nathan Jackson refers to his son's Kaats' house post as "postmodern." Certainly, the acquisition of his Kaats' house post, *Nearing Completion* (fig. 8.6), has brought the Burke Museum's collections a giant leap forward into the twenty-first century.

In 2009 the exhibition *AYP: Indigenous Voices Reply* was held at the Burke Museum to mark the one hundredth anniversary of the Alaska Yukon Pacific Exposition in Seattle. We invited contemporary indigenous artists to submit works for exhibition that responded to the way their ancestors had been put on display at that World's Fair. Sixteen artists were selected, and their responses ranged from traditional works inspired by objects that had been displayed at the AYP to pieces with cutting political and social commentary. We were pleased to be able to add a number of these pieces to the Burke's collection. Nicholas Galanin donated his video piece "Who We Are," an appropriation of the Holm/Wright videodisk created in 1996 to disseminate the research slides taken by Bill Holm and me of Northwest Coast art from over 180 museums and several private collections around the world. Galanin's video loop copy, set to fast-play still images originally intended to be viewed as still frames, was first exhibited in *Changing Hands: Art Without Reservations 2* at the New York Museum of Arts and Design in 2005. According to Galanin, "for me this work sums up a feeling I experience when walking into many institutions housing Native America." In gifting this piece back to the Burke Museum, Galanin has generously allowed us to "re-appropriate" it into our collection of contemporary art.

As this book was going to press, we acquired Nicholas Galanin's 2009 *Inert* for our permanent collection (fig. 1.7). The Burke Museum is the Washington State Natural History and Culture museum, which has many preserved animals in its mammology department. Because of this, *Inert* seems both a poignant and an appropriate addition to the Ethnology collection. *Inert* presents

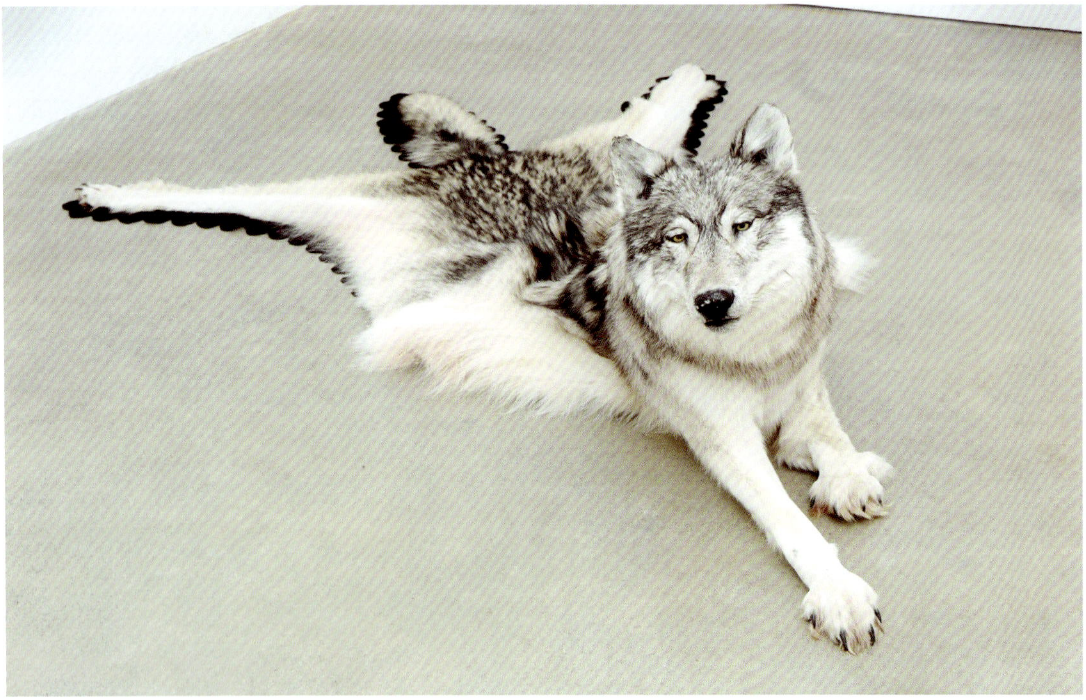

FIGURE I.7 Nicholas Galanin (Tlingit/Aleut). *Inert*, 2009. Wolf hide, felt. 72 × 48 × 30 in. Burke Museum #2012–83/1. Photograph by Wayne Leidenfrost.

a deliberately disturbing and ambiguous view of a wolf caught between being a rug and coming back to life—or is it going the other way? Just as the Holm/Wright slide collection captured images of objects housed in the world's museums, and Galanin's *Who We Are* reappropriated them, *Inert* challenges our comfort level. Galanin says: "The inability to progress or move forward was the basic concept. . . . I look at this piece in cultural terms. Mainstream society often looks at Indigenous or Native American art through a romantic lens, not allowing a culture like my Tlingit community room for creative sovereign growth. The back half of this piece is contained, a captured trophy or rug to bring into the home, while the front continues to move. It is sad and the struggle is evident."[5]

As Holm pointed out in his Foreword, museums and attitudes are changing. This book acknowledges and celebrates this change. We hope to continue to build a contemporary Native art collection that will encompass the full spectrum of media and messages that are of importance to Native artists today.

As we build our twenty-first century collection, we are also repatriating cultural materials in appropriate cases from the nineteenth-century collection and continuing our productive relationship with Native communities and artists. It is the mission of the Bill Holm Center for the Study of Northwest Coast Art to foster the appreciation and understanding of Native art of the Pacific Northwest region, and to promote broad access to the museum's resources, including images of Northwest Coast art from museums around the world. We are pleased that these resources have so often proven to be inspirational to First Nations artists, and we salute and respect those who continue to work "in the spirit of the ancestors."

NOTES

1 This volume is the first publication in "Native Art of the Pacific Northwest: A Bill Holm Center Series." The Bill Holm Center was established at the Burke Museum in 2003 to continue Curator Emeritus Bill Holm's legacy at the Burke Museum, which has made it one of the premier centers for the study of Native arts of the Pacific Northwest Coast. Bill Holm Center projects are funded by grants and through three endowments, the Bill Holm Center Endowed Research Fund, the Bill Holm Center Endowed Graduate Fellowship, and the Bill Holm Center Endowed Professorship. We use the distributed interest to fund projects that include research on, access to, and appreciation of Native Art of the Pacific Northwest Coast with the goals of establishing a globally accessible learning center at the Burke Museum, promoting scholarly research on Northwest Coast Native art, increasing Native and public access to research resources, and fostering appreciation and understanding of Native art of the Northwest Coast of North America.

Over the past ten years we have supported exhibitions and new web resources on Northwest Coast art, sponsored public programs, and funded Native speakers in University of Washington classes. We have supported University of Washington graduate student research, and awarded visiting research grants to scholars and artists. Now we are embarking on a publication program that will provide a permanent record of many of the research projects and exhibitions sponsored by the Bill Holm Center.

2 In 1979 a grant from the Canadian Museum of Civilization led to interviews with Northwest Coast print artists, and the resulting five volumes of transcribed interviews with artists, dealers, and printmakers accompany the Blackman Hall Collection.

3 In hindsight, Holm has indicated that a more appropriate title would have been "Northern Northwest Coast Indian Art: An Analysis of Form."

4 The shirts were designed by Sonny Assu (Kwakwa̱ka̱'wakw), Rick Bartow (Wiyot), Philip Charette (Yup'ik), Joe David (Tla-o-qui-aht), Jerrod and Nicholas Galanin (Aleut/Tlingit), Anna Hoover (Aleut), John Hoover (Aleut), Brad Kahlhamer (Lakota), Richard Kereopa (Te Arawa, Ngati Tuwharetoa, Tainui, Nga Phui), Larry McNeil (Tlingit/Nisga'a), Da-ka-xeen Mehner (Tlingit), and Tanis Seiltin (Tlingit). The exhibit was created as part of the requirements for Anna Hoover's master's degree in art history at the University of Washington (Hoover 2011).

5 Nicholas Galanin, artist's website, at http://galan.in/post/13976734736/by-combining-two-pre-taxidermied-wolves-into-one, accessed May 21, 2012.

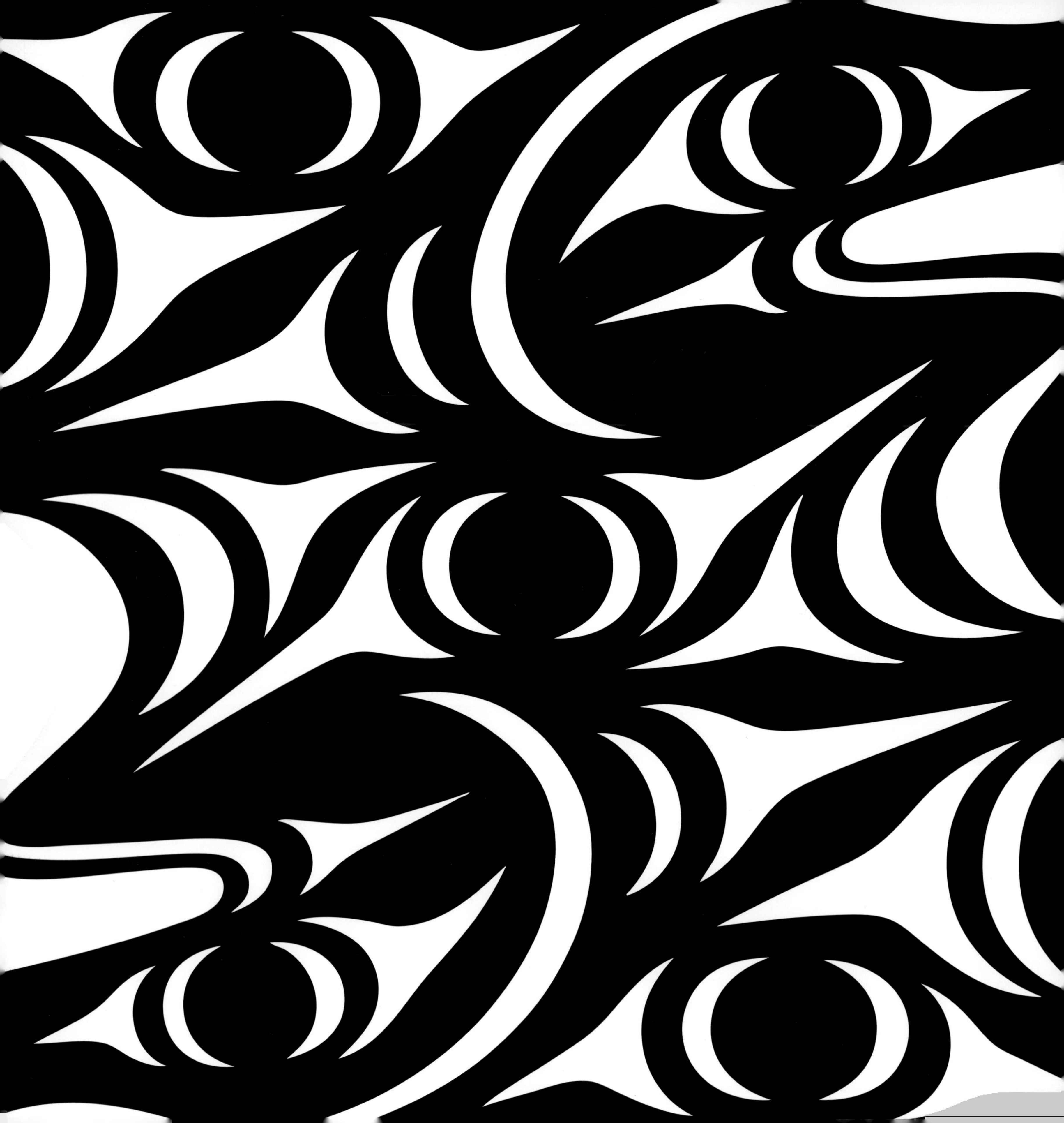

ONE

COAST SALISH DESIGN

An Anticipated Southern Analysis

SHAUN PETERSON

Over the years several volumes have been published about art of the Northwest Coast Native peoples. This region, from western Washington to southeast Alaska, has great diversity in styles despite a common root in the design principles. Studies of Northwest Coast art styles have suggested design terms that are now quite familiar to observers of the arts (Holm 1965). What has been overlooked, however, is that these terms and even their complex manner of examining design are not easily applied to all of the coastal styles from Puget Sound to northern Vancouver Island. Despite this, many authors and art historians have tried to do so. The focus of this chapter is to provide a much-needed analysis of the specific elements of Coast Salish design.

The term "Salish" refers to a language group of which the peoples of the Puget Sound are one branch, speaking a language known as Lushootseed. The Coast Salish territory also covers the Strait of Georgia and southeastern Vancouver Island. The art style discussed in this chapter is primarily the Central Coast Salish style of the Halkomelem language group and the Puget Sound peoples, both Northern and Southern Lushootseed–speaking tribes. I use the terms "Coast Salish" and "Salish" interchangeably.

A STYLISTIC ANALYSIS

Among the many tribal styles of the Northwest Coast, the Salish style is unique. The Salish two-dimensional works are particular to our region of the Northwest Coast, differing from the northern Northwest Coast formline design system. Contrary to popular assumption, the term "formline" does not lend itself well to discussing the two-dimensional Coast Salish art style. In 1965 the author and acclaimed art historian Bill Holm published *Northwest Coast Indian Art: An Analysis of Form*. He took an in-depth look at objects of the northern Northwest Coast and examined their commonalities. Simply stated, the art form—at least in two-dimensional aspects—was comprised of two main shapes, the ovoid (fig. 1.1a) and the U-form (fig. 1.1b). Before Holm's book, authors and art historians had struggled to name these shapes with practical terms; since then, Holm's terms have become a part of mainstream vocabulary for those examining the art of this northern style. Sometimes overlooked, however, is the fact that his book does not set out to examine the regional tribal groups of the Northwest Coast as a whole. Rather, Holm (1965: ix) offers terms for the practices of the northern Northwest Coast design tradition.

The term "formline" is defined as a bandlike element that tapers and swells and joins itself in a continuous grid delineating the design (Holm 1965: 29). The term is appropriate in the cases where a continuous positive (that is, painted) design field is composed using the ovoid, U-form, and other positive and negative formline shapes to create a design (fig. 1.2). Although these northern-style shapes have appeared in the creations of contemporary Salish artists, the use of the northern formline elements actually departs from the historical Salish art tradition. Explanations of why this occurs are discussed later in this chapter.

This formline practice is shared by some other tribal groups. In the process of creating formline art, as Holm has described, the designs are commonly achieved by outlining shapes (ovoids, U-forms, and so on) and filling them in by painting. He has characterized formline art as having "calligraphic characteristic," and to call it line alone would minimize its importance (Holm 1965: 35). By observing the isolated shapes of the formline art, one could look upon a design composition of this artistic tradition and see the pieces distributed about. In the eagle example (see fig. 1.2), one can see the large portion of the bird head is an ovoid variation with a U-form above to define an ear and to the right to create the beak. The wing appendage is a large ovoid with a single U-form followed by two smaller variations to distinguish feathers. The design is made up of shapes that are painted.

WHY NOT FORMLINE?

Why is the term "formline" not appropriate for discussing Coast Salish art? Northern formline designs are composed using a continuous line with U-forms and ovoids connected to define the form (fig. 1.3a). In the Central Coast area (among the Kwakwa̱ka̱'wakw and Nuu-chah-nulth) formline-type elements are used to create designs that are unconstrained from the conventions that guide northern artists. In the Nuu-chah-nulth-style eagle (fig. 1.3b) we see a bold formline creating the bird's beak and head. In the Salish design tradition the "positive space" (the painted area) is not a formline in the northern sense. The relationship between the positive and negative elements is different: it is the negative areas rather than positive formlines that initially define the composition. The Salish eagle design (fig. 1.3c) is characterized by the cutout negative areas, rather than by a formline framework of consistent design shapes. In the Salish example the cheek area behind the mouth is defined by two negative crescent relief shapes, followed by a trigon. The trigon shape has been called many things, including wedge, cuneiform, and T-shaped relief. Although each of these terms can work in particular design contexts, for this discussion I use the word "trigon" to describe this shape.

Additional negative trigons define the oval-shaped eye of the bird. The trigon is used two more times, above the brow and behind the crescent that defines the nostril in the beak. What is characteris-

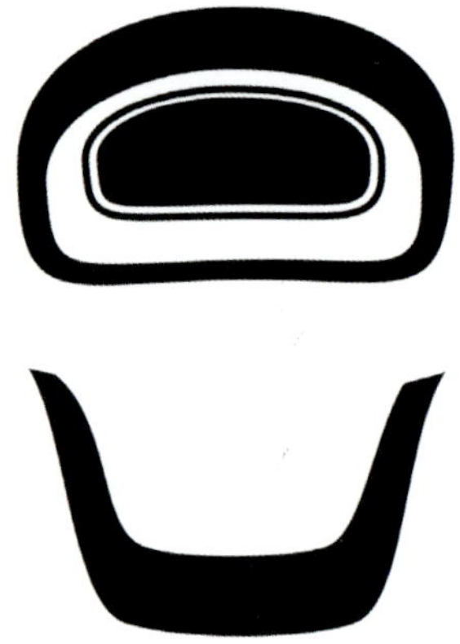

FIGURE 1.1A-B Ovoid (a) and U-form (b) diagrams. Illustration by Shaun Peterson (Coast Salish—Puyallup, Tulalip).

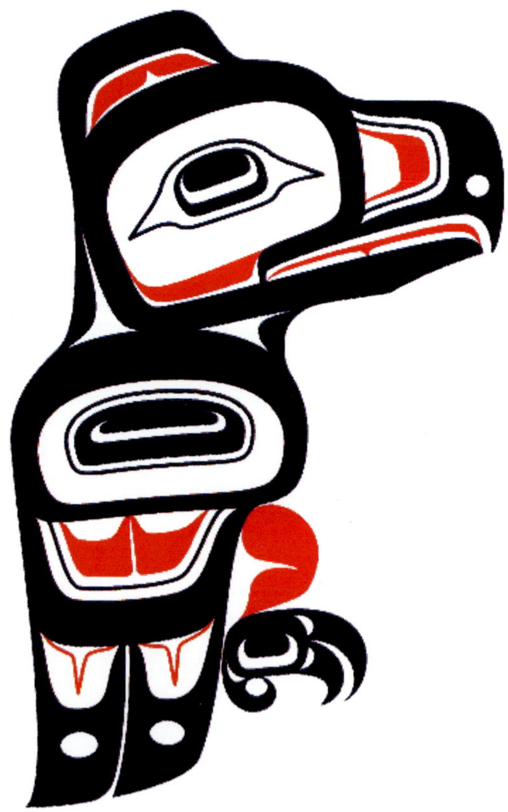

FIGURE 1.2 Example of formline design. Illustration by Shaun Peterson (Coast Salish—Puyallup, Tulalip).

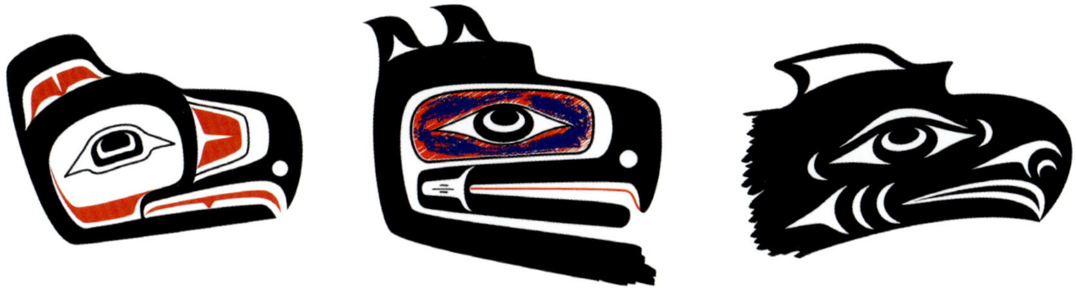

FIGURE 1.3A-C (a) Northern formline-style eagle; (b) Nuu-chah-nulth-style eagle; (c) Salish eagle. Illustrations by Shaun Peterson (Coast Salish—Puyallup, Tulalip).

tic of the Salish design tradition is how the placement of these negative (unpainted) design elements throughout the composition suggests movement. Some of the most common compositional devices in Salish art are the crescent and trigon elements that emanate from the back of the mouth (again, see fig. 1.3c). Likewise, from the center of the eye on both sides, the crescent follows the trigons. Though the positive design area is continuously interconnected, it is not composed of consistent positive design shapes with negative (unpainted) spaces between them, and because of this it seems impractical to use the term "formline."

The difference in the northern and southern systems can be partly explained by the emphasis on the two-dimensional painting tradition on the northern Northwest Coast. The northern painting tradition grew away from the common artistic roots of the ancient proto-formlines into the northern style with a changed ratio of balance between positive and negative space (Brown 2005: 8; Brown 1997: 67–69). Moreover, the northern painted designs call for color to be used in a hierarchical manner with secondary formlines nested within the primary formlines (Holm 1965: 26–35). In addition to differences in color and form, the function of northern art was fundamentally different than art in the south. In the Haida, Tlingit, and Tsimshian cultures the purpose of art was to be publicly displayed, serving as a marker of one's identity by the crests represented.

In the Coast Salish tradition, however, very few objects were made for public display. This has to do with our beliefs and ceremonial system. We are not a crest-based society, and therefore have no need to create and display objects that reflect a particular being personified in painting or sculpture. In fact, for generations it was believed that if one publicly displayed objects that depicted specific animals, they might be regarded as beings associated with one's spirituality, thereby striking against a cultural value to be humble. For this reason much of the work remained ambiguous as these were very private objects. Today, the need to identify with one's culture has sparked an explosion of artistic expression; a way for many artists to maintain and foster their cultural identity.

A DIFFERENT DIRECTION

The works of early twentieth-century Salish artists show a departure from the work of their nineteenth-century predecessors. Artists from the Puget Sound region, including William Shelton (Tulalip) and Joseph Hillaire (Lummi), were among a small group of carvers to see the power and influence that monumental sculptures had to offer. This generation witnessed a radical shift, one where the way of life, stories, and sculptural style of the people were at risk of disappearing entirely except for the efforts of a few innovative artists. During these difficult years the artists parted from traditional practices to create what is known as a story pole (fig. 1.4). Unlike the northern totem pole tradition, where sculptures included a family or crest identity, the story pole was a new way to preserve oral histories using a house post sculptural format not unlike ones that had existed in earlier plank house structures on the Puget Sound.

The draw of the Northern-style totemic art captivated newcomers to the Pacific Northwest. Witnessing this power, Salish artists who sought to preserve a cultural perspective began carving monumental works. Carved from western red cedar, some more than seventy feet tall, the story pole took an existing tradition of sculpture and literally expanded on it. This was the beginning of breaching a divide between the past and present. Often these sculptures depicted men and women with feather headdresses or buckskin clothing, which was clearly not a part of the Coastal culture before that time but directly mirrored what was happening in the region during the period. During the later 1800s, many groups from the Plateau and inland regions played a role in influencing the Coastal societies, as the image of an Indian wearing a headdress carried great influence and prompted some of the indigenous Salish communities to adopt this practice for a time. Photos from the mid-twentieth century record families in regalia far different from the mountain goat wool blankets and cedar bark capes or vests that had been customary in previous decades. The skills and processes required for making these had largely disappeared. This in part explains the unique appearance of the sculptures from those decades and how the combination of influences from regions north and east of the Puget Sound resulted in story poles with Plateau- and Plains-type imagery being carved by Salish artists. Today a handful of Puget Sound Native artists are exploring this expression in hopes of revitalizing the story pole tradition, bringing to it a new expression full of potential and promise.

SETTING A PATH

Despite the commercial market demand and the challenges posed during the 1980s, Susan Point, Rod Modeste, and Stan Greene persevered as artists of Coast Salish heritage. They forged a path for a new generation of Salish artists to meet the world of consumers with less resistance to this once unfamiliar traditional design system. Their efforts to create a body of work based on the Coast Salish tradition brought the Salish style into the public realm. Point's early prints (such as Burke Museum #2.5E/1829) were important as they closely followed nineteenth-century objects that captured the strong features of Coast Salish design. My illustration (fig. 1.5) is based on that same comb from the Peabody Museum of Archeology and Ethnology at Harvard University.

This object has served as inspiration for a number of works by several Salish artists as it is a prime example of successful design work that defines Salish two-dimensional art. In looking at the overall design, we see two heads, the upper right and the lower left. The design illustrates the use of rotational symmetry, which appears in many Salish designs. We can find five black, positive oval shapes that are created by the white, negative crescents. Each oval is followed by a trigon extending away from its positive oval shape. This is highly characteristic of the Salish design tradition whereby the elements are distributed throughout the design field, creating a rhythmic movement that suggests emitting energy. The negative spaces flow outward from the central positive element, like the ripples of a pebble dropped in calm water. Like the earlier example of the eagle (see fig. 1.3c), the serpent heads have a negative element that follows from behind the opening of the mouth.

However, in this highly advanced design, the element that would normally be a single crescent or trigon flows into a larger crescent just below, thus creating an asymmetrical S-shape. A trigon flanks the upper half of the S-shape, and both a crescent and a trigon echo the lower half of the

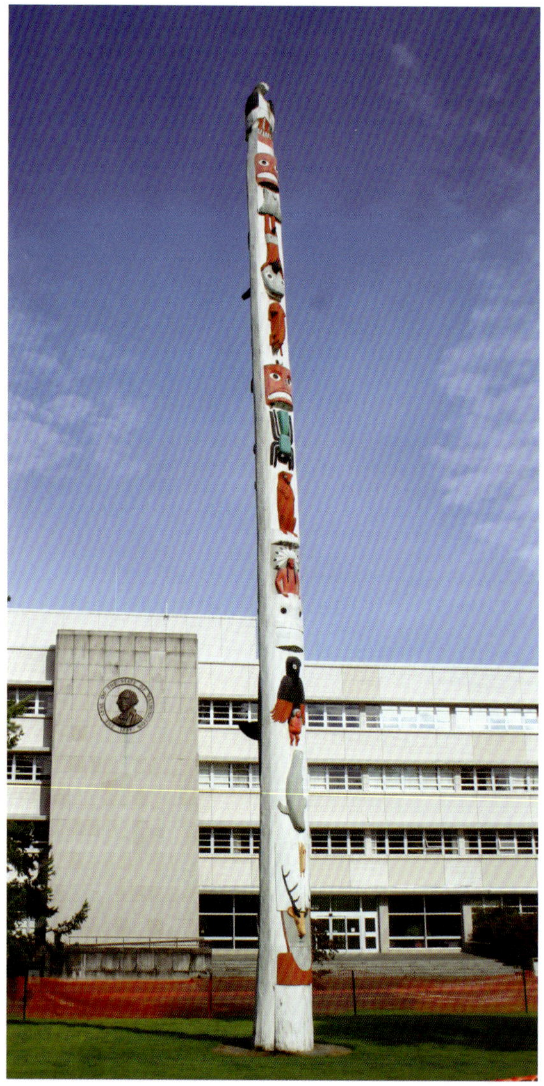

FIGURE 1.4 William Shelton (Coast Salish—Tulalip). *Story Pole*, Olympia, Washington, 1940. Wood, paint. Photograph by State of Washington.

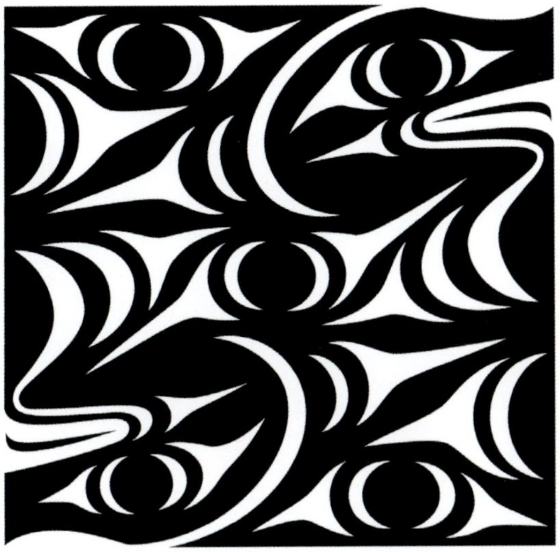

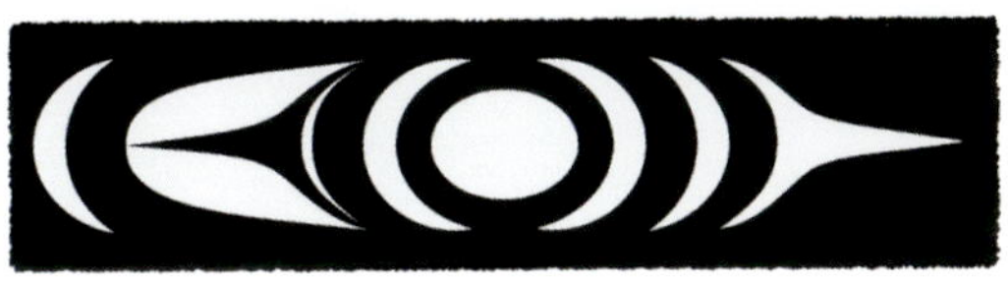

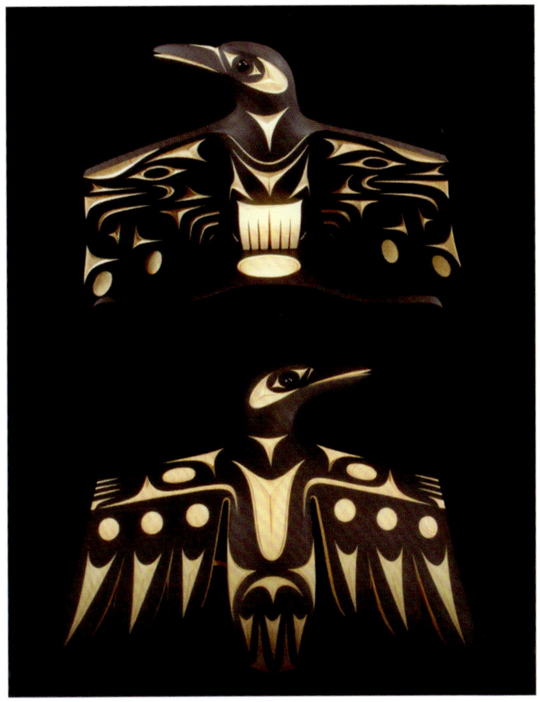

FIGURE 1.5 Coast Salish comb, nineteenth century. Peabody Museum of Archeology and Ethnology #48393. Illustration by Shaun Peterson (Coast Salish—Puyallup, Tulalip).

FIGURE 1.6 Coast Salish design elements, including oval, crescent, extended crescent, and positive and negative trigon. Illustration by Shaun Peterson (Coast Salish—Puyallup, Tulalip).

FIGURE 1.7 (front and back) John Marston (Coast Salish). *Raven*, 2008. Wood, paint. Collection of Edgar and Linda Marcuse.

S-shape. We see a suggestion of movement in these grouped elements. The central positive oval is created by crescents followed by a trigon on either side. In this design the tendency of the shapes to give way, or yield to one another, is particularly pronounced, especially when looking at the trigons. The tapers of the points appear to make room for one another rather than overlapping or merging. This example also illustrates the absence of a positive line made up of conventionalized design shapes—a "formline"—that would be central to a discussion of a Northern artwork. It focuses instead on the defining characteristics of the negative elements, rather than the positive ones.

SPOTLIGHT ON ELEMENTS

After having talked about how design components or elements are used in composing a design, it seems only appropriate to devote some attention to the components themselves. Over my career I have used various terms—circle/oval, crescent, and trigon to explain the design shapes—that have become familiar in discussions of Coast Salish art. I would like to add to this discussion the term "extended crescent," where a trigon is contained within that crescent. This derives directly from the incised carvings seen on Salish objects, such as spindle whorls, rattles, or combs. In the past I have used the term "U-form," but I have come to realize that this term is more appropriate to the Northern design system, not the Salish system. One common Salish distribution of the elements is where the circle or oval is central and crescents and/or trigons extend from it as if a radial energy is present (fig. 1.6). To the right are two crescents followed by a negative trigon. On the left, however, is a single crescent followed by an extended crescent, which is then filled with a positive trigon. This positive trigon in the two-dimensional print or painted form is representative of a carved negative (3-D) trigon within the extended crescent. It is rare that an extended crescent is not divided by a trigon. An example can be seen in John Marston's *Raven* (fig. 1.7), which we examine in further detail later in this chapter. In print form the trigon relies on the positive and negative relationship: the black trigon simulates the shadow that would occur in the carved version of the design (as can be seen in on the bird's back in Marston's piece). The left side is then ended with a crescent.

These same elements are found in the ancient proto–Northwest Coast design system on objects several thousand years old (Brown 2005: 10). This system predates the Northern formline system as we know it today and gives us a window into a much different practice, in which both Northern and Southern artists employed shared design elements to create mammal, bird, and human designs in bone, wood, and antler objects. These components have all been used in discussing Central Coast Salish works of the Halkomelem people, and it is important to know that this shared format was widespread long ago. Artists in the Puget Sound today have taken up these design practices and applied them to their works. Although many artists directly translate nineteenth-century spindle whorl motifs and similar objects from Central Salish territories, they have equal right to use these elements, which stem from the more ancient proto–Northwest Coast objects. Examples of the design elements used for such work can be seen in the comb collected at Restoration Point, on Bainbridge Island in Washington (fig. 1.8). Decorated objects of this kind can be found in many areas of the coast from the Makah in northwestern Washington to the Tsimshian of Prince Rupert, British Columbia, and demonstrate this wider use of common-root design principles.

THE TRAJECTORY

Today many Salish artists work using variations of the northern formline system. There are several reasons for this. First, there is an issue of readily available content from which one could draw examples for study. Few objects were made for, or made available to, museum collections for public display, given their ceremonial and private nature. Artists trying to familiarize themselves with Coast Salish examples have greater exposure to other tribal groups whose artworks were collected and displayed, whereas Salish items—even in public collections—are not easily accessible, rendering them less influential. Second, the southern and central Northwest Coast design traditions, including those of the Nuu-chah-nulth and Kwakwaka'wakw, do not lend themselves well to a northern-style formal analysis and therefore are more difficult to teach. Third, artists who are the children of intertribal marriages have tended to make artwork in the tradition of the non-Salish parent, for reasons listed in this chapter as well as others. Fourth, the demands of the commercial market in which the Northern style is more familiar was once a disincentive to work in the less well-recognized Salish style.

When European trade first took place on the Northwest Coast, the objects that left these shores were the first to represent this region to the broader world. Museum collections feature a much greater percentage of Northern work and far fewer examples of Salish work for at least two reasons: (1) there were simply larger numbers of works produced in Northern communities, where public crest display was a priority; and (2) by the time museum collectors made their largest collections in the late nineteenth century, the Salish communities had already suffered major disruption to their lands and social practices. Salish cultural practices that demanded the production of artworks were carefully guarded; those objects were not considered appropriate for sale or display. The older Salish society perceived the public display of one's spirit power in sculpture or painting as a sacrilegious act that might result in the loss of one's privileges. These factors, although much simplified here, help to explain the disparity between the public availability of Salish material and material from other parts of the Northwest Coast in museum collections.

As a whole, the Southern Northwest Coast groups have a system that is much less contained by "rules" or conventions and is therefore difficult to analyze with consistency; the personal nature of many Salish designs have challenged art historians and anthropologists alike. Because of the consistency of the conventions within the Northern formline system, it has been easier to describe both design elements and whole compositions in

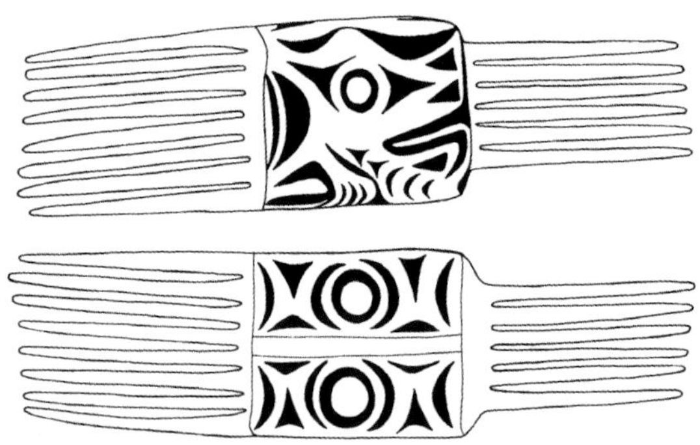

FIGURE 1.8 Coast Salish comb. Collected in 1792 at Restoration Point, Washington. British Museum #VAN219. Illustration by Robin Wright.

writing. In addition, these conventions have made the Northern system easier to teach and to learn (but perhaps no easier to master).

Since time immemorial, we (the Coast Salish people) have warred with, traded with, and intermarried with other tribes. To this day, there are Salish artists who practice Northern formline styles as part of their inherited rights. Often a child who has a Salish parent and a parent whose people have a more public design tradition will likely follow the non-Salish tradition. This is due in part to the point made earlier: there are more teachers of the Northern style because it is an integrated part of their cultural practice to create works to identify their clan. There are far fewer Salish artists teaching their cultural style because of cultural conventions that discourage public display. Contemporary Coast Salish public works are in an early phase within the culture; it will take time for the generations to come to define a healthy balance for public display and ceremonial privilege. This is not to say the Salish tradition is not respected or continuous within the communities, but historically fewer families have been able to connect with that two-dimensional design practice and, through no fault of their own, have been influenced by other regional styles and have employed those for their creative works.

The commercial market is also a contributing factor to why some Salish artists have practiced other design traditions. When Northwest Coast silkscreen prints first hit the market in large numbers in the 1970s, there was only a small number of artists making Salish prints. Almost all the active artists, Native and non-Native alike, produced works based in a formline system, choosing the northern style as their approach. Many Salish sculptors and painters found that the demand for the arts of other regions made it more lucrative to produce, and they therefore followed that demand, although they may have been capable of producing Salish art. Until recent years this has been a familiar situation for Salish artists entering the commercial market. It has only been with recent publications and efforts from the Salish communities themselves that the demand for Salish art has come to the forefront. For those whose parents practiced other regional arts, it would explain how one could perceive the formline practice as his or her inherited tradition and the challenge this would pose to the individual artist.

LOST IN TRANSLATION

In the time that I was transitioning from the northern formline system to a better understanding of the Coast Salish style, I made some decisions that hindered my progress. Perhaps the most important error I made in interpreting Coast Salish art is that I approached the Salish style as if I could simply swap out ovoids for circles or ovals and the U-forms for crescents and trigons. Although this is a common mistake, it is important to cite why this is *not* productive if the goal is to better understand the Salish design system. For one, basing an art tradition on another's principles is like attempting to translate written languages word for word without accounting for grammar, conjugation, or cultural relevance. Art—in this case Northwest Coast Native art—is a visual language, and the analogy of swapping elements out is a crucial error. Although one might experience some success by using this method, it hinders true creativity because it calls for one to derive content from outside the cultural style, essentially plagiarizing the creative works of others. Even when I experimented with creating original northern-style designs and then switching out the elements for Salish ones, it did not work because the two systems are so different in compositional terms.

Another misinterpretation of the Salish style appeared in my early works. Despite my growth in understanding the Salish principles of elemental distribution, for some time I persisted in creating wing forms with an oval as the main focus and rows of feathers coming from it with crescent and trigons placed within; this was analogous to the northern wing form composed of an ovoid and attached U-forms (fig. 1.9a). Equally influential is that of the Kwakwa̱ka̱'wakw example (fig. 1.9c) that demonstrates another formline style using its variation of ovoid and U-form shapes to compose a design. My decision to change the wing compositions came directly from observing not only Salish artworks but southern Northwest Coast objects.

Since then, my approach has generally kept closer to historical examples (fig. 1.9d), where the wing has rows of feathers off a main appendage that is not oval or circular but closer to the weight or thickness of the feathers that branch away from it. These feathers are then relieved by rows of crescents and trigons. One would be hard-pressed to find historical examples where the Coast Salish wing form mimics the approach of either figure 1.9a or figure 1.9c. This was a turning point for me, as it marked a realization that in order to practice Salish design, I would truly have to understand what set it apart from other styles and leave my reliance on what had become familiar by exposure to the marketplace and art publications.

Of course there are other approaches aside from this. In the work by Coast Salish artist John Marston (see fig.1.7), we see that through the placement of the negative design elements on the underside of the wing another animal is created: wolflike creatures face outward away from the bird's body with the design elements below elaborating both feathers and the legs of the wolf. On the opposite side, the top of the wings include outstretched arms with hands created by the flanking trigons. These examples show us the variety of ways in which the trigon shape can be used. Likewise, the tail feathers include relief-carved trigons—a less common but versatile use of this element. Just as important to note in this example are the extended crescents in the central body just behind the bird's eye and below the head. Here the extended crescent is relieved by the incised trigon, rather than a painted positive trigon. Marston successfully applies the design elements to create a sculpture with applied two-dimensional relief carving and painting that continue the discipline of his ancestors, while creating new work to inspire the coming generations of Salish artists seeking direction.

NEW DAY, NEW CHALLENGES

Although Coast Salish art is finally getting the recognition it deserves, there are still challenges on the horizon for those working in the practice.

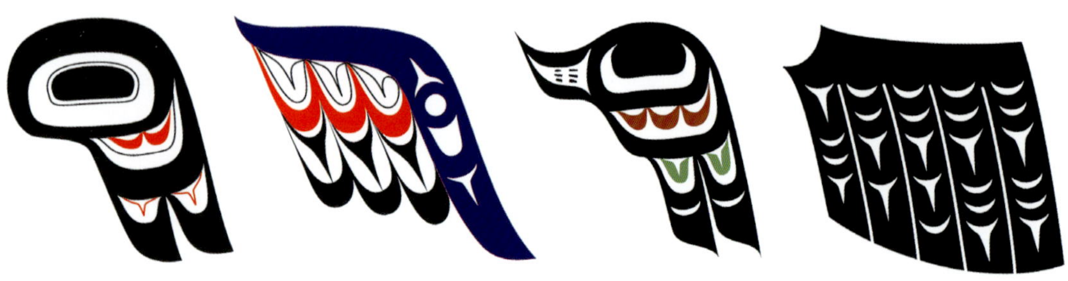

FIGURE 1.9A-D Wing designs: (a) Northern formline style; (b) Nuu-chah-nulth style; (c) Kwakwa̱ka̱'wakw style; (d) Salish style. Illustration by Shaun Peterson (Puyallup/Tulalip, Coast Salish).

Artists like Stan Greene, Susan Point, and Marvin Oliver have played a crucial role in establishing the path for a new generation of artists working in the Salish style. Today's artists have an equally important role in challenging current expectations for the art form. In the 1970s some artists who produced prints encountered prejudices against what was considered an "untraditional" medium; similarly, today's artists are breaking barriers with a variety of new media. With the continual depletion of such resources as western red cedar, artists are seeking out other new—and renewable—media for their work.

For some time Marvin Oliver (Isleta Pueblo/Quinault) and Susan Point (Musqueam) have incorporated glass and metal into their commissions and public works. Glass has now made its way into the accepted arenas of Northwest Coast galleries, and the next generation of artists has made it a staple in their tricks of the trade. Andy Peterson (Skokomish), Andrea Wilbur-Sigo (Squaxin Island), and Jason Gobin (Tulalip) have made glass their primary medium in public art installations within their tribal communities. In my own experience working on a commission for the Puyallup tribe, I was surprised when the elders committee requested specifically that I use more glass and cedar panels as well as traditional two-dimensional designs to demonstrate our changing world. The artists in this field (myself included) are also making use of digital technology in installations and printmaking. Today we live in a digital world, and we are just as eager to use modern innovations and technologies as were artists of earlier generations, to be relevant to our time. Some of the tools we use may have changed—some have not—but overall the underlying principles of design remain unaltered.

There may be continued resistance to the use of digital technology and other "untraditional" media from a public that wants to confine Native artists to outdated standards of authenticity. But we know from our oral histories that sometimes it is the aspect we resist the most that teaches us the greatest lesson. Thus I encourage both patrons and artists to ask about the art, to pose questions, to listen, to learn. It is a great responsibility to produce art, and as artists we must understand the work that we produce. Much contemporary Salish art is based on narrative, and the stories that inspire these works must be examined for original meaning rather than simply quoting from earlier motifs or sculptures. The works we produce have a life of their own that we must honor. In doing so, we truly continue in our ancestors' traditions.

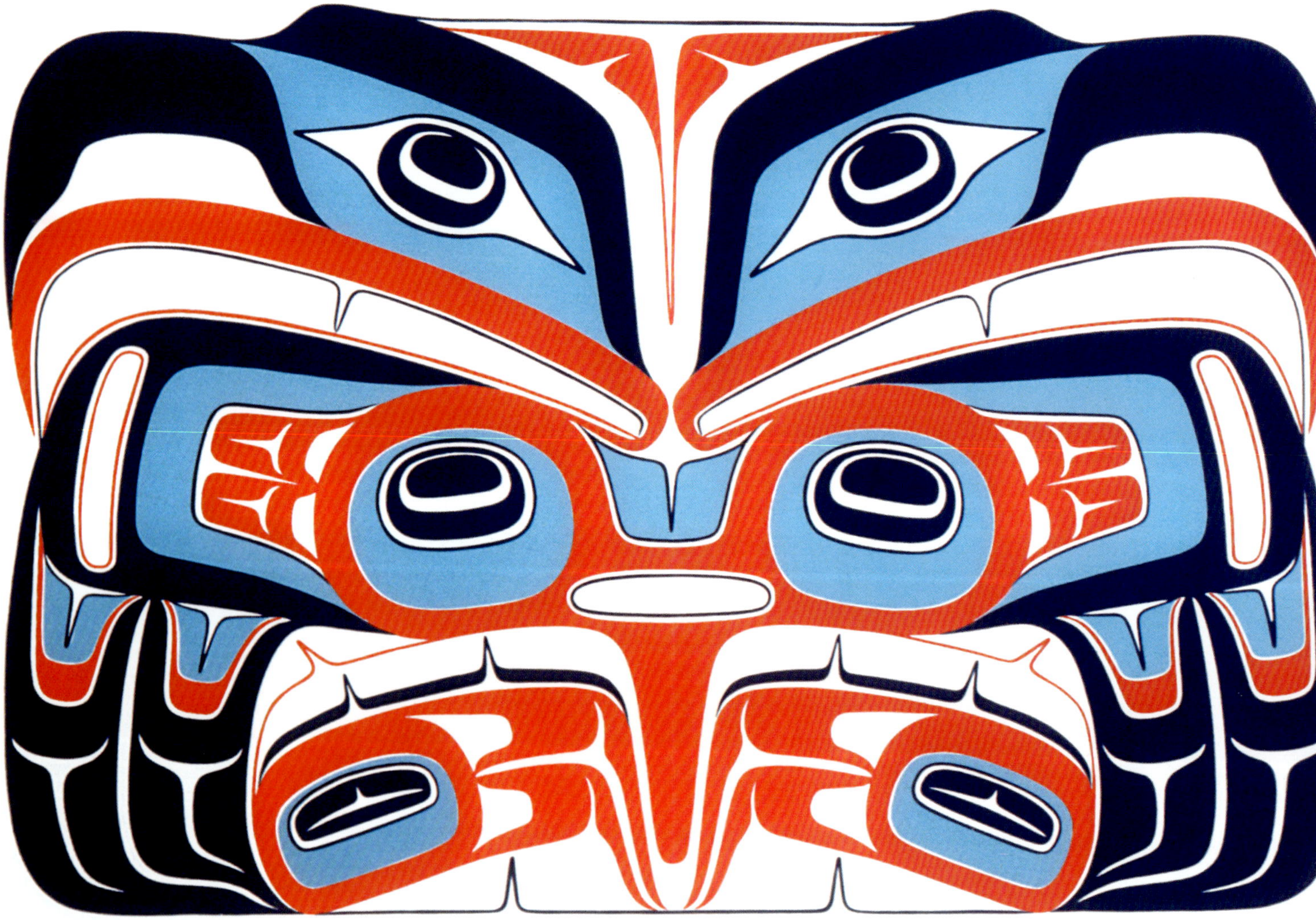

TWO

BEHIND THE "SCREENS"

A Collection, the Collectors, and the Art

MARGARET B. BLACKMAN

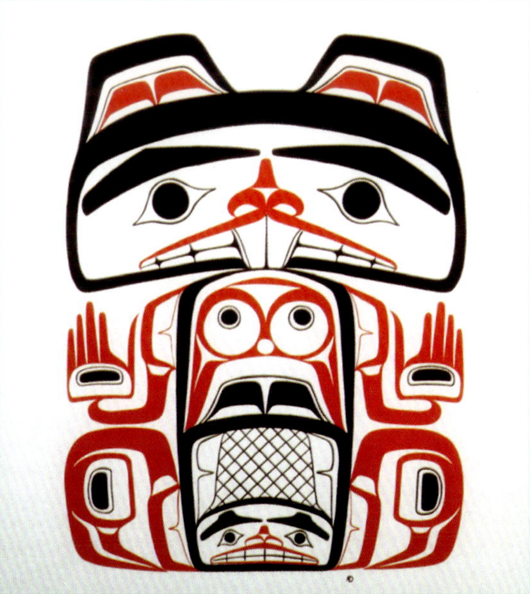

FIGURE 2.1 Robert Davidson (Haida). *Beaver*, 1969. Serigraph, 17 × 13 in. Blackman Hall Collection, Burke Museum #1998–90/148.

In 1970, while doing the research for my doctoral dissertation in Haida Gwaii (the Queen Charlotte Islands), I had the good fortune to attend a memorial potlatch for Robert Davidson Sr., held at the home of his widow, Florence Edenshaw Davidson, in Old Massett. I had recently met their grandson, Robert Davidson, his brother Reg, and was living next door to Robert and Reg's parents on the Haida reserve. At his grandfather's potlatch, Robert gave out silkscreened prints of a Beaver design. I was thrilled to get one (fig. 2.1). My very first piece of Northwest Coast Indian art! In the village I had seen the totem pole Robert had carved in 1969 and heard the story of its raising. I was witness that year on the coast to what would soon be called the renaissance in Northwest Coast Indian art. I acquired a couple of other prints that field season from Robert, one commemorating his totem pole raising in Old Massett, and my very first Northwest Coast Indian art purchase—a thunderbird print Robert was marketing for seven dollars (Burke Museum #1998–90/150). I especially liked the design because I had come across the inspiration for it, a tombstone in the Old Massett cemetery carved in 1912 by the legendary Haida artist Charles Edenshaw. I bought two thunderbird prints, actually—one for myself and one as a gift for my dissertation adviser, Ed Hall. A collection was born.

Collectors—and I do not claim to be one—and their activity, collecting, are a source of endless fascination. Collecting is a passion, a hunger. It is about acquiring and possessing. If you are truly a collector, you cannot collect too much. Psychoanalysts are fond of searching for the roots of collecting in unfulfilled childhood needs (Muensterberger 1994). Books have been written about the odd things that people collect and the odd people who collect them (Alsop 1982; Elsner and Cardinel 1994). Collectors themselves have enthusiastically reflected on what it means to be a collector (Benjamin 1968).

Consider George Heye, whose collection of Native American artifacts now comprises the

National Museum of the American Indian (King and Little 1986). A wealthy New York businessman, he acquired his first piece of Native American art in 1897, when he worked as a civil engineer in Arizona. He bought a rawhide shirt for five dollars from the Navajo woman he watched make it and was, then and there, he later confessed, bitten by the collecting bug. Heye filled whole railroad cars with his purchases and rented a series of lofts in New York City to house his growing collection. He then went in search of a museum to house his collection, bringing it first to the University Museum at the University of Pennsylvania and then to the museum in New York City that came to bear his name—the Museum of the American Indian, Heye Foundation, completed in 1916. His collection totaled a million artifacts; he spent his entire fortune on it. Heye, with his vast wealth, is perhaps an extreme example, but his story serves to remind us: museums are built on the habits of collectors. To put it another way, had the Blackman Hall Collection of silkscreen prints, acquired by the Burke Museum in 1998, depended on the bent of my personality, the "collection" would have consisted of only as many prints as could be hung on the walls, perhaps 66 instead of 1,166. Surely not worth the attention of the Burke.

Ed Hall, however, has always been an irrepressible collector. When he was a boy, he collected stamps. Later, as an anthropologist, he collected books, especially rare ethnographic and archaeological works from his area of interest, northern Alaska and the Arctic. Before we married in 1977, he collected shells. Not the wave-worn kind you pick up on the beach, but the shells you read about in publications like *Molluscan Digest* and the *Journal of Conchology* (both of which he subscribed to). Cowries and crown shells. Rare shells, expensive shells. Like all collectors, Ed needed a place to put his collection. He was teaching at Ohio State University at the time, and he had seen some collection cabinets he liked at the nearby Ohio Historical Society, so he decided to order one. He lined the fifteen graduated drawers with black velvet and put down wooden grids he built himself and spray-painted black. Then he filled all the drawers with his shells. In time, the shells would be removed, boxed, and consigned to the loft of our barn. The cabinet drawers would be relined with acid-free cardboard, and filled with more than eleven hundred Northwest Coast serigraphs (fig. 2.2).

Actually, the prints weren't just simply collected; we had an academic interest in Northwest Coast graphics. I was fledged as a cultural anthropologist on the Northwest Coast, doing field research with the Haida, as noted earlier, and I was vitally interested in contemporary Northwest Coast art. Ed, an Alaskan archaeologist, was also interested in Native American art and had built a modest but carefully selected collection of old and new artworks. Study of Northwest Coast graphics gave us a scholarly project to collaborate upon while nourishing our hunger for Northwest Coast art. It gave Ed license to follow his collector's instinct, and it justified for me the periodic purchases, the pile of prints (roughly sixty-five a year) that were accumulating in the cabinet drawers.

The late 1970s was an exciting time to launch a study of Northwest Coast Indian graphics. A number of Northwest Coast Indian artists as well as some non-Indian artists had been working in the medium for a decade. A growing market for the art existed. Visitors to Victoria, Vancouver, and Seattle found serigraphs an arresting and affordable art form. Several artists had produced a sizable body of work: Kwagiulth artist Tony Hunt, for example, had done thirty-three prints by 1977, Nuu-chah-nulth artist Art Thompson, forty-eight. In northern British Columbia, near Hazelton, a distinctive graphic style had developed at the

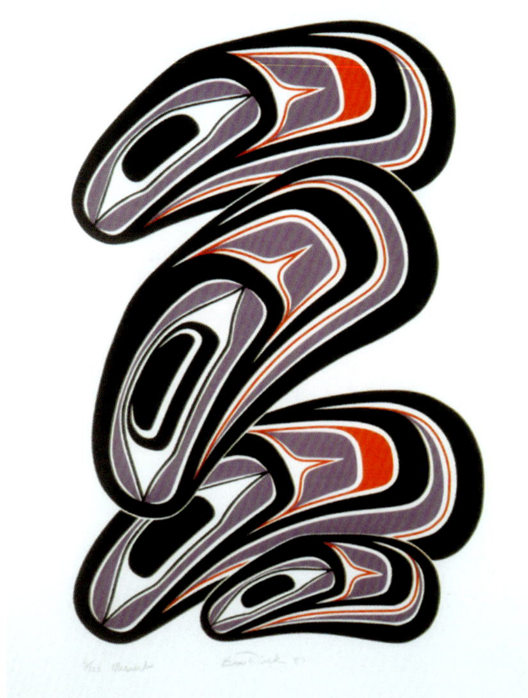

FIGURE 2.2 Beau Dick (Kwakwaka'wakw). *Mussels*, 1987. Serigraph, 20 × 14.7 in. Blackman Hall Collection, Burke Museum #1998–90/256.

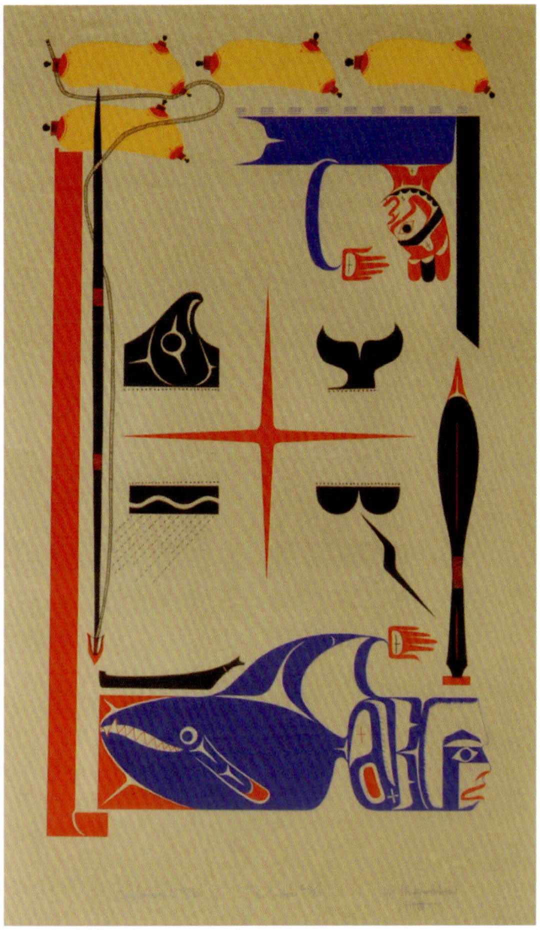

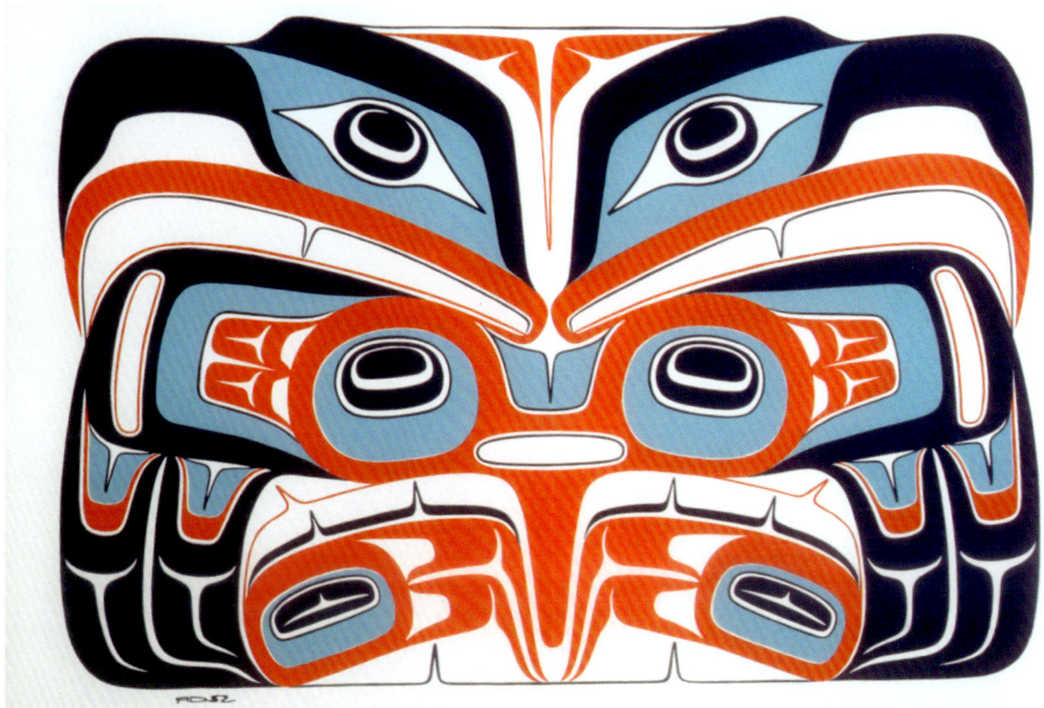

FIGURE 2.3 Ron Hamilton (Nuu-chah-nulth). *Poo'witsa (Whaler's Dream)*, 1977. Serigraph, 36.75 × 24.5 in. Blackman Hall Collection, Burke Museum #1998–90/347.

FIGURE 2.4 Robert Davidson (Haida). *Double Headed Eagle with Baby*, 1982. Serigraph, 7.5 × 10.5 in. Blackman Hall Collection, Burke Museum #1998–90/187.

Kitanmax School of Northwest Coast Indian Art at the cultural heritage center of 'Ksan. And, in 1977, the Northwest Coast Indian Artists' Guild had formed in an attempt to raise and set standards for the art and to call attention to Northwest Coast Indian graphics as fine art. The guild produced two collections, one in 1977 (fig. 2.3) and another in 1978 (Canadian Indian Marketing Services 1977, 1978).

Just as the guild was forming, Ed and I launched a full-scale study of Northwest Coast Indian graphics, interviewing artists, wholesalers, printers, and retailers. Several of these people we returned to over the years to interview again. Our project brought us in touch with Vincent Rickard, owner of Open Pacific Graphics—now Pacific Editions—in Victoria. Rickard is a printer, wholesaler, and retailer of Northwest Coast silkscreen prints. He has printed for more Northwest Coast artists than any other printer. At that time he was thinking of producing an introductory guide to Northwest Coast prints; we were thinking of writing a book on the art as well. The three of us ended up collaborating on a book, *Northwest Coast Indian Graphics*, published in 1981 by the University of Washington Press (Hall, Blackman, and Rickard 1981). The book was never the bestseller we all hoped for, but it did document the beginning and development of an art form that has continued to evolve and flourish.

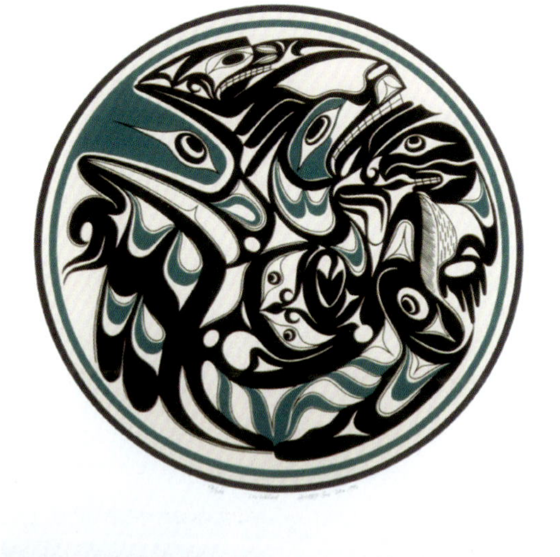

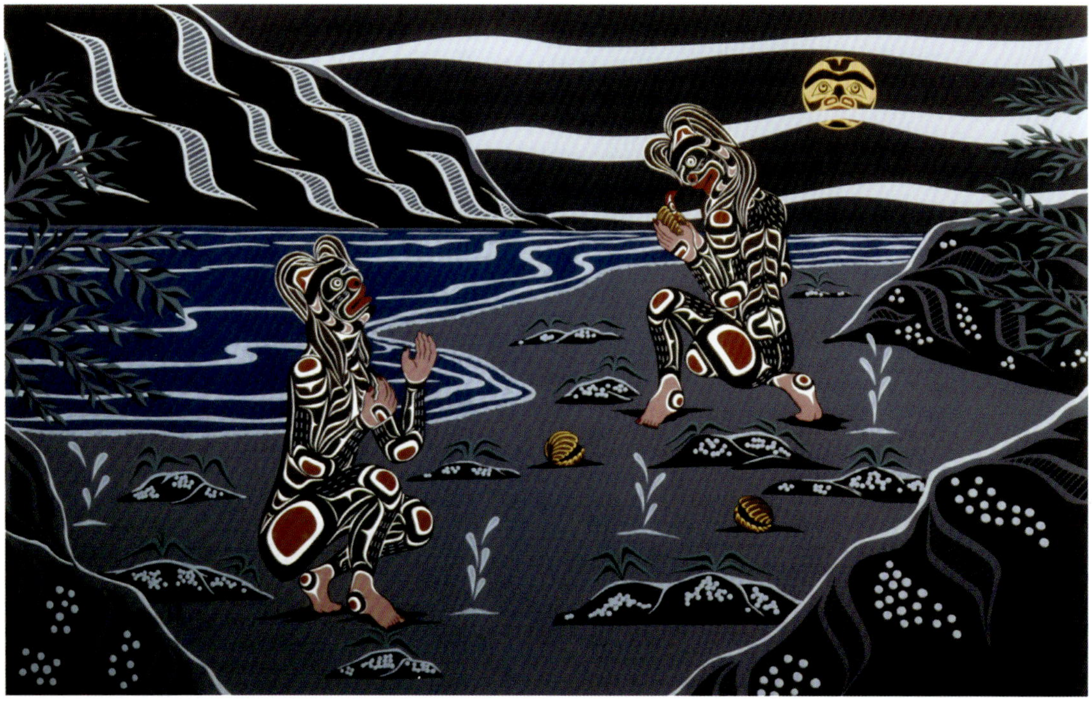

FIGURE 2.5 Art Thompson (Nuu-chah-nulth—Dit-i-daht). *Untitled*, 1992. Serigraph, 21 × 9.5 in. Blackman Hall Collection, Burke Museum #1998–90/1007.

FIGURE 2.6 Mark Henderson (Kwakwaka'wakw—Wei Wai Kum). *Cockle-Hunters (Bookwus)*, 1985. Serigraph, 19.5 × 29.4 in. Blackman Hall Collection, Burke Museum #1998–90/423.

Just as Northwest Coast serigraphs became part of our professional lives as anthropologists, so they became intertwined with Ed's and my personal lives. When we married in 1977, it seemed only appropriate that our wedding announcement be a Northwest Coast graphic, so we commissioned Tim Paul of the Hesquiat Band of Nuu-chah-nulth to create a print featuring Eagle and Killerwhale. The two figures combined into one represent crests of opposite moieties of the Haida, marriageable crests. The eagle was my adoptive crest. When our daughter, Meryn, was born five years later, we asked Robert Davidson to design her birth announcement (fig. 2.4). The resultant design shows the double-headed eagle, the adoptive crest of her mother, the anthropologist, with the fetal eagle inside. Meryn, like her older brother, Justin, had a childhood one-sidedly recalled as a sorry blur of being dragged from gallery to art shop. But as a teenager, she had the pleasant astonishment of seeing her very own birth announcement framed and on the wall of a Vancouver art gallery bearing a price tag of $450. Gallery hopping with one's parent has its rewards after all.

Professionally, Ed and I collaborated on several articles in addition to the book on silkscreens (Blackman and Hall 1981, 1982a, 1986b, 1988). We also delivered papers at professional meetings with fun titles like "The Fuzzy Formline" (1982b), reflecting on who does the art and in what tribal styles, and "Calculating Killerwhales" (1986a)—our limited attempt to crunch numbers. There are, for those who might inquire, ninety-nine killer whale prints in the Blackman Hall Collection.

A collection of serigraphs raises questions about distinctiveness, as serigraphs are not one-of-a-kind items. A collection of prints is similar to a collection of coins or stamps in that prints are produced in multiples—in editions of as few as ten to several hundred. What makes a print collection

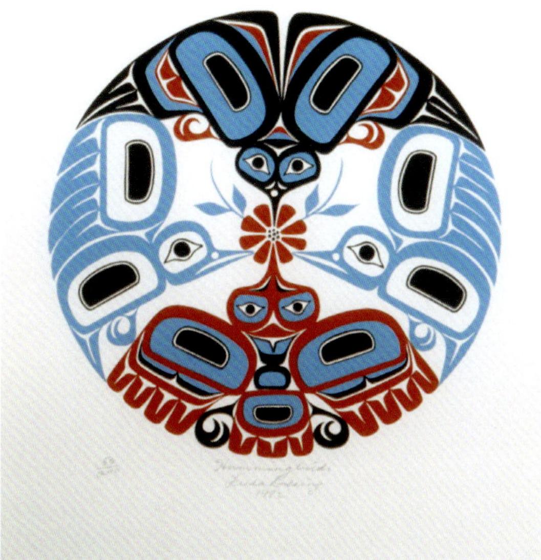

FIGURE 2.7 Frieda Diesing (Haida). *Hummingbirds*, 1982. Serigraph, 14 × 14 in. Blackman Hall Collection, Burke Museum #1998–90/282.

distinctive is its breadth—many works by many different artists, coupled with rare, very limited-edition prints either not commercially sold or not widely offered for sale, such as potlatch gifts and wedding and birth announcements. Commissioning one or more exclusive special editions from an artist bestows uniqueness on a collection. Like any collection, ours is biased toward the tastes of its collectors. There are, for example, no Bill Reid prints in the collection while there is every Art Thompson print that was available for purchase (fig. 2.5). We bought prints that we regarded as works of art; we bought prints that we thought were ugly (and violated the rules of Northwest Coast two-dimensional design) but nonetheless had lessons to offer in their transgressions. We bought prints done by non-Natives knowledgeable about and working in the art style. We collected old prints that documented the early days of silkscreening in Northwest Coast design; we collected prints that we liked because they represented experimentations in design or because they told stories or offered social commentary (fig. 2.6). We collected prints of every tribal style that was available; and we followed the evolving careers of selected artists.

Technology is a wonderful handmaiden to collecting, for it can tell you things about your collection that you might otherwise not know. Like the simple fact that ours contains 1,166 prints. Or that there are more prints by Nuu-chah-nulth artists, 276, than any other tribe; that there are 122 male artists represented in the collection and only 12 female artists (fig. 2.7). We did what scholars typically do to keep track of so much information; we put it in a database, which by today's standards was primitive but in the late 1980s was state of the art.[1] Our record-keeping and the database extended beyond our own collection. We entered all the other Northwest Coast serigraphs we had seen in the course of our research, which by the time we quit in 1988 numbered almost seventeen hundred.

The first version of our database was actually typed on five-by-seven notecards in 1977–78. The fields were ones we thought important as we began the project.[2] But, as we quickly discovered, there were problems in the recording of this information. Most obvious was the difficulty in accurately describing design colors and paper colors. If there was one color of red, there were ten. Was the paper color best described as buff, tan, manila, or cream? Was the dominant design color the color of the primary formline or the color that took up the most space on the paper? Were we even consistent in our labeling? Those problems we left the Burke to wrestle with as they acquired the database with the collection of prints.

A collection not only reveals some of the life history of the collector; it tells other histories as well. The Blackman Hall Collection does not include what is likely the very first silkscreen done by a Northwest Coast Native artist, a Kwakwaka'wakw woman named Ellen Neel. Neel screened simple designs onto scarves in the late 1940s. But the collection does include an example of Charles Gruel's attempt at rendering Northwest Coast design. Gruel was a non-Native whose black designs on white rice paper sold very cheaply in tourist venues in the 1960s and 1970s and whose—I think one can safely say—dreadful renditions of the art form nudged more than one Native artist into silkscreening just to show what "real Northwest Coast design" should look like. The earliest works of "real Northwest Coast design" in serigraphs consisted of single figures, often in single colors, floating on an expanse of paper. Multiple figures followed in time; some designs depicted stories; some artists experimented with perspective and color. Backgrounds and horizons appeared in the work of some artists, and others experimented with the paper surface itself.

Our collection documents the rise of women artists: Haida artists Freida Diesing, who began working in the 1960s, and Sharon Hitchcock, who began in the 1970s; Coast Salish artist Susan Point, the most prolific of the women artists; and younger artists like Kwakwa̱ka̱'wakw Frances Dick, whose first print appeared in 1986.[3]

Spanning more than twenty-five years of Northwest Coast silkscreening, the collection also offers a look at the careers of individual artists. Ken Mowatt's work from 'Ksan is one of the most striking examples (fig. 2.8). His style has developed from the traditional, static two-dimensional formline style, to an explosion of form into freedom, to highly abstract creations.

The collection reveals the personal histories of some artists. Wedding and birth announcements, housewarmings, potlatch invitations, and potlatch gifts are among the prints.

When a museum purchases and then exhibits a collection, it gives that collection a visibility and an authority that it didn't previously have. Elevating the personal collection to the realm of public museum exhibit renders the ordinary extraordinary, validating both the collection and the collectors. In 1998 the Blackman Hall Collection went from the living room print cabinet to the gallery walls of the Burke Museum. And it felt good to see it there.[4] It is both a curious and exciting experience to have your collection curated and exhibited by someone else. I cannot help but see these prints differently than I did when they lay in drawers, than when Ed and I were studying and writing about them. Looking at a two-story wall of 182 massed, framed prints in the gallery, I saw them for the first time *as a collection*. For me, the best thing about this personal collection going to a museum was that it could be studied again and again by others who have a scholarly or artistic interest in Northwest Coast graphics. And now, twelve years later, that indeed has happened. However, simply touring the exhibit at the time,

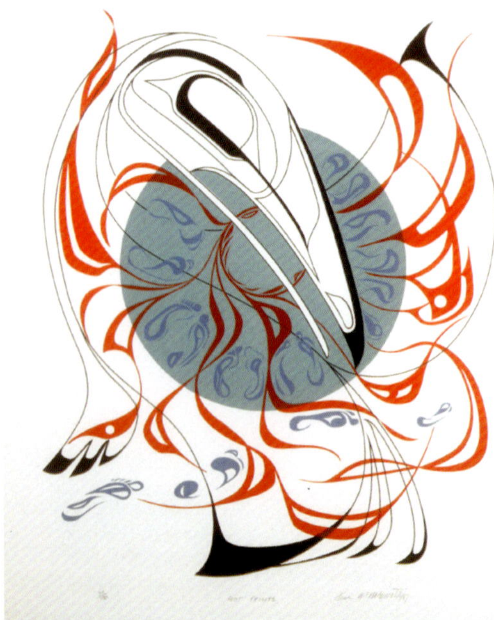

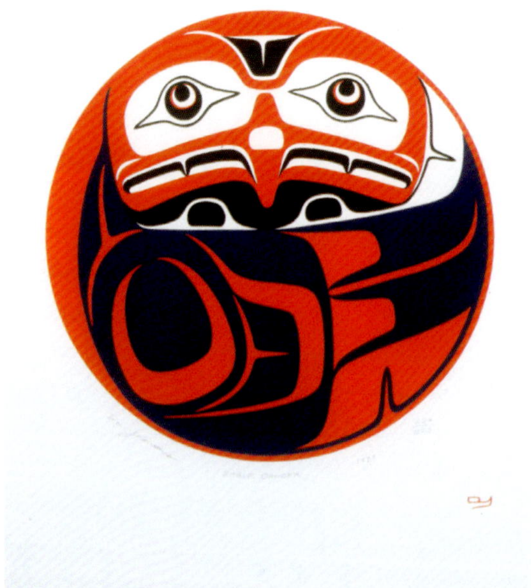

FIGURE 2.8 Ken Mowatt (Gitksan). *Foot Prints*, 1987. Serigraph, 22.5 × 15 in. Blackman Hall Collection, Burke Museum #1998–90/700.

FIGURE 2.9 Donald Yeomans (Haida). *Eagle Dancer*, 1980. Potlatch gift, serigraph, 13 × 11 in. Blackman Hall Collection, Burke Museum #1998–90/1152.

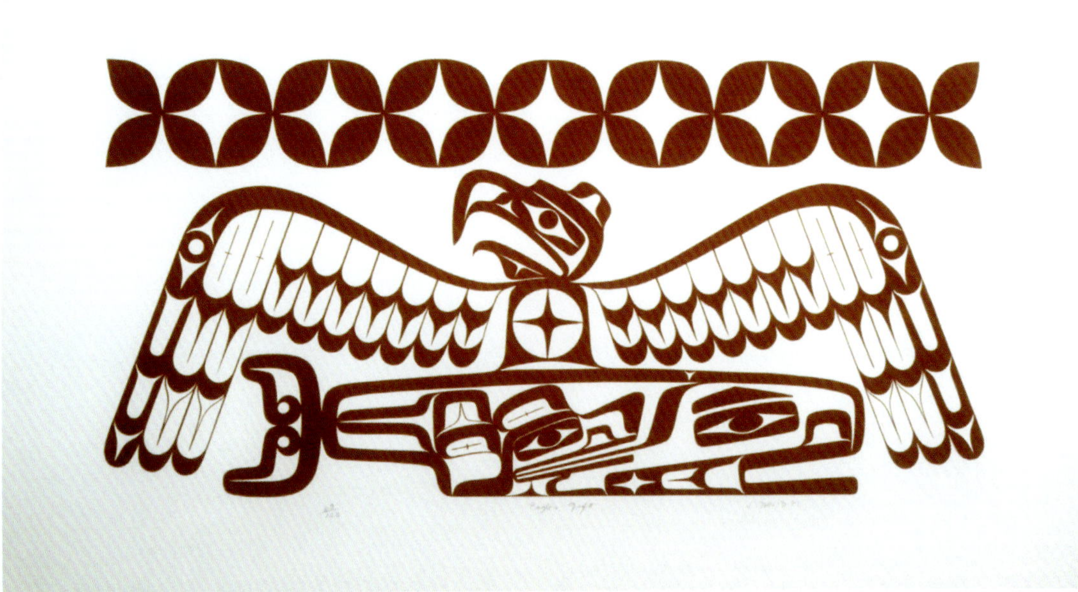

FIGURE 2.10 Joe David (Nuu-chah-nulth—Tla-o-qui-aht). *Eagle's Gift*, 1981. Serigraph, 18 × 28 in. Blackman Hall Collection, Burke Museum #1998–90/115.

I saw something of what others might pull from this collection that Ed and I did not.

Take, for example, the connection between ceremony and Northwest Coast graphics. It is obvious that potlatches inspire the creation of silkscreen prints—as invitation cards, as potlatch gifts, and even as fundraisers for the potlatch itself. But until the exhibit I was not aware of how interconnected such influences might be. Two potlatches, hosted by Robert Davidson, one in 1980 and the other in 1981, resulted in the creation of at least six prints by four different artists. The family dance curtain (Burke Museum #1998–90/967), which was the model for a print by Art Thompson, was used at Robert's 1980 potlatch, "Celebration of the Living Haida." A print titled *Eagle Rising* (Burke Museum #1998–90/966), by Art Thompson, was inspired by that potlatch. The title is a referent to Robert Davidson's crest and Haida name. The inspiration for Don Yeomans's print *Eagle Dancer* (see fig. 2.9) was Reg Davidson's performance at the 1980 potlatch of an eagle dance in which he wore an eagle headdress.

Robert's Davidson's 1981 potlatch, *xa•adaa 7laa git'lang 7isis*, "Children of the Good People," was announced with a card bearing the design of Raven and Eagle, the two matrilineal divisions representing the Haida Nation. A circle of human faces surrounds the central figures. A print of the same design was given to potlatch guests (Burke Museum #1998–90/185).[5] At his 1981 potlatch, Robert Davidson adopted into his eagle clan Nuu-chah-nulth artist Joe David. David, in turn, commemorated his adoption with a print titled *Eagle's Gift*, showing a supernatural eagle or thunderbird surmounting a whale with a wolf inside its body (fig. 2.10). The cycle was completed ten years later, in 1991, when Joe David reciprocally adopted Robert Davidson. A print depicting the wolf robe Robert had been given was handed out as a gift at the potlatch (Burke Museum #2002–20/6).

It has been twelve years since the Burke exhibit *Graphic Culture: Northwest Coast Prints from the Blackman-Hall Collection*, twelve years since I have seriously thought about silkscreen prints as I and my research have moved on to other areas. In revising the essay that I read at the opening of that exhibit for this edited volume, I revisited the Blackman Hall Collection of prints and viewed two other collections of Northwest Coast prints at the Burke, all online from home.[6] A total of 1,876 prints—a number conferring on the Burke the distinction of being the world's second largest holder of Northwest Coast silkscreen prints. Quite a few of these prints postdate the most recent ones from the Blackman Hall Collection, which date to 1992.

From the Burke my virtual journey took me to galleries in Seattle, Portland, Ottawa, Vancouver, and Victoria searching for graphic works of Northwest Coast artists who had begun printmaking in the years following our record-keeping of Northwest Coast silkscreen artists. The number was impressive. I counted more than fifty artists

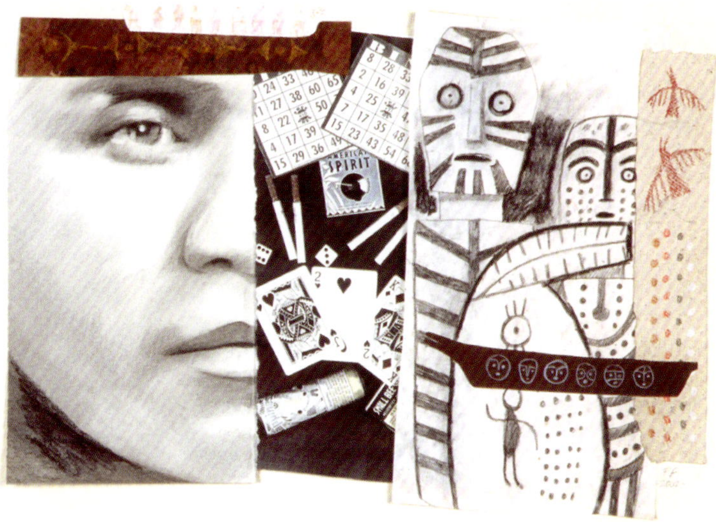

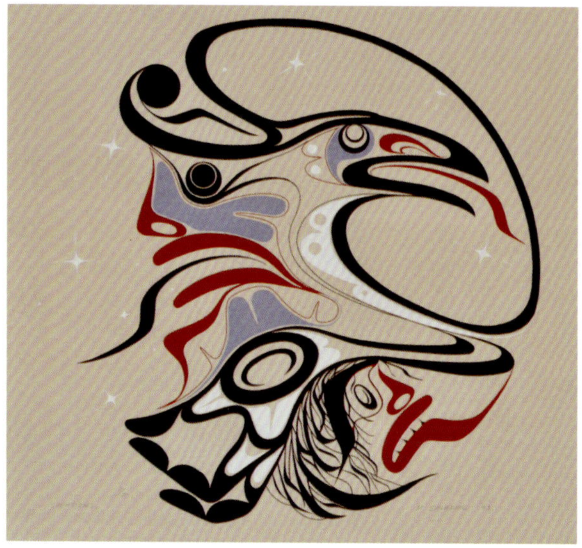

in addition to the 134 represented in the Blackman Hall Collection, almost all of them still male. Appearing in their works, rendered in traditional colors and recognizable tribal styles, were familiar figures from tribal traditions—*sisiutls*, lightning serpents, thunderbirds, frogs, salmon, and eagles as well as designs drawn from well-known Native narratives. Though the thematic content of these prints are by and large traditional, a few, like their predecessors, have used graphic arts as political commentary. In his collage *New Spirit Journey*, S'Klallam artist Roger Fernandes questions Native peoples' relationship with the spirit world in the new casino economy (fig. 2.11). These more recent artists, like others before them, continue to push the boundaries of the formal graphic design style (fig. 2.12). Along with these mostly younger artists, the first generation of silkscreen artists like Susan Point, Richard Hunt, Mark Henderson, and Robert Davidson continue to produce exciting graphic works (figs. 2.13 and 2.14).[7]

A virtual journey through the contemporary Northwest Coast print market invariably raises the question of the impact the online presence of so many Northwest Coast graphic works, in both museums and art galleries, is having on artists in respect to the communication of designs and ideas. And what is the impact on the scholarly study of the art form? The online wealth of images is overwhelming. Do an online search for Susan Point, or Richard Hunt, or any of the other artists mentioned here and you will get pages of images, artists' websites, and the galleries and museums that house their works.

Forty-plus years after the first Northwest Coast silkscreen prints appeared, it is exciting to see this medium continuing to evolve in the hands of a new generation of printmakers. It is both refreshing and reassuring that Northwest Coast silkscreen prints continue to provide the collector of modest means with a quality piece of art at an affordable price.

FIGURE 2.11 Roger Fernandes (Coast Salish—S'Klallam). *New Spirit Journey*, 2002. Collage, 20.25 × 25.75 in. Gift of Simon Ottenberg, Burke Museum #2005–61/1.

FIGURE 2.12 Manual Salazar (Coast Salish—Cowichan). *Creations*, 1993. Serigraph, 20 × 22 in. Gift of Simon Ottenberg, Burke Museum #2004–141/25.

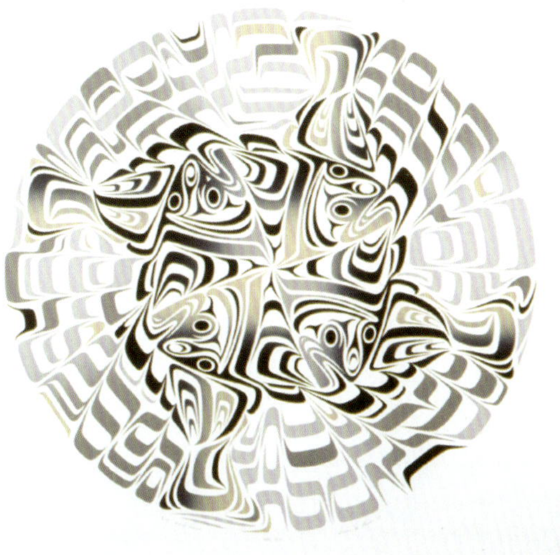

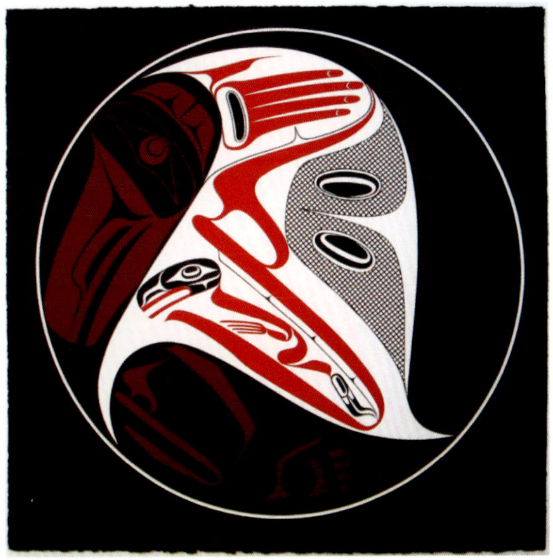

FIGURE 2.13 Susan A. Point (Coast Salish—Musqueam). *Halibut*, 2007. Serigraph, 30 × 30 in. Burke Museum #2007–12/1.

FIGURE 2.14 Robert Davidson (Haida). *Innocent Bystander*, 2000. Serigraph, 25.6 × 25.4 in. Gift of Arthur B. Steinman, Burke Museum #2004–2/385.

NOTES

1 That information from our personal database has been incorporated into the Burke's collection database.

2 The categories included the following: Artist, Tribal Affiliation, Date of Print, Title of Print, Design, Total Run, Proof Number of Print Seen, Print Size (height and width, in centimeters), Design Size (height and width, in centimeters), Paper Color, Print Colors (in order of dominance), Printer, Location of Print, Date of Entry, Price, and Comments.

3 Point's work is more fully represented in the Burke Museum's Simon Ottenberg Collection of Salish prints.

4 The exhibit *Graphic Culture* featured the Blackman Hall Collection along with other prints from the Burke Museum's collection

5 This design is now used on the flag of the Haida Nation.

6 The other two collections are the Simon Ottenberg Collection and the Arthur B. Steinman Collection.

7 Kwakwa̱ka̱'wakw artist Doug Cranmer (1927–2006) was also in the first generation of serigraph artists (see pl. 31 in the portfolio) (Kramer 2012).

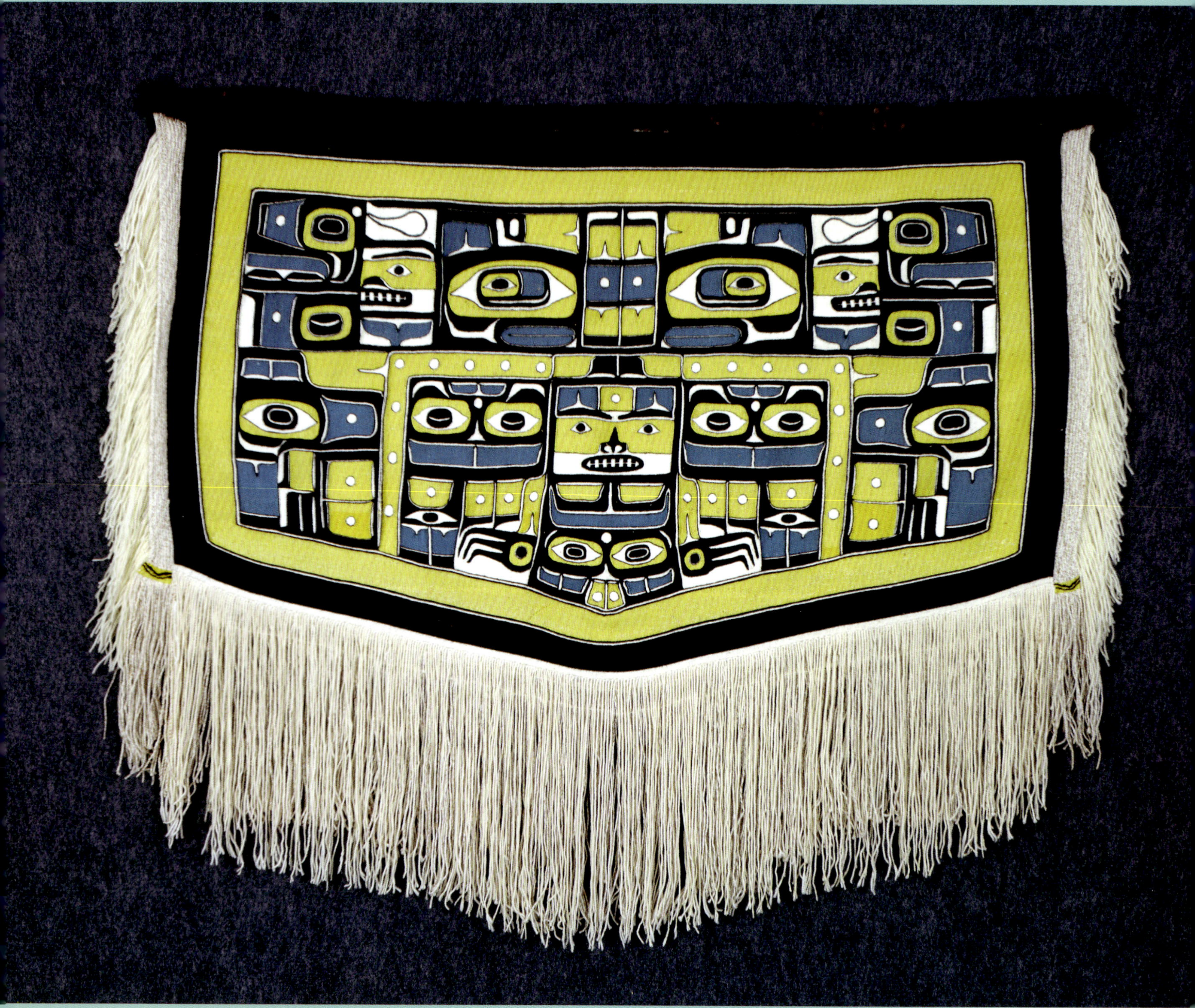

THREE

THE *NAAXIIN*

Robe of Sacred Honor

EVELYN VANDERHOOP

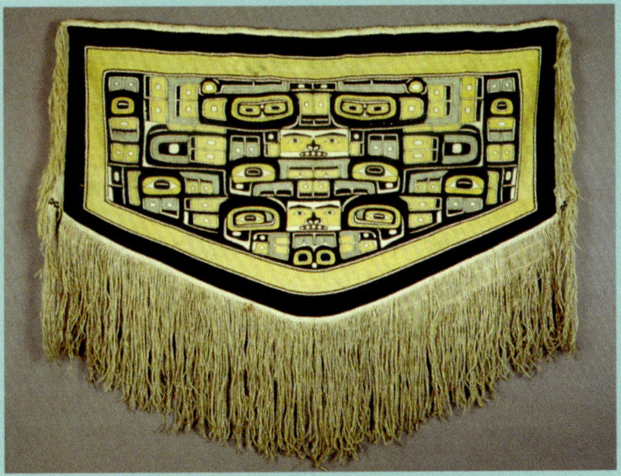

FIGURE 3.1 *Diving Whale Design Robe* (Tlingit), nineteenth century. Cedar bark, mountain goat wool. 63.4 × 53.2 in. Walter Waters Collection, Burke Museum #1–1587.

THE islands, fjords, and mountainous coastline of the Pacific Northwest are host to more than twenty First Nations, speaking distinctly different languages and dialects. Out of the rugged environment and diverse population emerged a complex, stylistic, and sophisticated art. Undulating formline designs wrap symmetrically around objects as grand as monumental totem poles, as simple as the elegant soapberry spoon. The designs served the ancestors of the coastal nations as an implicit language. Unlike the spoken languages that kept secrets from each neighboring tribe, this language of visual art used bold statements to be understood by all—warriors, wanderers, and traders—within the broad Northwest Coast range.

The language of Pacific Northwest Coast art manifests in the exquisite *naaxiin* textiles. *Naaxiin* is the word used by the Haida and Tlingit for the formline-designed chiefs robe now commonly referred to as "Chilkat" (fig. 3.1). The designs of *naaxiin* regalia display the identity, prestige, and power of the owner. Woven formlines of black, blue-green, and yellow create symbolic, abstract images of clan crest figures. Kinsmen as well as members of neighboring tribes are able to distinguish where each person fits within their social hierarchy. Clan membership and social position is stated by design. Women of the Tlingit, Haida, and Tsimshian cultures weave the regalia as dictated by painted pattern boards. Men would paint the boards with images inherited by the chiefs and nobility. Ancestral privileges gained by interaction with natural phenomena and supernatural beings were recounted in stories and symbolized in crest designs. The *naaxiin* regalia beautifully illustrates these prerogatives.

Aprons with designs created from shamans' visions and executed in the weaver's twill-twine techniques are thought to be some of the first objects woven in the *naaxiin* style. Power from the spirit helpers was channeled through the shaman. While dispelling evil spirits and curing the sick, the shaman was aided by the woven image

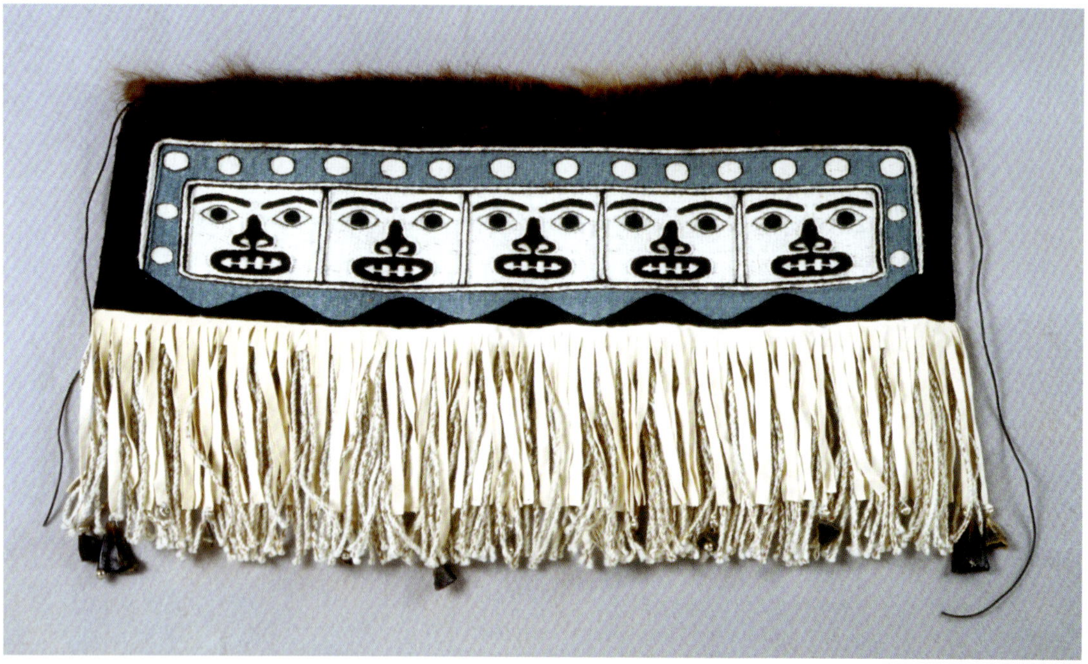

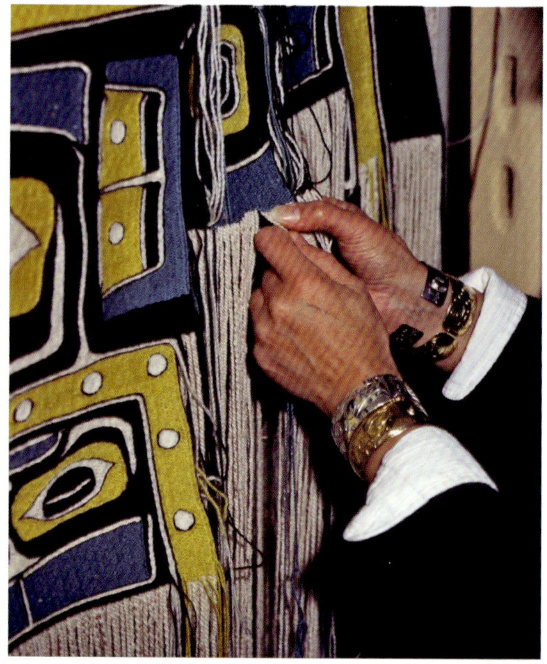

along with spirit songs and sounds. Woven regalia could display messages of intention as they did when they were designed for warfare. The wives of Haida warriors would weave war belts out of whale sinew. Figures of human beings were woven into the belts, which represented the spirit of future war captives (fig. 3.2) (Swanton 1905a: 55).

The visual language of the arts was intended to extend beyond the comprehension of humans. Its messages were composed also for the natural and supernatural worlds of sky, forest, and sea. Travelers and warriors, wearing designs honoring the sky and sea spirits, were assured safe and victorious canoe expeditions. Donning a woven pattern honoring the forest and sea beings guaranteed a triumphant hunt. The weavers of the woven regalia held a specialized position within their community. They were transformers, converting raw material—inner red and yellow cedar bark, mountain goat wool, nettle fiber, deer hooves, puffin beaks, martin and sea otter fur—into woven objects of communication amid spiritual and natural realms. Mountain goat wool was one of the primary fibers that made up *naaxiin* weavings. Mountain goat spirits were shaman helpers. Hunters inherited or earned the right to pursue the elusive mountain goat.

In the spring the goat shed its winter coat, and privileged gatherers picked the wool from towering mountain paths. Women from villages close to the mountain ranges produced the thin, twisted weft of mountain goat wool: *lis* is the Haida word for this trade item. Cooperative trade was essential for the *naaxiin* weavers of the Pacific Northwest Coast. Northern Tlingit such as the Chilkat had to trade for the cedar that does not flourish in their region. Mountain goats do not reside on the mountains of Haida Gwaii, so the Haida needed to trade for the wool. The copper often used for producing the blue dye was a prestigious trade item as well, and Coastal weavers had to trade with people who lived further inland for the wolf lichen that is necessary for the rich yellow hue of *naaxiin* regalia.

FIGURE 3.2 Evelyn Vanderhoop (Haida). *Spirit Belt*, 2008–9. Mountain goat wool, cedar bark, leather, beaver fur, deer hooves, beads. 15 × 27 in. Purchased with funds donated by Lawrence Christian, Burke Museum #2009–183/1.

FIGURE 3.3 Evelyn Vanderhoop weaving, 2000. Photograph by Helen Carlson.

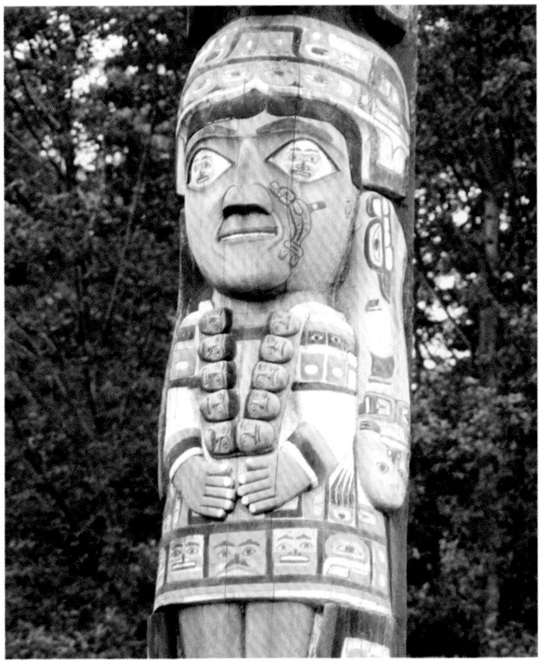

FIGURE 3.4 John Wallace (Haida). *Master Carpenter* pole, Totem Bight Park, Ketchikan, Alaska, 1941. Burke Museum negative #2008–18/275. Photograph by Adelaide de Menil.

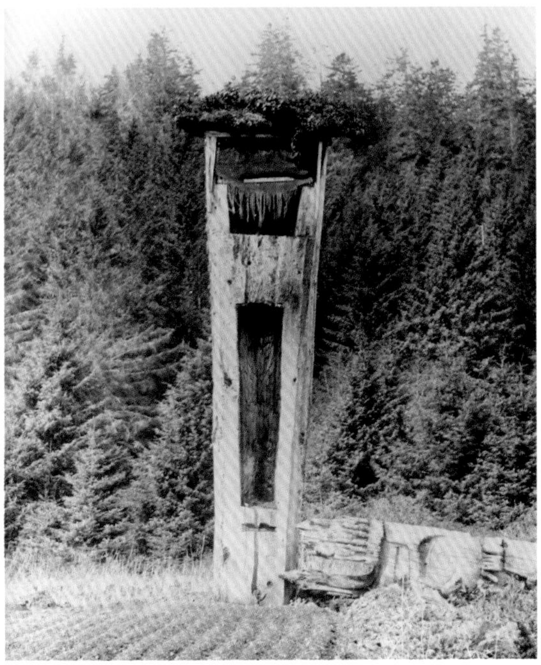

FIGURE 3.5 Chief Skidegate's grave monument with robe. Image PN5163, courtesy of Royal BC Museum. Photograph by Maynard, 1884.

The warp yarn used for *naaxiin* weaving is composed of thinly shredded yellow cedar bark strips joined together with the mountain goat wool. These two fibers, cedar and wool, are rolled down the thigh into Z-twisted ply. The inner bark of the yellow cedar adds a stiff core to the warp. This prevents bunching up of the soft goat wool warps when twined with the wefts into circles, U-forms, and ovoids. Only the hands of the weaver work the *naaxiin* woven garment: there is no other tool, no heddle, and no shuttle (fig. 3.3). The warp is hung from a simple gravity-weighted bar loom. It is up to the weaver's fingers to produce the correct tension and placement of warp and weft yarns. The cedar-stiffened wool aides in attaining the proper tension, but there may have been another reason that cedar was incorporated into *naaxiin* regalia. In stories set during mythical times, cedar bark woven garments had purifying and restorative powers. Often a legend's hero brought a companion back to life by rubbing him with a cedar bark garment. The *naaxiin* mantle with its mystical elements—mountain goat and cedar—was a sacred object of esteem.

The five-sided *naaxiin* chief's robe is wrapped with martin or sea otter fur along its top edge. The sides have an attached plaited, folded braid. This side braid and the shallow V-shaped bottom edge have an added layer of mountain goat wool fringe. The inner design is surrounded with broad black and yellow borders. Borders within basket designs were intended to keep spiritual elements contained. The wide *naaxiin* borders, woven before the inner pattern, allude to the spirit core of the central design of Killer Whale, Eagle, Wolf, Beaver, Raven, or Thunderbird. In the Tsimshian language, the robe is called a *gwis-halait*. During winter ceremonies of the past, a tsimshian chief filled his clan's spiritual role of a *wi-halait* (great dancer). In this role he would distribute power to initiates of secret societies. The robe, with its bold iconography and swaying fringes, must have added greatly to the dramatization of this power transfer.

The Haida had secret societies also, and chiefs had the role of initiating novices. Eagle and Raven are the moieties for the Haida. The two groups fulfilled reciprocal roles during life's milestones, such as puberty rites, house erecting, funeral rites, and chief inauguration feasts, as well as secret society initiations. The *naaxiin* robe was an important part of the chief's apparel for his role in the ceremonies conducted for these momentous events.

Winter ceremonies among the Tlingit centered on the veneration of ancestors. Clans own the *naaxiin* robes as part of their ancestral treasures called *at.oow*. Handed down from one generation to the next, *at.oow* are brought out during memorial potlatches to display affluence and status. The robes could also be held as individual property among both the Haida and the Tlingit. Early photographs show robes attached to grave houses as well as on totem poles; some poles even include carved images of *naaxiin* weavings (fig. 3.4). An 1880s photograph of Chief Skidegate's mortuary pole shows a robe attached behind the missing panel that enclosed the coffin (fig. 3.5). Robes displayed in this manner memorialized an individual's honor during his life and identified him in the spirit world.

Wealth, power, and social standing was of utmost importance among the Northwest Pacific Coast cultures. Hosting feasts and gifting guests established and upheld honor for the clans and chiefs of all the coastal nations. Often a hosting chief would cut a *naaxiin* robe to pieces and distribute the fragments to show his extreme wealth. Distribution of blanket sections was an element in Haida winter ceremonies; these remnants were called "spirit belts" (see fig. 3.2). They were handed out as restitution to guests who had been injured by secret society initiates during their spirit dances (Swanton 1905a: 164, 165). Remnants were later pieced into headdresses, dance leggings, purses, dance shirts, and aprons. In turn, these too became clan treasures.

The ethnologist John Swanton collected stories from the Haida and the Tlingit in the early twentieth century. These were recollections of myths, legends, and clan origin accounts that had been passed from generation to generation by trained oral historians. Through these ancient adventures, knowledge is gained of how apparel was used within a cultural context. In a story collected from Massett, two Haida chiefs clashed over a gambling debt. Because of this debt owed, one insulted the other by using his image in a disrespectful manner. To reestablish his honor, the one insulted prepared to show wealth by giving property away. *Sangaada* is the Haida word for this face saving event. *Tinaah* (copper shields), fish oil, and bentwood treasure boxes were assembled. Songs were composed and practiced. One of the first preparatory activities was the weaving of a crest robe for the chief. In this same story the chief wears an earring: "And Hai'yas had in one ear a long earring made of strung abalone-shell. But on the side where he was going to speak to Lk!ukaslas, he was not going to wear one. And when the chiefs and the chief's sons spoke to him, he was going to turn the side on which he wore the earring towards them" (Swanton 1908: 756–70). This short excerpt contains the intention of one chief to insult the other by not facing him with his earring-adorned side. This story highlights the power of adornment to communicate.

This clan story provides insight into certain designs. For instance, a robe in the Peabody Harvard Museum, in Cambridge, Massachusetts, has two different geometric designs on each half of the rectangular woven robe. This robe—named the *Swift Robe*, made from pure mountain goat wool of white, yellow, and black geometric designs—is an early precontact chief's robe, predating the *naaxiin* (fig. 3.6). When the robe is draped over the shoulders, the designs are divided down the center of the back. Viewed from one side, the design is totally different than when viewed from the other side. The meanings of the robe's geometric symbols are lost in history. The clan story, together with this unique robe, gives us clues into additional purposes for donning a robe of unspoken messages.

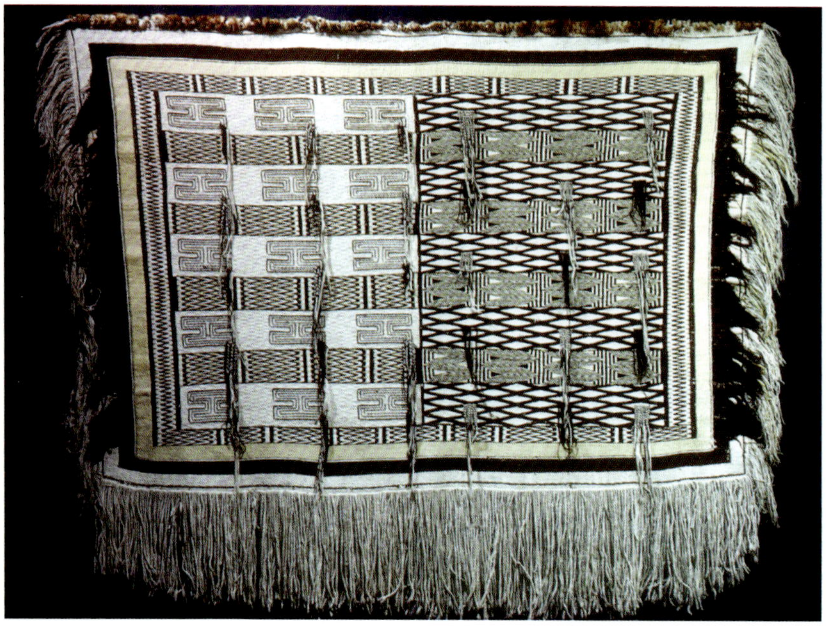

FIGURE 3.6 *Swift Robe* (Tlingit). Mountain goat wool. Courtesy of the Peabody Museum of Archaeology and Ethnology, Harvard University #09–8–10/76401.

Because there are no archaeological remnants of *naaxiin* robes, it is believed to be a relatively recent development, evolving from cedar bark robes and the earlier style geometric-patterned robes, now referred to as Ravenstail (figs. 3.6, 3.7, 3.9). By the time the first explorers to this coast arrived, the *naaxiin* textiles of cedar and wool were already highly developed. Diaries and journals from these early expeditions clearly described the indigenous apparel. The earliest explorer to

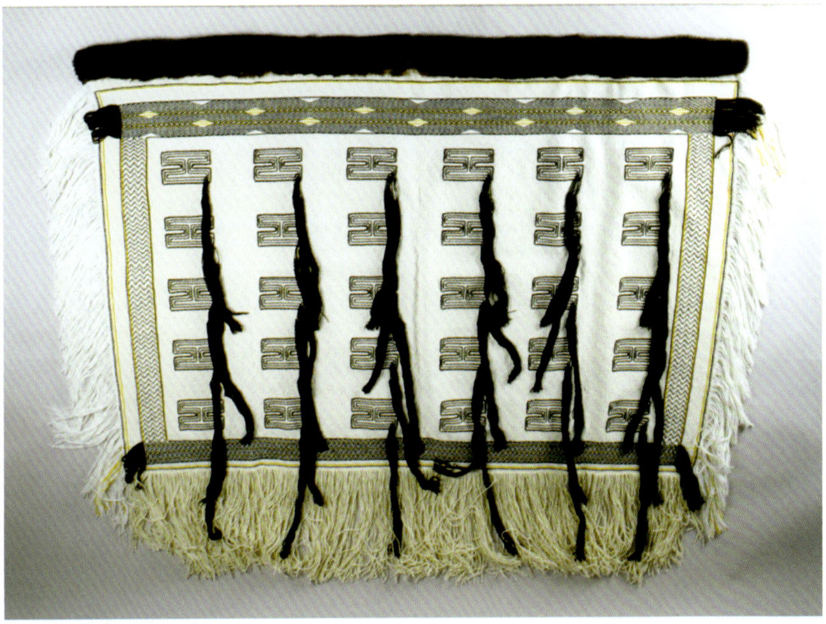

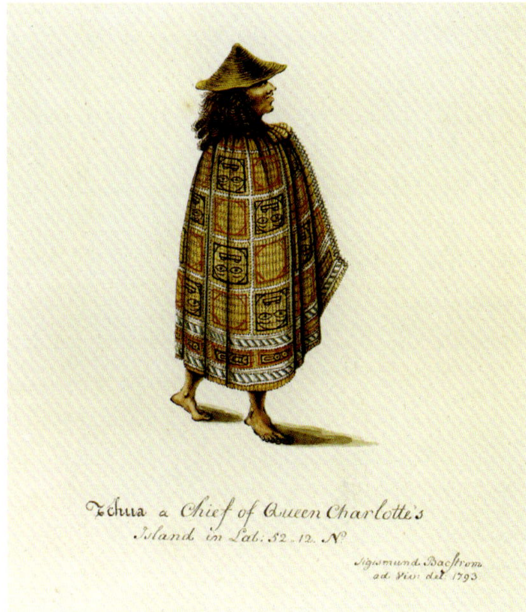

FIGURE 3.7 Marie Oldfield (Haida/Tsimshian) with William White (Tsimshian). *Ravenstail Robe*, 2002. Merino wool, sea otter fur. 52 × 74 in. Gift of Arthur B. Steinman, Burke Museum #2004–2/417.

FIGURE 3.8 Sigismund Bacstrom, *Tchua a Chief of Queen Charlotte's Island in Lat. 52, 12N*, 1793. Watercolor, 10.7 × 7.4 in. Courtesy of Paul Mellon Collection, Yale Collection of Western Americana, Beinecke Rare Book and Manuscript Library.

Haida Gwaii was Juan Pérez aboard the Spanish vessel *Santiago*. At Langara Island, during his trading expedition in 1774, he wrote in his ship's journal the following observation: "All their commerce amounts to giving animal pelts as seals, sea otter and bears. . . . They also have a kind of white wool, which they extract from an unknown species of animal that produces it. They weave beautiful blankets, of which I acquired four. They are not large, but woven and wrought nicely" (Beals 1989: 77).

Fray Juan Crespi, a chaplain with the same exposition, states in his diary: "All appeared with the body completely covered, some with skins of otter and other animals, others with cloaks woven of wool, or a hair which looked like fine wool, and a garment like a cape and covering them to the waist, the rest of the person being clothed in dressed skins or the woven wool cloths of different colors in handsome patterns. Some of these garments have sleeves others have not" (Griffin and Cutter 1969: 192; Wright 2001: 25; De Laguna and Emmons 1991: 235). Artists such as Sigismund Bacstrom, E. F. Burney, José Cardero, and John Webber accompanied early explorations and with pen, ink, and pigments produced portraits of the indigenous people of the coast wearing geometric and formline-patterned wool and cedar bark clothing (fig. 3.8).

Unlike the indigenous tribes of the Eastern Seaboard, contact with European customs did not cause an immediate demise of the Northwest Coast First Nations cultures. The primary intention of the early visitors was trade, not domination. The first seventy-five years brought about a flourishing of the indigenous way of life. With the coming of the *yaatsxaadee*—iron men, as the Haida call them—better tools were available. The new tools allowed easier carving of canoes, monumental heraldic and memorial poles. Hunting and trading sea otter pelts brought many new goods to the Northwest cultures. Ceremonial feasts were lavish with abundant and novel objects of wealth. The European mass-produced blankets were adopted as an important trade item with a set value; they became an early currency among the different villages of the coastal range. Worn over the shoulders, the blanket-turned-robe was embellished for ceremonial wear with sewn appliqué red cloth and shell buttons. These replaced cedar capes and robes that had been painted in the past with red ocher crest designs. The new blanket robes were further adorned with dentalia shells, mother-of-pearl buttons, and abalone shell pieces. The use of the blue-green color and the blue abalone shells were the prerogative of nobility. This may explain why blue, not red, is a standard color within designs of *naaxiin* chief regalia.

First Nations people assimilated the new materials and ideas into their cultures. These changes were reflected in the art of the coast. Human figures with jackets and top hats carved in cedar posts spoke of adventures in such cities as Victoria and Seattle. Egyptian sphinx and circus elephants were carved motifs adopted from book illustrations and newspapers (Wright 2001: 170–71, 204, 277, 290). Sailing ship imagery carved in argillite told of meetings with traders. Imported sheet copper replaced native copper in the prestigious *tinaah*. Cotton twine replaced animal sinew for cordage. Blue military jackets were soaked to bleed the new blue color for dyeing the *naaxiin* weaving wefts. Commercial knitting yarns eventually replaced the *naaxiin* mountain goat weft fibers.

With the coming of settlers and missionaries, a vastly different worldview was introduced to the coast nations. European diseases devastated the population of all the villages of the Pacific Northwest. Shamans were ineffectual against the new sicknesses. First Nation peoples were encouraged to adopt the monotheistic Christian religion. Winter ceremonies did not retain the spiritual rituals of the past. European-style cottages replaced large clan houses. Gone was the stage on which the *naaxiin* robe danced its message of spirit and prestige. Wealth was defined differently by the newcomers' economic system. Trade and barter was replaced with wage jobs and monetary gain. Creating art for curio collectors engaged the traditional skills of carving, painting, and weaving. Weavers made miniature versions of the large utilitarian clam, seaweed, and storage baskets for the growing tourist trade. Men carved miniature totem poles and canoes. It was the northern Chilkat Tlingit who continued to weave the full-size *naaxiin* robe for this latest audience. The Chilkat Tlingit women continued weaving the *naaxiin* into the early 1900s, and because of this, these robes are currently called "Chilkat."

As fluid and flexible as the defining formline, the Pacific Northwest Coast art continues into this current age of dynamic change. Artists span the realms of the mystical past to the innovations of the future to produce art that speaks of the present. For the Northwest textile weavers there has been a recent renaissance. Due to such researchers as Cheryl Samuel and Bill Holm, forgotten techniques have been rediscovered. Weavers are again producing the once extinct Ravenstail regalia (figs. 3.7 and 3.9). Traditional weavers such as Jenny Thlunaut and Delores Churchill as well as Cheryl Samuel have mentored a new generation of textile weavers. This revival has caused some weavers to go further and learn the complex iconography and techniques of the *naaxiin* textiles as well. Unlike the Ravenstail, the continuity of weaving the *naaxiin* has never been broken. Because of the complex design and weaving techniques, *naaxiin* robes demand more than a year to execute, and only a handful of contemporary weavers have taken the challenge to complete a full robe (fig. 3.10). The Ravenstail and *naaxiin* robes continue to be rare and prestigious garments worn by clan leaders and traditional chiefs.

Teaching and passing on the techniques is a very important goal for present-day *naaxiin* weav-

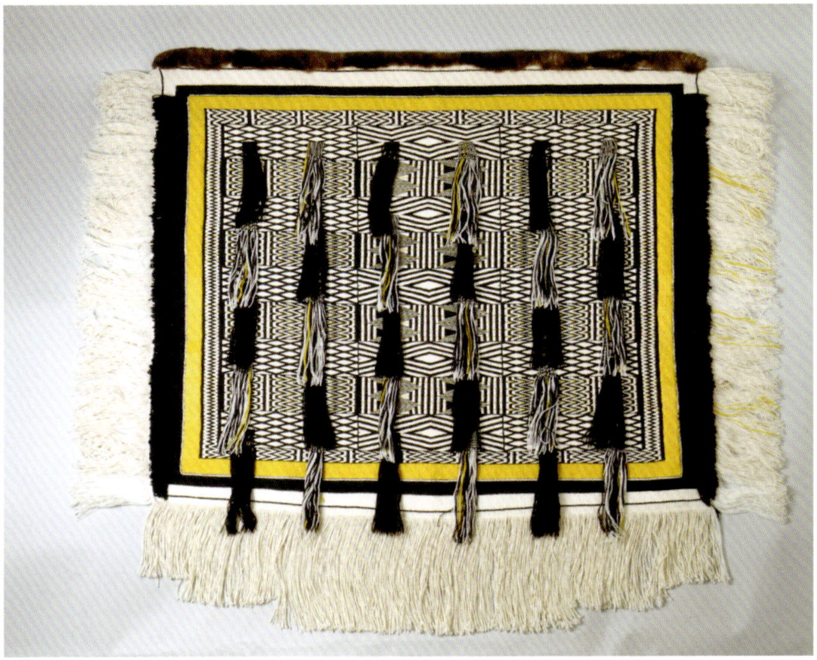

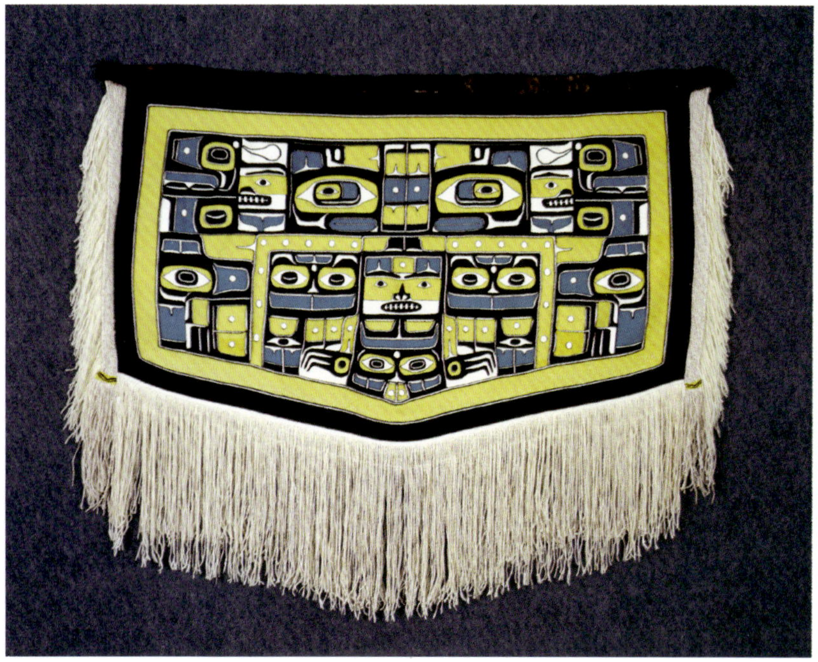

FIGURE 3.9 John Beard with Dawn DiGregorio, Dodie Gannett, Carol Griesmeyer, Eileen Jacobs, Alene Linehan, Fran Mazzara, Darlene Peters (Coast Salish—S'klallam), Paula Sauvageau, Delores Schnitzer, Betty Swinkel, and Shelly Tarbet. *Damascus Three Panel Robe*, 1998. Merino wool, fur, leather. 61 × 66 in. Gift of Damascus Ravenstail Weavers, Burke Museum #2005–124/1.

FIGURE 3.10 Evelyn Vanderhoop (Haida). *Naaxiin Robe*, 2002–3. Merino wool, yellow cedar bark, sea otter fur. Collection of Gayle and Charlie Pancerzewski. Photograph by Jerry McCollum.

ers. Through workshops, classes, and mentoring programs young weavers are practicing the art. Challenged by the standards set by our ancestors, we take up the threads of traditional skills to weave with fresh new ideas. Designs are inspired by ancient clan crests as well as by contemporary stories from our interactions with the constantly changing world of today. Ancient techniques are followed, but because of using new materials such as the commercial S-twisted plied wefts, some weavers have started to S-twine those wefts to maintain the look of ancient patterns. Others choose to keep with the ancestors' Z-twining hand movements. All *naaxiin* woven objects of the past were worked with the Z-twisted weft and twining. The contemporary weavers have many choices with new colors, materials, designs, and object forms, all creatively produced to tell of today's evolving traditions.

Once again, regalia such as leggings, headdresses, pouches, tunics, and dance aprons are being used in the vibrant present-day performance arts of First Nations' song and dance. The *naaxiin* robe with its fluent crest art continues to speak of the everlasting spirit of the people and cultures of the Pacific Northwest Coast.

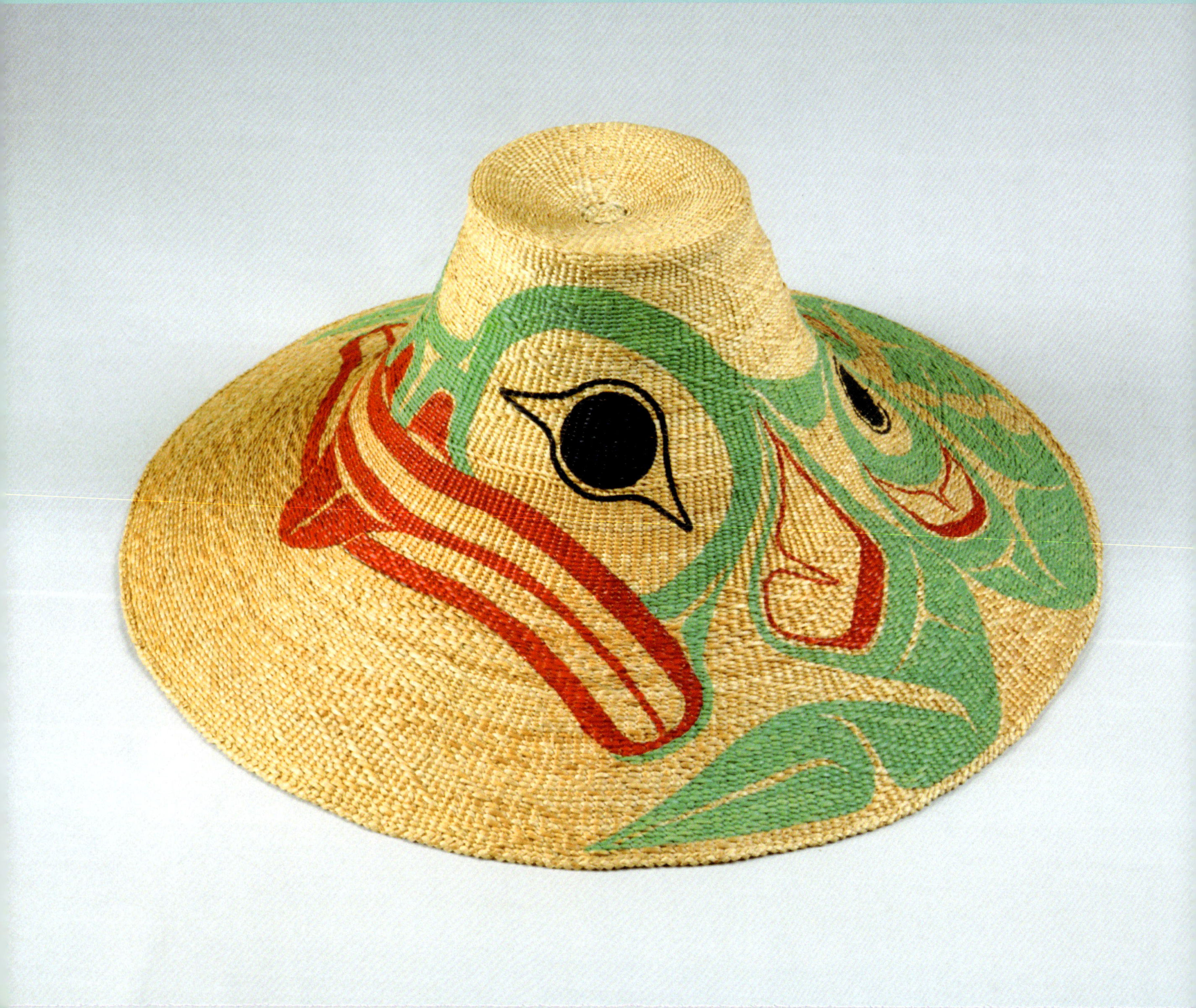

FOUR

WEARING IDENTITY

The Strength of Expression through Personal Adornment

KATHRYN BUNN-MARCUSE

"WHAT shall I wear?"—that age-old question. What considerations does this question engender? We dress for the occasion; we dress to fit in; we dress to stand out; we dress to express; we dress for success. Clothing has always communicated. In cultures without a written language, clothing was a means of expression: of clan or tribal identity, of wealth and power, of resistance to colonial authority. "For our people," says Haida chief 7Idansuu, Jim Hart, "what we wear is who we are. Our jewelry and our clothing represent where we come from. We wear our history" (Chalker, Dubin, and Whiteley 2004: 16).

This chapter explores how both historical and contemporary choices in dress and body adornment—for ceremonial and everyday occasions alike—signal personal allegiances to clan, family, or nation. Examining contemporary choices must include reference to their historical precedents because, as Hart noted, items of personal adornment clothe the wearer in his or her own history, linking past generations to the events of the present. This essay illustrates the shifting roles that personal adornment can play in public displays of identity as well as in the personal construction of identity and social relations. In contrast to much scholarship on Native American adornment that focuses on ceremonial regalia and the expression of rank and status within that context, this chapter compares the use of regalia in ceremonial contexts with the use of personal adornment in nonceremonial moments, illustrating the connections between them. The essay also examines how the value and function of an object may be transmutable depending on context and individual interpretation.

CEREMONIAL REGALIA

Northwest Coast ceremonial regalia is experienced within a defined set of parameters—displayed within the context of the potlatch, feast, dance, funeral, or other ritualized occasion. Historically, it represented the status of the wearer: one's dress articulated a particular social position within clans or moieties; adornment was an additional layer indicating social status—class or rank. The ensemble that chiefs and other high-ranking individuals wear represents all the wealth and family connections available to them. The painted, appliquéd, or woven designs on the regalia can signify clan affinities, such as the raven design seen on the apron by William White (fig. 4.1) or the frog painted by Alfred Adams on a spruce root hat by Primrose Adams (fig. 4.2).

Today the basic parts of ceremonial ensemble remain similar to that worn in the nineteenth century. High-ranking individuals continue to wear crest hats (among the Tlingit) or headdresses with carved frontlets. This chief's headdress is (and was) often worn on the central and northern Northwest Coast during a welcome dance to greet visitors to the village, although they are and have been worn during other ceremonial occasions as well. The carved wooden frontlet typically represents a family crest and fronts a headdress (fig. 4.3). Carved and painted, the frontlet is often surrounded by inlaid pieces of abalone and, on the northern coast, topped with a row of red-shafted flicker feathers. This carving is attached to a frame that itself is covered in cloth, and the sides and back of the frame are ornamented with fur or swan skin thick with down; numerous ermine skins trail from the rear of the frame, draping the dancer's back with the white pelts that sway in time with the rhythm. The headdress is crowned with sea lion whiskers that often hold a loose stuffing of bird (preferably eagle) down, meant to float out and around the dancer. Nineteenth-century frontlets expressed concerns of the time, illustrating chiefly prerogatives; today's frontlets often follow older forms, while some play on contemporary politics or issues (fig. 4.4).

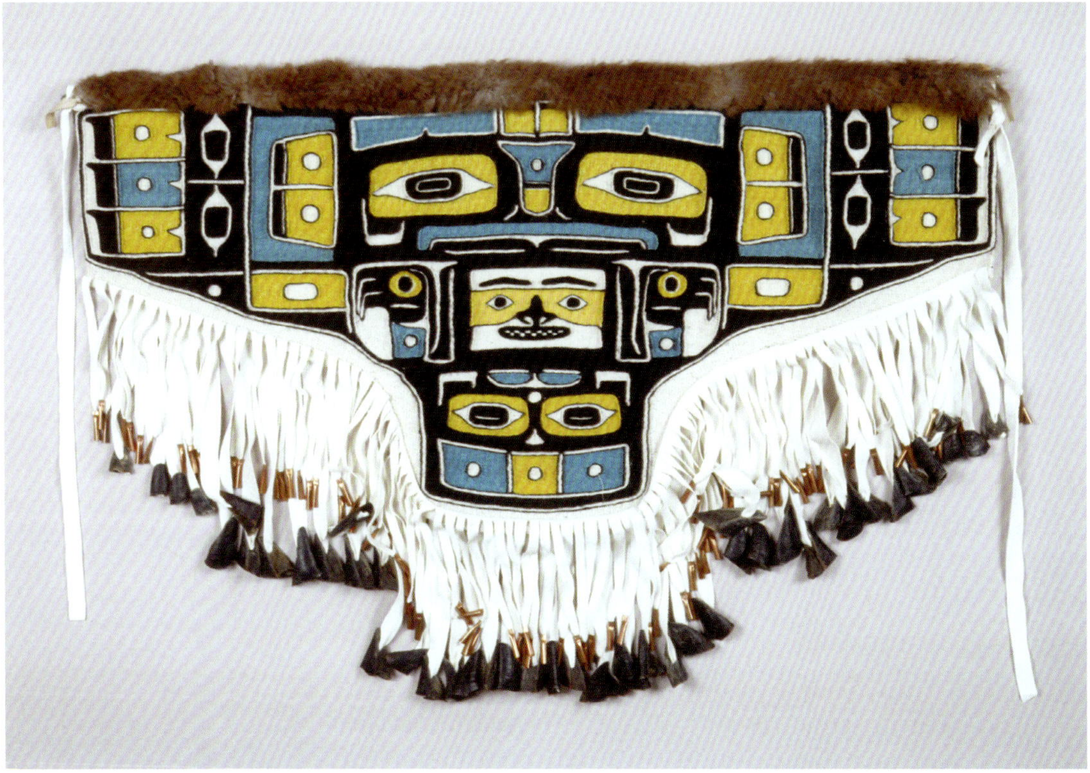

FIGURE 4.1 William White (Tsimshian). *All My Ancestors Are Raven* apron, 2000. Wool, cedar bark. 21.3 × 33.1 in. Gift of Arthur B. Steinman, Burke Museum #2004–2/103.

In addition to the headdress, a speaker or dancer may wear a woven robe or tunic known as *naaxiin* (often called "Chilkat"), although button blankets are used as well, especially in the central coast region. Ravenstail robes, worn by chiefs in the late eighteenth century, are now being worn again on ceremonial occasions (see figs. 3.6, 3.7, and 3.9). A truly rich ensemble would include a beaded or painted apron and leggings (see figs 4.1 and fig. 4.5). The Tlingit alone included unique elements, such as beaded collars and eight-tabbed, beaded octopus bags in a ceremonial ensemble. Then, as now, ceremonial clothing engaged more than just the visual sense. Many blankets, tunics, and aprons were adorned with items that would augment the aural presence of the wearer. Deer hooves and puffin beaks would rattle as the dancer or speaker moved. With the introduction of trade metals, embellishments

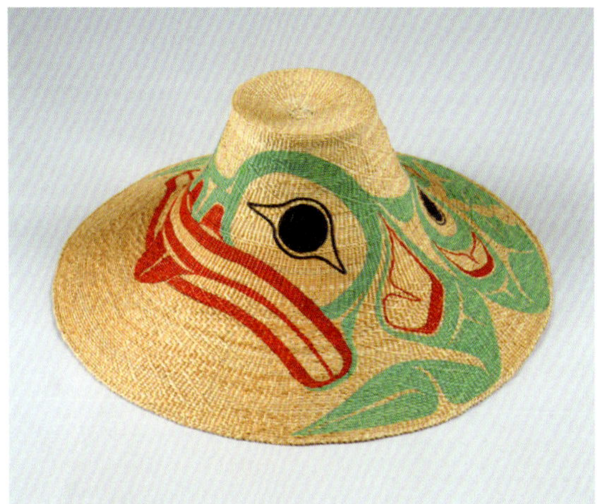

FIGURE 4.2 Primrose Adams (weaving) and Alfred Adams (painting) (Haida). *Hat*, 1990s. Spruce root. 15 × 6 in. Gift of Arthur B. Steinman, Burke Museum #2004–2/47.

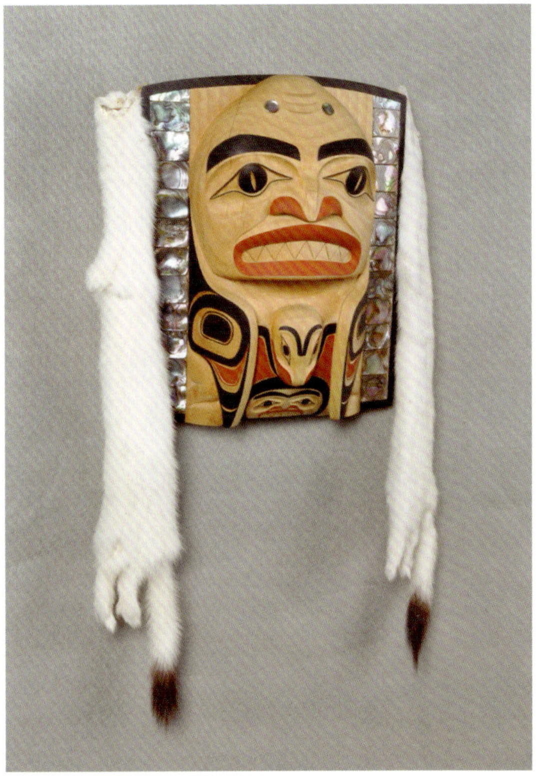

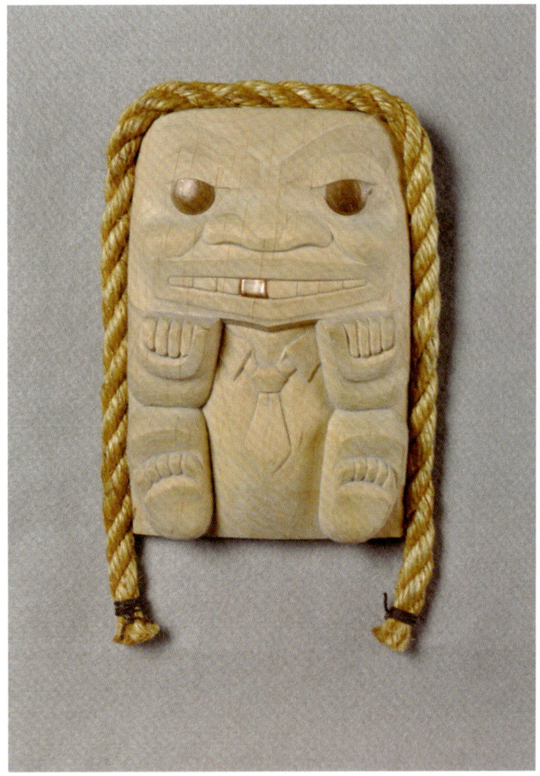

FIGURE 4.3 Dale Marie Campbell (Tlingit/Tahltan). *Shark and Killer Whale Frontlet*, 1999. Wood, paint, abalone, ermine. 9.1 × 7.5 in. Gift of Arthur B. Steinman, Burke Museum #2004–2/149.

FIGURE 4.4 Isaac Tait (Nisga'a). *He's Seen the Queen Twice*, 1999. Wood, Canadian coins, copper ore, rope, string, leather. 8.2 × 6.2 in. Gift of Arthur B. Steinman, Burke Museum #2004–2/157.

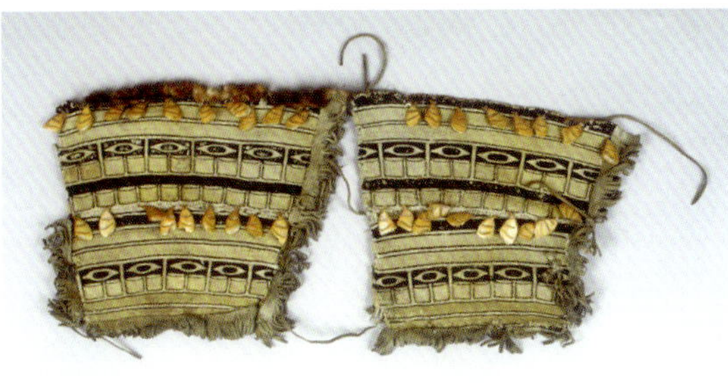

FIGURE 4.5 *Naaxiin Leggings*, Tlingit, early nineteenth century. Collected by George Emmons. Mountain goat wool, puffin beaks. 33 × 9.8 in. Burke Museum #1954.

such as thimbles, tin tinklers, or locally made miniature coppers were added.

In addition to the static display of visual wealth on potlatch participants, the kinetic qualities of ceremonial regalia further enhanced the effect of the spectacle. As alluded to earlier, the bird-down that had been placed within the circle of sea lion whiskers of a headdress would float down around a dancer from the quick and deliberate movements of the dance, creating a maelstrom of white against the darkness of a big house. The swaying of cedar bark regalia or the fringe of a Chilkat blanket blurs the edges of the dancer's profile and emphasizes the fluidity of his or her movements.

In the nineteenth century the use of jewelry, piercings, and tattooing all denoted rank as well as clan affiliation throughout the Northwest Coast. The anthropologist Sergei Kan has written that high-ranking children had to have every major stage of life marked by specific types of adornment expressed through clothing, jewelry, and physical alterations to the body. The ceremonies that celebrated changes in age and rank "involved marking the child's body with the signs of aristocratic status and bringing it into physical contact with wealth" (Kan 1989: 87). Adorning the body with wealth objects underlined the high rank of the wearer and made the body "heavier," a concept emphasized among the Tlingit as well as other groups.[1] Kan asserts: "The marking and decoration of the bodies of aristocratic children could be seen as an imposition of society's control on the natural (i.e., uncontrolled) body. In addition to being more controlled, the bodies of aristocrats were made heavier by being brought into contact with wealth (i.e., heavy objects). . . . The same role was played by the special clothing worn by the aristocracy. It not only decorated their bodies but made them heavier by placing a layer of valuable objects on them" (ibid.: 89).

Kan emphasizes the intimate connection between aristocrats' clothing and their bodies and their adornments—nose rings, earrings, and bracelets—that were made of heavier and more valuable materials reserved for use by the upper classes, including precious metals, shark's teeth, and abalone shells (fig. 4.6) (ibid.: 89). In 1794, Captain Roberts of the *Jefferson* recorded a pole raising that included lip piercing done with great ceremony; he describes much singing and lavish payments as a part of the festivities (Wright 2001: 72). Jewelry has always been a critical part of ceremonial regalia. In the early twentieth century, Alfred Adams, a leading figure in Massett, reported that "some people like to have bands or rings for ears, nose and arms. These were used because [they were] identified with the highest rank in society" (Barbeau 1916–54: 249.16). Then, as now, an armful of silver or especially gold bracelets provides the final expression of wealth and respect on the part of potlatch participants. Today armfuls of bracelets and other jewelry on mothers, aunts, and grandmothers denote their role as cherished caretakers of families, and the silver jewelry seen on even the youngest children signify that they are the precious treasures of the clans.

The ensemble just described is typical of ceremonial regalia in general. However, some ceremonies called for specific types of adornment that symbolized particular social meanings. During the Kwakwaka'wakw *qautē'x•a* (also spelled *kutixa*), or bride price repayment ceremony, jewelry was a critical part of a woman's regalia. All participants were encouraged to dress in their finest but the bride's adornments, such as an abalone nose ornament, were a physical symbol of the wealth being transferred to her husband and were specific to the marriage regalia (Boas and Hunt 1897: 422). This appearance of the bride was a key moment in the ceremony: "the great dance of the occasion was hers when she displayed her jewelry" (Benedict 1989 [1934]: 206).

In volume 10 of *The North American Indian*, the ethnographer and famed photographer Edward Curtis recorded the status-enhancing marriage repayment procedure and noted that a women's high status could be marked by specific types of personal adornment—in this case the wearing of abalone earrings (fig. 4.7): "There is especial honor in being many time married and released by payment of the marriage debt. Thus, a woman who has been four times wedded, whether to the same man or to different men, and freed by the payment of property, bears the honorable title of *ó'ma*, and she alone is permitted to wear a painted hat and abalone-shell earrings" (Curtis 1970 [1915]: 131). Some types of jewelry are seen more frequently in a ceremonial context; for example, silver nose rings were most often seen on ceremonial occasions (De Laguna 1991: 244) both in the past and today. The wider social acceptance of facial piercings today means that nose rings and lip pins are being seen in quotidian settings more frequently. All of these examples attest to the function and value of jewelry as a social and ceremonial signifier (Bunn-Marcuse 2007).[2]

In addition to clan affiliations and the expressions of rank or social status, adornment can express a connection between the human and supernatural or natural worlds, presenting spiritual or extraordinary experiences in a concrete form. For example, tattoos have been ascribed operative as well as symbolic or amuletic powers. In 1864 a Haida woman told Francis Poole that her halibut tattoo with the face of her chief on its tail would protect her and her kin from drowning in the sea (Niblack 1888: 258). Regalia also records

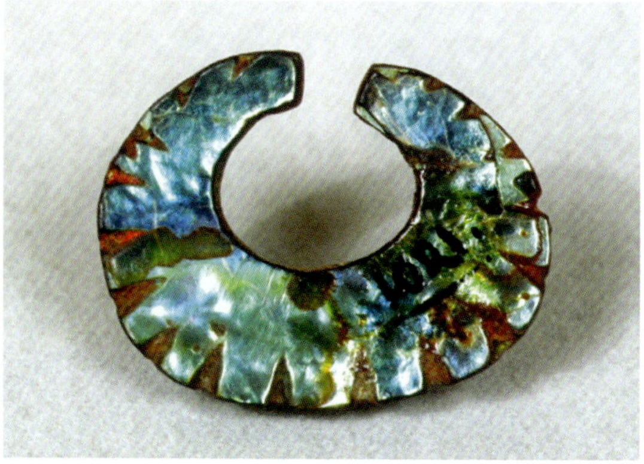

FIGURE 4.6 *Nose Ring*, Tlingit, abalone, nineteenth century. Collected by George Emmons. 0.8 × 0.6 in. Burke Museum #1021.

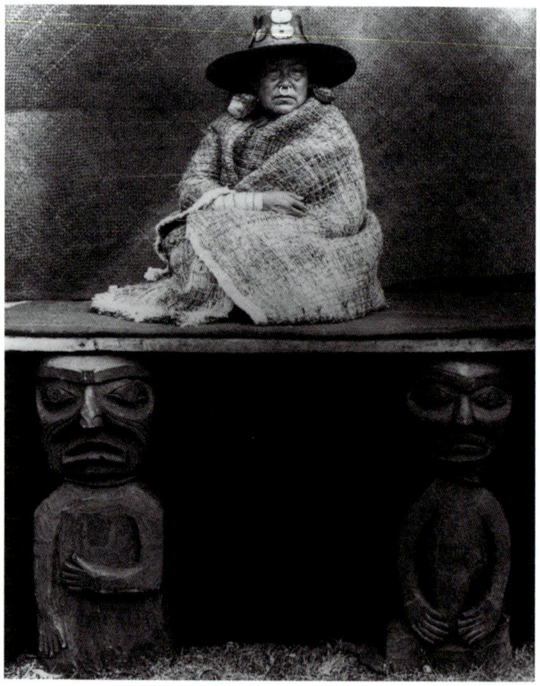

FIGURE 4.7 Edward Curtis. *Chief's daughter—Nakoaktok* (Francine Hunt), 1915. Curtis 1915: vol. 10, plate 364.

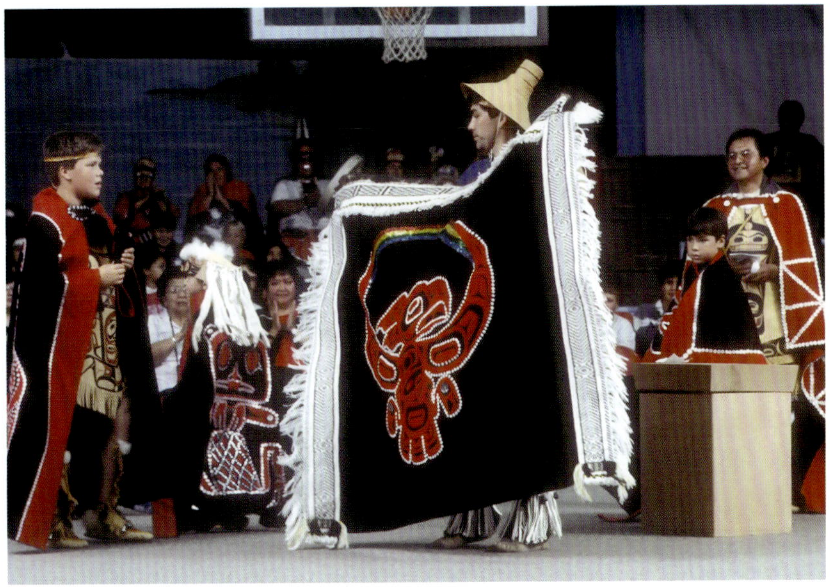

FIGURE 4.8 Evelyn Vanderhoop (Haida). *Button Robe*, commemorating David Boxley's *Eagle and Rainbow* pole, Metlakatla, 1994. Photograph by Lawrence Migdale.

and connects to the experiences of clan ancestors, such as the many pieces of regalia belonging to the Tlingit Naanya.áayí clan that reference their ancestors' interactions with a grizzly bear at the time of the great flood (Holm 1987: 192). Experiential references in clan images are not a relic of the past, confined to the realm of ancestral adventuring. Contemporary regalia also illustrates personal experiences that align clan affiliations with modern events such as David Boxley's button blanket (fig. 4.8) commemorating the *Eagle and Rainbow* pole he raised in front of the Metlakatla Senior Center in 1994 (Hoyt-Goldsmith 1997: 23).

SECULAR EXAMPLES

Even in the nineteenth century, not all adornment was reserved for ceremonial occasions. Some crest displays, such as tattoos on the hands and faces, were by their very nature displayed in all settings, both quotidian and ceremonial. In fact, although the *application* of tattoos was a part of the ceremonial marking of high-ranking children, the tattoos themselves, unlike other ceremonial regalia, were obviously permanent bodily adornments. Likewise, although the *presentation* of silver and gold jewelry is often a part of potlatch proceedings, jewelry is worn on both ceremonial and mundane occasions. While in the mid- to late-nineteenth century most tattoos would be covered by the daily clothing and might only be revealed on ceremonial occasions (Swan 1886: 70), this was *not* true of tattoos on the hands of women.[3] It was emphatically not true for bracelets, which were a part of both ceremonial and daily wear.[4]

Nineteenth-century photographs and written accounts patently illustrate jewelry—labrets, earrings, rings, and bracelets—as part of the everyday clothing for women on the Northwest Coast. The Haida weaver Ilshilay, photographed at Massett in 1881, wears silver earrings and a wide silver bracelet with her cotton dress as she works on her basket (fig. 4.9). Travelers to the coast describe women wearing silver bracelets as a matter of course starting in the 1860s. In the mid- to late nineteenth century, high-ranking women adorned their arms with precious metals bracelets and thus achieved a display of rank, even as European clothing threatened to level the outward class distinctions of women throughout Native communities. Their silver- and gold-bedecked arms echoed the older practice of tattooing the hands, a prerogative reserved for those of high rank. During the years before missionary influence (pre-1876), crest designs would have been doubled as women's bracelets reemphasized the tattoos that were on their arms.

As Northwest Coast women navigated the cultural crosscurrents of the late nineteenth and early twentieth centuries, bracelets and other silver jewelry provided a substitute for tattoos displaying one's crest that was more acceptable to Victorian standards of dress and decorum. During the years of the potlatch ban, "tattooing of clan and crest on the body was frowned upon and viewed as primitive, so objects such as gold and silver bracelets became alternate resting places for this secret language of ancestry; aunties and grandmothers wore clan symbols on bracelets, which were easily removed when the church minister came to visit. These adaptations became icons of survival and continuity" (Jones 2006: 35). Photos from the early twentieth century suggest that silver jewelry was a part of everyday wear; rings, bracelets, and brooches were worn with calico dresses and woolen coats. Haida filmmaker Marianne Jones's suggestion—that bracelets with clan designs were removed at the arrival of the minister—complicates the premise that bracelets were acceptable adornment in the late Victorian era. Did they need to be hidden, just as women from that generation hid their tattooed hands under gloves (Blackman 1982: 149)?

The clergy's condemnation of these expressions of clan (or simply Native) identity—such as crest jewelry or tattoos—is, sadly, not limited to the nineteenth century. Although it might be assumed that religious objections to tattooing would be an artifact of a bygone era, overt symbols of cultural identity still threaten some representatives of the church.[5] Tsimshian scholar Mique'l Dangeli reported that a clergy member approached her in Metlakatla, touched the eagle tattoo on the back of her neck, and said, "You can just feel the devil" (Mique'l Dangeli personal communication, 2007). Similarly, in the late 1980s an evangelical preacher objected to the crest jewelry worn by Nisga'a carver Mike Dangeli, his mother, and grandmother and insisted their bracelets be relinquished to him (Dangeli personal communication, 2007).

These experiences underscore the continuing conflicts that can arise when belief systems collide. To many First Nations individuals, tattoos and jewelry represent personal and cultural identity—familial and clan ties—independent of Western religious beliefs. To the clergy, however, these symbols of culture represented something threatening to their current mission. Dangeli noted that speaking to someone of this mind-set was like "going back in history" (Dangeli personal communication, 2007). These contemporary anecdotes illustrate the potency of objects to "act as vehicles for bringing past time into the present" (Weiner 1985: 210). The importance of objects from previous generations is inherent in heirlooms and prized family possessions in many cultures.

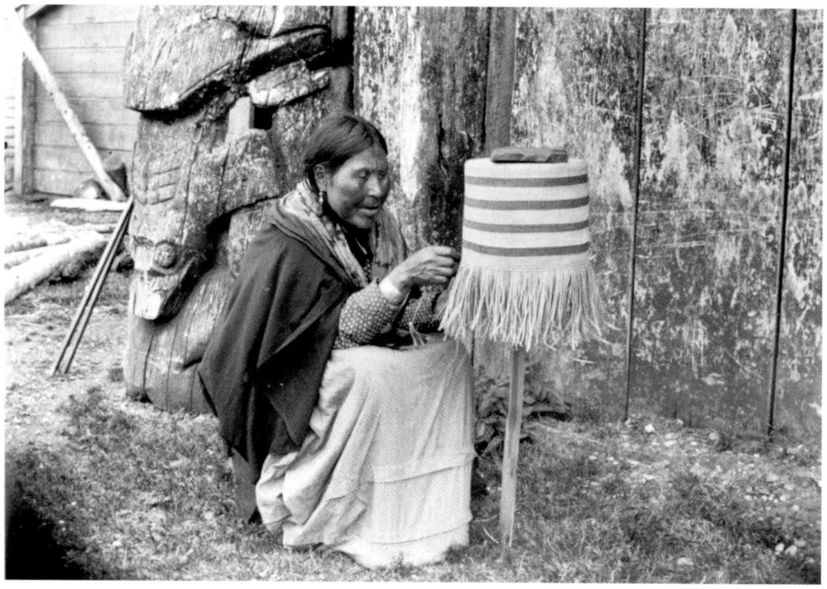

FIGURE 4.9 Haida weaver, Massett, 1881. The Field Museum negative #CSA854. Photograph by Edward P. Allen.

In her article on the concept of inalienable wealth, the anthropologist Annette Weiner (1985: 210) noted that "age adds value, as does the ability to keep the object against all exigencies that might force a person or a group to release it to others. The primary value of . . . these objects [is] to define who one is in a historical sense. [They] bring . . . past time into the present, so that the histories of ancestors, titles, or mythological events become an intimate part of a person's present identity. To

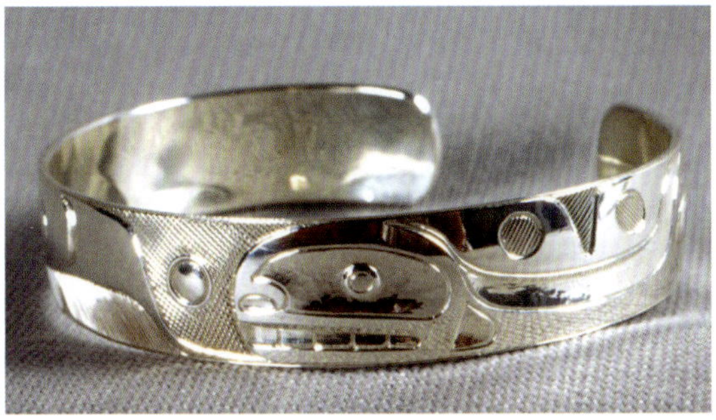

FIGURE 4.10 Gerry Marks (Haida). *Raven Bracelet*, 2008. Silver, 2.3 × .5 in. Gift of Mark Kernaghan in honor of William and Sandra Dunn, Burke Museum #2010–170/1.

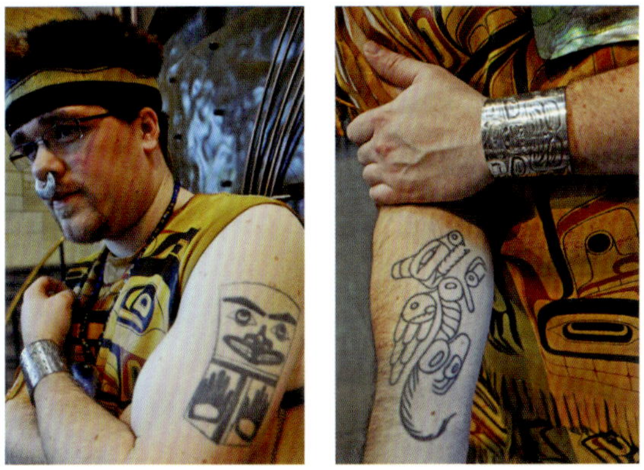

FIGURE 4.11 David R. Boxley (Tsimshian) with bracelet and tattoos, 2011. Photograph by Molly Stephey, Smithsonian's National Museum of the American Indian.

lose this claim to the past is to lose part of who one is in the present." Keeping an object through "all exigencies" can be especially potent for cultures that are or have been under colonial and religious pressure to jettison all markers of indigenous identity.

Jones wrote that physical objects connected to the past provide inspiration for the current generation. Her grandmother, Agnes Russ, was one of the last of her generation to be tattooed. Jones (2006: 35) has written: "I am honored to have one of her bracelets because it reminds me that she was one of the few who survived invasion and pandemic; even through that, she managed to retain her connection to her clan and to being Haida, so that many years later I might have that same chance." Haida artist Robert Davidson also wrote of the importance of remaining connected to previous generations: "My grandparents' generation, they were the last generation to understand and to know the origins of our clans. And so we have this generation gap that we need to reconnect with. In order for us to understand where our grandparents left off, the work that they were carrying and doing for us, we need to bridge that gap" (Jones 2006: 30, 35). It is not surprising that the physical presence of a family heirloom, such as a bracelet, can help to bridge the gap between past and present, to bring the emotional connection forward, and to inspire the work that Davidson and Jones suggest is the calling of this generation of Haida artists and scholars.

Many First Nations artists have commented on their commitment to expressing family pride through the regalia they make for members of their communities. Dan Wallace, Kwakwaka'wakw jeweler, discussed the current importance of adornment and how adorning his elders with jewelry raises their status and increases their "visual wealth." "I like to see the old ladies walking into a ceremony wearing their bracelets," he says, "their arms all dressed up. You can tell that they just feel good. They know who they are" (Chalker, Dubin, and Whiteley 2004: 108). Bracelets engraved with crest designs are ubiquitous among First Nations—worn as an expression of one's crest and as a continual reminder of intergenerational connections (fig. 4.10). Mique'l Dangeli spoke of the critical function of bracelets in her community of Metlakatla, Alaska, where many of the older attributes of clan identity were rarely seen during the twentieth century, but children were regularly given crest bracelets early in life (Askren personal communication, 2007).

Tsimshian carver and silversmith Corey Moraes echoes Wallace's sentiments in discussing how members of his community today are using bracelets and tattoos to convey their clan affiliations.[6] "I look at jewelry, contemporary jewelry today, almost like body adornment," he says, "it's like a tattoo. In our own community, the native women are interested in obtaining things that are going to display their crest. Or subcrests. Much in the same way that we would get body tattoos done that were permanently on our bodies" (American Museum of Natural History 2003). Jewelry and tattoos, unlike button blankets and headdresses, are not limited to a ceremonial setting. Tattoos, of course, are living documents of affiliation inscribed on the body, a symbolic record of personal connections. In fact, the preferred ink used in nineteenth-century Tlingit tattoos was a combination of the ash from the blueberry bush mixed with the mother's breast milk—providing a bodily connection to the matrilineal origin of the applied crest design (De Laguna and Emmons 1991: 253). In the twenty-first century, many First Nations individuals are returning to the practice of tattooing their clan identity on their bodies with designs commissioned from prominent Northwest Coast artists (fig. 4.11). Whether revealed or concealed, tattoos are a continual affirmation of the choice of the individual—the decision to be forever marked with a graphic of identity

The choice to visually pronounce one's affiliations does not have to be as serious a decision as being tattooed. The most casual of everyday dress—the T-shirt—can also be a record of tribal affiliation, community involvement, or simple admiration of Native art styles. In the past forty years, T-shirts have been one of the standard payments given out at potlatches and feasts. As such, they testify to both the actions of the host and the involvement of the recipient (fig. 4.12). Like ceremonial regalia, these shirts attest to certain affiliations or relationships with a community; unlike regalia, these are not limited to First Nations members of particular clans or moieties. Non-Native people with connections to Native communities may announce those affiliations by wearing the shirts they have received at potlatches or feasts. The booming business of clothing sporting designs by Native artists allows anyone with an admiration for Native art to express this interest in attire.

The popularity of Dorothy Grant's Feastwear designs across a varied set of consumers attests to the success of Native-inspired clothing at the high end of the fashion spectrum as well (fig. 4.13). Grant notes that it takes a certain confidence to wear her unique designs: "Feastwear is for people who are really, really attracted to it and not afraid to wear it. You have to feel good about it, good that you're wearing something that you really, really love and that you identify with. You appreciate the craft in it, the artwork on it, and maybe you identify with that certain creature on it" (Blackman 1992: 56). Grant describes her patrons as a people "who have a real connection, or want to have a connection to Haida art or Northwest Coast art."

In 1991 anthropologist Margaret Blackman commissioned Grant to make a coat in honor of Florence Edenshaw Davidson, whom Blackman called "my teacher, collaborator, and surrogate grandmother (*nani*)" (Burke Museum, Collection notes, Burke Museum #2003–83/1). The design tells of their collaboration over many years, culminating in the biography *During My Time: Florence Edenshaw Davidson, A Haida Woman* (Blackman 1982). Davidson is symbolized by the raven telling the story and Blackman by the frog receiving it. Blackman wore this coat to Davidson's memorial potlatch in October 1994. Grant celebrates such connections between cultures that her clothes embody. "When they buy my clothing," she notes, "it's a statement about their alignment to Haida culture, their acceptance of it. And it's a really good thing to bridge our cultures like that, through clothing" (American Museum of Natural History 2003).

CONCLUSION

Throughout this chapter the use of personal adornment in a ceremonial context is contrasted to the roles that jewelry plays as an everyday marker of connections to family and clan. Personal stories from the present and the past, by artists and others, illustrate the subjective nature of both function and value, and the idiosyncratic ways that cherished objects can symbolize either personal identity or valued relationships between people. The examples show the overlap between public and private, ceremonial and secular, and between the past and the present. On ceremonial or secular occasions alike, adornment is a public testament to identity. First Nations traditions demand an awareness of public action and appearance, and the function of regalia and adornment is to reflect clan history.

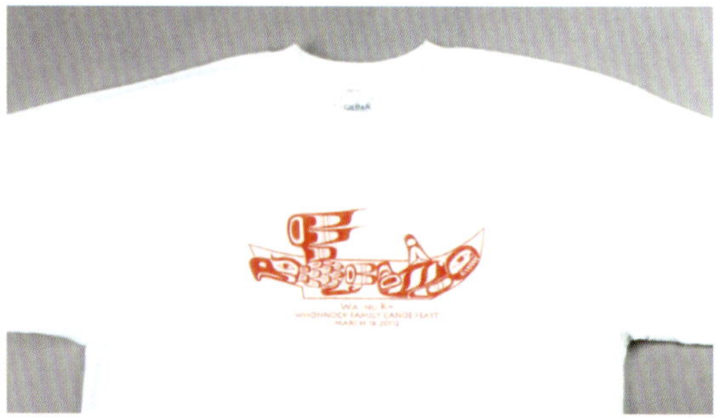

FIGURE 4.12 Whonnock Family (Kwakwaka'wakw) Canoe Feast T-shirt, 2002. 31 × 23 in. Gift of Sean Whonnock, Burke Museum #2002–23/1.

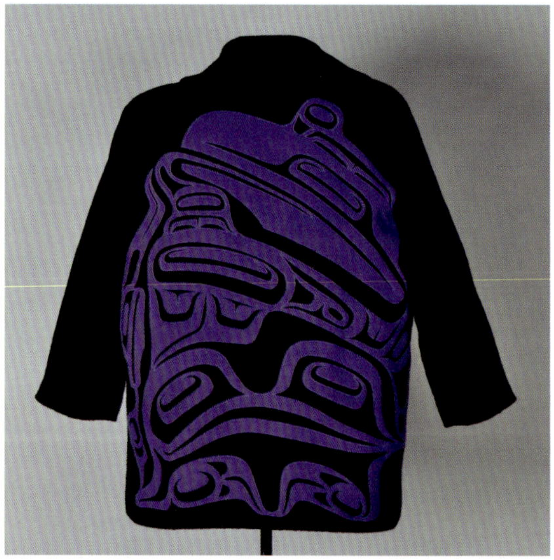

FIGURE 4.13 Dorothy Grant (Haida) and Robert Davidson (Haida). *Nani Coat*, 1991. Wool, silk, 35 × 58 in. Gift of Margaret B. Blackman, Burke Museum #2003–83/1.

Artists have long been cognizant of how wearing the proper ceremonial adornment can clothe them in the pride of their history. “The regalia, including the jewelry, is not just adornment,” Jim Hart stated, “it’s old, old history. So, it’s a lot more than just standing there looking good. You’re standing there as a pinnacle of all that’s behind you. . . . The regalia can be passed on, generation to generation” (Chalker, Dubin, and Whiteley 2004: 78). When one’s personal adornment can carry the weight of generations, the question of “what to wear?” can be a serious matter. For people confident in their identity, the physical expression of heritage is a matter of pride.

NOTES

1 The Tsimshian used the concept of weight to signify status as well. The anthropologist Jay Miller (1997: 42) noted that the labret represented “the heaviness of royal status.”

2 The use of jewelry at marriage ceremonies to express the wealth of the bride’s family was not exclusive to the Kwakwa̲ka̲'wakw. The missionary Reverend Myron Eells described a Cowlitz woman whose wedding regalia—including dentalium jewelry and brass and silver bracelets and an apron of money and glass beads—was “worth perhaps a thousand dollars” (Castille 1985: 292).

3 Once missionary values took hold, many adults who had been tattooed as children went to great lengths to hide those tattoos (Blackman 1982: 68).

4 James G. Swan, ethnologist and Indian Agent at Neah Bay, wrote that the Haida were careful not to admit white persons or strangers to their ceremonies; consequently, few outsiders had ever been present at times when the tattoo marks were shown (Swan 1886: 71).

5 This is not the case everywhere. In many communities members of the clergy take important roles in some cultural practices, offering a communal prayer and other services at appropriate occasions.

6 Robert Davidson and others have discussed the important link between tattooing and jewelry (Seattle Art Museum 1995: 128).

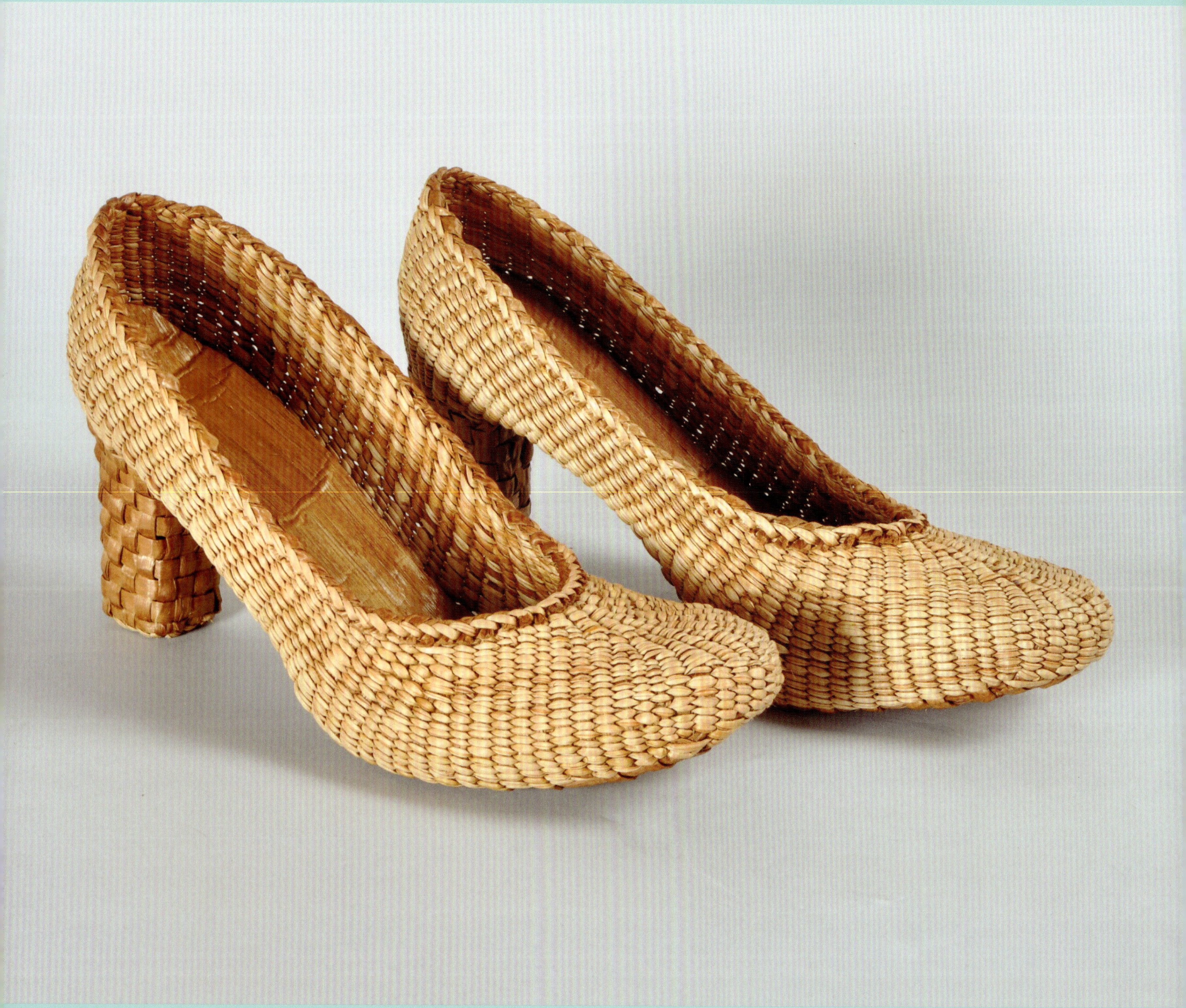

FIVE

INTERTWINING

Learning for the Future from Our Past

LISA TELFORD

I AM a Gawa Git'ans Git'anee Haida weaver, born in Ketchikan, Alaska, in 1957. I come from a long line of weavers, including my grandmother, mother, and aunt. The knowledge of weaving has also been passed to my cousins, daughter, and granddaughter. I learned traditional techniques of Haida basketry from my aunt, Delores Churchill, and the techniques of making Haida cedar garments from my cousin, Holly Churchill. While growing up, my family lived in many different states. My stepfather was an ironworker, and we went wherever the next big job was. When I was thirteen, my mother and I went to stay with my grandmother, Selina Peratrovich, for six months. Every morning my grandmother would rise early and start weaving at the kitchen table. One morning, when I came down the stairs to head off to school, my grandmother said, "Come here, I want to show you something." I knew that she wanted to show me how to weave, and I replied, "Nonie, I don't have time for that." My grandmother never offered again. She passed away in 1984. As I grew older, I often thought of that missed opportunity.

In 1986, I moved to Washington State, and at that time there was an awakening of our culture. Dance groups were forming all over Puget Sound, and I joined the Alaska Native Cultural Heritage Association (ANCHA) dancers. When I danced, I wore a cedar hat my grandmother wove years ago. The other dancers would wonder where I got it. Weaving was always part of my life, and I was surprised to see so many people desiring a hat of their own. I assumed everyone's grandmother wove. Hearing constant inquiries on my hat, I realized that weaving was a part of Haida culture not often seen in 1986 or used by urban Haida in Washington State. I started to think about the art form I had always taken for granted. I decided I wanted to learn to weave. When I mentioned this to my mother, Jane Adams, she said, "Let me talk to your Aunt."

I had my first basic weaving lesson in 1992. Weaving seemed to come naturally to me, and the next year I received a grant from the Washington State Arts Commission to apprentice in Haida basketry with my aunt Delores Churchill. Our first lesson was to travel to Massett, British Columbia, and gather spruce roots—the traditional weaving material of the Haida. For my next lessons my aunt would travel to Washington to stay with me for a week; each time I would count the days until her next visit. During her absence I would look at old photographs and books, so I could dream about what I wanted to learn at my next weaving lesson. This was up to Delores to decide. The books and photos would inspire me to have my weaving material prepared and ready to start weaving. I have been weaving ever since.

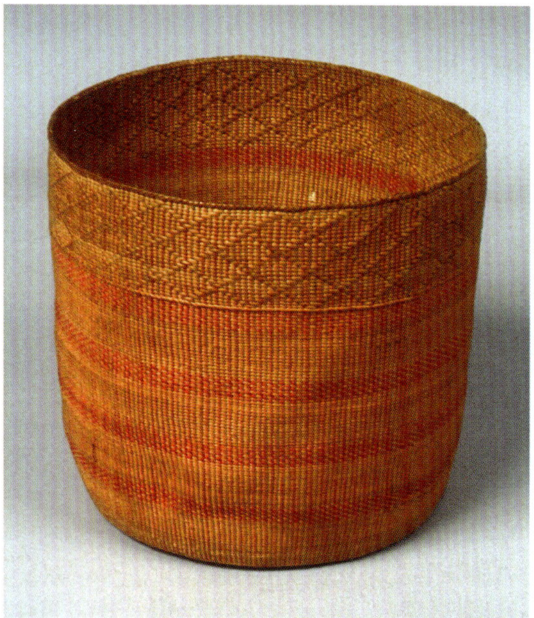

FIGURE 5.1 *Basket.* Haida, late nineteenth century. Twined spruce root, 6.7 × 7.1 in. Walter Waters Collection, Burke Museum #1–1520.

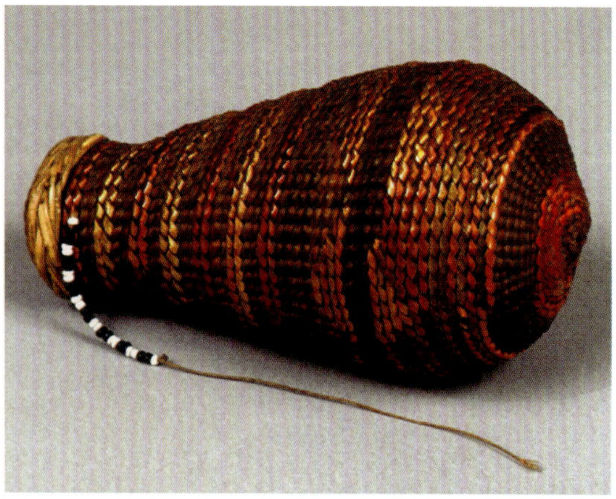

FIGURE 5.2 *Basketry Covered Light Bulb.* Tlingit, early twentieth century. Twined spruce root, 4.25 × 2.25 in. Walter Waters Collection, Burke Museum #1–1548.

My cousin Holly Churchill was instrumental in reviving the tradition of making cedar clothing out of pounded cedar bark. Enjoying basketry so much, I knew the next step was to move to cedar clothing. I asked Holly if she would instruct me, and she agreed. I was awarded another grant from the Washington State Arts Commission in 1994 to apprentice in cedar clothing. During my trip to Massett in 1993, I had collected yew wood to make my cedar bark pounder. It is a piece of hard wood that is used to pound the bark to soften it for clothing. I made my pounder the way I thought it should look based on a description I read from Holly. I had read it wrong, though; my pounder was incorrect. Northwest Coast art scholar Bill Holm fixed my pounder and taught me how to pound bark the correct way. When I started to pound bark, I wet the bark and pounded it to mush. The correct way is to pound it dry. If hit correctly, it layers and fluffs up rather than breaking down. I currently use cedar bark as my medium to create clothing, hats, and baskets.

In the days of my grandmother's grandmother, basketry was essential to life. It was used for food gathering, storage, cooking, shelter from the rain, for hats and clothing, and even for trade with

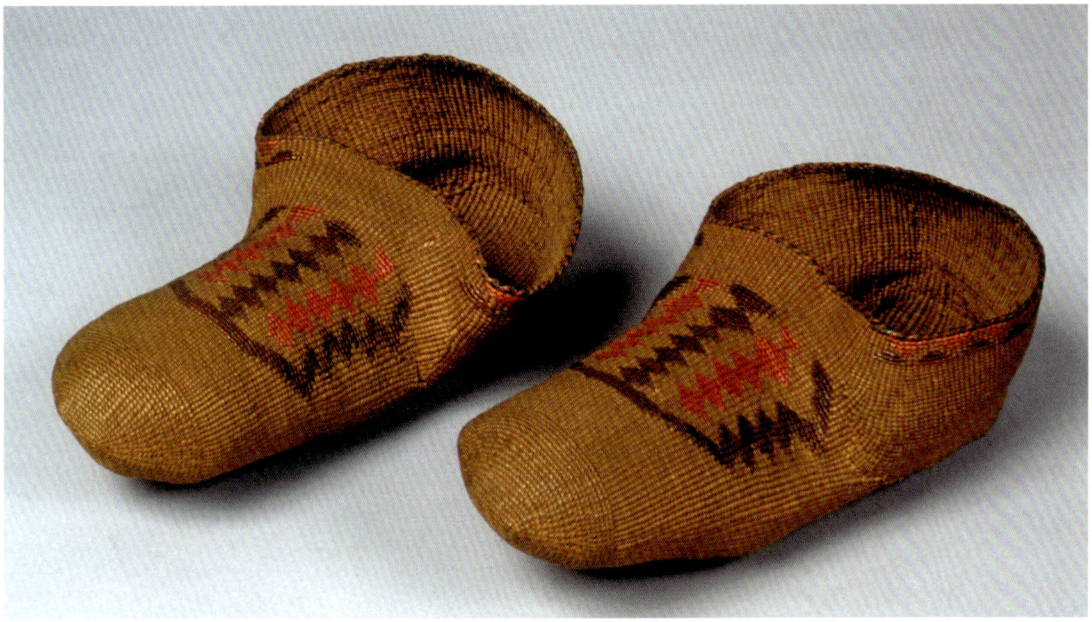

FIGURE 5.3 *Shoes*. Tlingit, late nineteenth century. Twined spruce root, 9.75 × 3.5 × 3 in. Gift of Mrs. Earl Morrisson, Burke Museum #1–860.

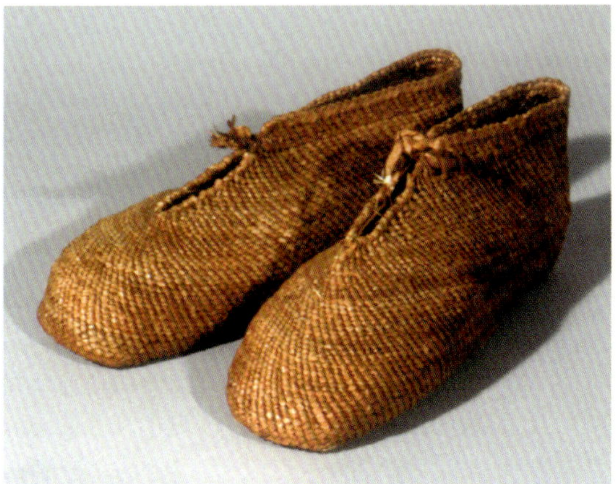

FIGURE 5.4 *Shoes*. Southern Northwest Coast (Makah?). Late nineteenth century. Twined and plaited cedar bark, 9.85 × 3.94 in. Purchased from Phoebe Condon, Burke Museum #1–2030.

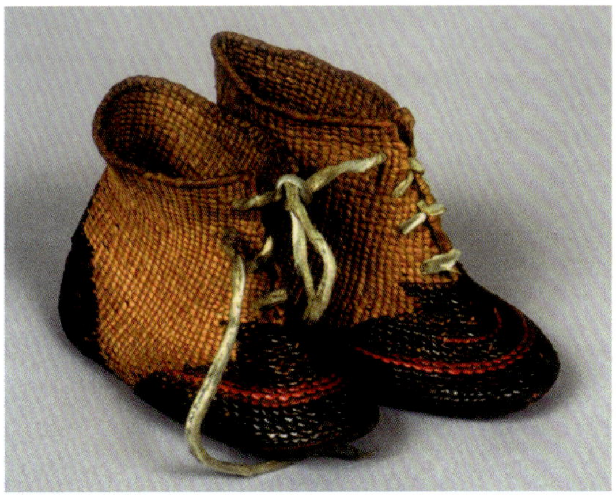

FIGURE 5.5 *Shoes*. Tlingit, late nineteenth century. Twined and false embroidered spruce root, 4.5 × 2 in. Burke Museum #1–1904.

other Natives. Haida baskets used for food gathering or storage always had a bit of beauty added during weaving. The beauty in the basket here (fig. 5.1) is the red bands and diamond self-weave design on the top portion of the basket. This bit of beauty was influenced by nature and incorporated into such everyday items as clothing and basketry. This basket would be used as a cooking vessel or for storage, folded when not in use, like a shopping bag. Tradition dictates the type of basket a weaver would create as well as the designs used. In other words, every basket created had a purpose or, as my cousin always states: form follows function. For example, a clam basket has small holes created by crossing the warp and creating a "fish eye" design. That way, the clams were trapped in the basket while the water could flow through to allow the clams to spit out all the sand. A clam basket would not be used for any other purpose.

Then tourism and commerce appeared in the form of collectors. Starting in the late eighteenth century, ship captains and sailors collected baskets as souvenirs of their foreign travels. A hundred years later, museum collectors and anthropologists bought baskets as part of their documentation of Native cultures. I have studied baskets at the American Museum of Natural History and the Brooklyn Art Museum in New York, the Burke Museum in Seattle, the Heard Museum in Phoenix, the University Museum at the University of Pennsylvania in Philadelphia, and the National Museum of the American Indian in Washington, D.C. Wandering around in the collections, one comes across basketry novelties—items seldom seen on display. To me, a novelty basket is one that does not adhere to the form-follows-function rule, such as the basketry-covered light bulb in the Burke Museum's collection (fig. 5.2). Are they novelties or the work of a trailblazing weaver looking into the future? Was the weaver trying to

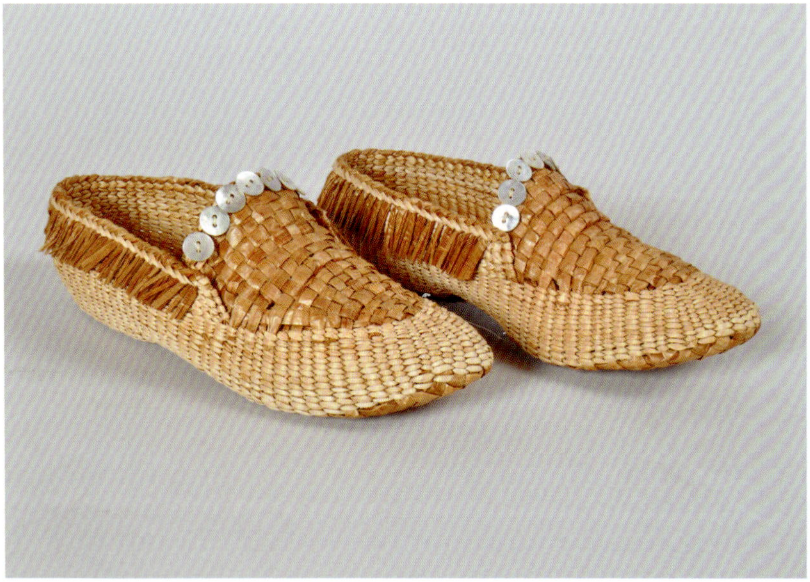

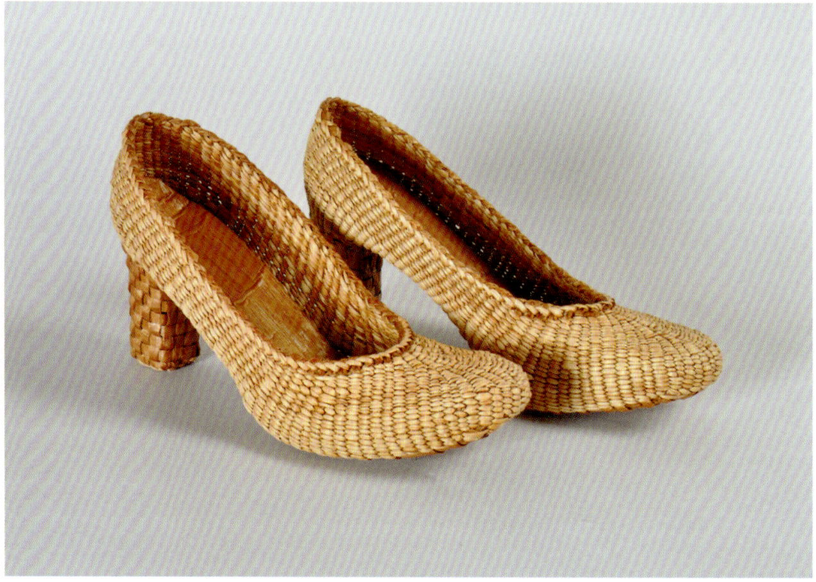

FIGURE 5.6 Lisa Telford (Haida). *Loafers*, 2006. Plaited red cedar bark, twined yellow cedar bark, abalone buttons, 9.5 × 3.25 in. Commissioned for *In the Spirit of the Ancestors* exhibition with funds donated by Lawrence Christian, Burke Museum #2007–7/2.

FIGURE 5.7 Lisa Telford (Haida). *High Heels*, 2006. Plaited red cedar bark, twined yellow cedar bark, 9.6 × 3.4 in. Commissioned for *In the Spirit of the Ancestors* exhibition with funds donated by Lawrence Christian, Burke Museum #2007–7/1.

capture the eye of the savvy collector looking for that one avant-garde piece to complete his or her collection? Possibly, living in the village, weavers might have enjoyed being the first to create such a piece, standing in the moment of fame. I think all of these reasons are possible, but only the weaver can answer that question. Nonetheless, we are the fortunate ones to gaze upon these unique creations and marvel at their creativity.

In 2006, I was asked to make a pair of shoes for the Heard Museum's *Sole Stories: American Indian Footwear*. I agreed, certain I would have my moment of fame by creating these shoes. I had one year to figure out how to do it. During that time I was awarded a Bill Holm Center Visiting Research grant with my apprentice, Shauna Colbert. Preparing to start my research, I looked through the Burke collection and I was surprised to find not one but three pairs of shoes. Two had been collected between 1900 and 1920, and the third had been collected in the 1950s. The first pair was a moccasin type that was all twined with false embroidery (fig. 5.3). The second was wrap-twined and shaped more like a large baby booty that tied at the top; the sole was plaited with a solid piece of cedar inserted and attached with sinew to reinforce the sole (fig. 5.4). The third pair were child's shoes or baby booties that looked simple but were probably the most difficult to weave (fig. 5.5).

Studying the three pairs, I decided to make a moccasin-type shoe. I have large feet, and I wanted to make a cute pair of shoes, so I chose a friend with small feet. I asked her permission to trace her feet and moved forward. I would combine the knowledge I had learned from these three shoes and weave flat shoes. I decided to have a plaited bottom, as I did not feel up to the challenge of a twined bottom. I started plaiting and, using the small-foot template, I shaped the sole of my shoe; easy enough. I started twining and it was going well, but mixing the plaiting and the twining did not do. I learned to weave with spruce roots, so I have a tendency to pull very tight. Upon drying, the result was a curved sole; I had worked on one shoe for twelve hours only to have something that looked like a curled slipper. I needed to think more on it, so I set the curled dashed dream on a shelf in the living room. I would gaze at it nightly to analyze my error.

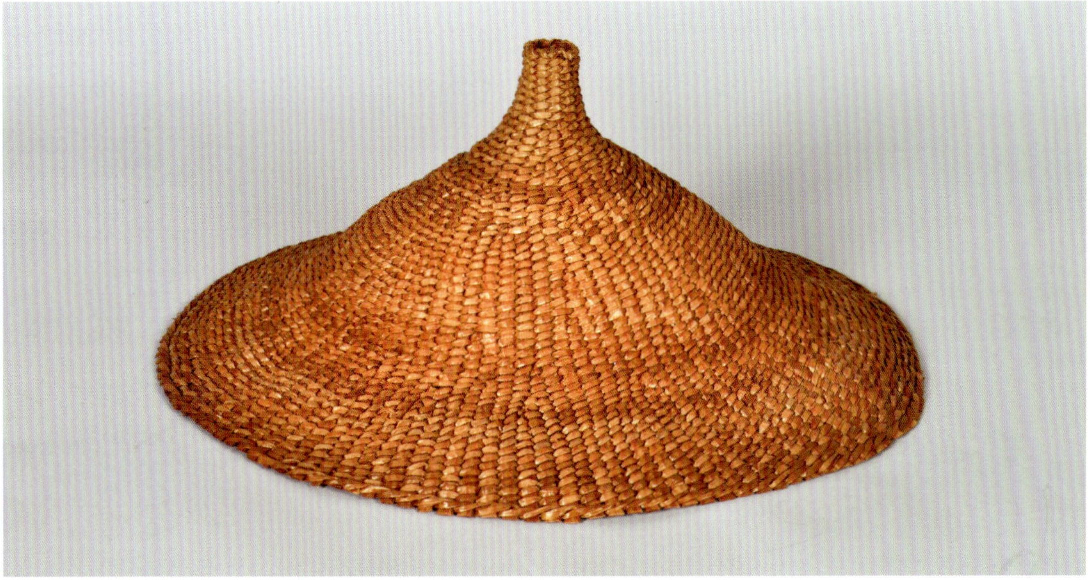

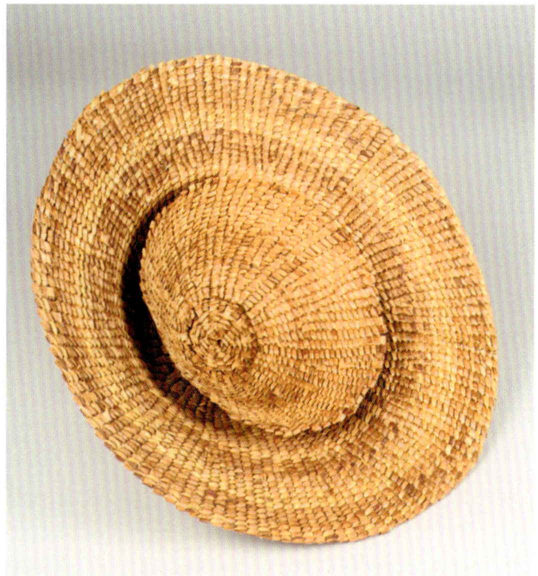

FIGURE 5.8A-B Karen Reed (Coast Salish—Puyallup/Chinook). *Hat*, 2000. Twined cedar bark, 5.5 × 13.5 in. Purchased with funds given by Lawrence Christian, Burke Museum #2000–124/1.

Two weeks later the light bulb finally came on! Rather than fight the curve, I decided to make it work for me—I made high heels. I would still use a plaited bottom but would use the curve to my advantage by putting a weight on one side to let the other side curl up for a heel. I would have never thought to weave shoes had I not been asked to—the very idea would have never come to me on my own. I have always thought of myself as a very traditional weaver: form follows function. I was happy to see the older shoes during my study at the Burke to use as inspiration for the shoes I ended up making for the exhibition *In the Spirit of the Ancestors: Contemporary Northwest Coast Native Art* (figs. 5.6 and 5.7). The technique used on the shoes from almost a hundred years ago is the one I used for my creations. Studying basketry from the past is invaluable to a weaver to reclaim or learn new techniques.

Weaving a basket is very time intensive, so I wondered at techniques found in certain baskets that seemed inconsistent with the careful, detail-oriented process of weaving. I would see baskets where it seemed the weaver ended the basket by just cutting off the warp. This made me curious since so much work had been involved in the weaving. Today, because weaving is so labor intensive, every warp is incorporated in the ending, folded over and locked in to ensure unraveling cannot happen. Looking at the cut-off endings on baskets at the Burke, I realized that they were not just cut off. In fact, every fourth or fifth stitch was incorporated in the ending to ensure against unraveling. Even though I have woven baskets for sixteen years and studied hundreds of baskets, I am always learning from every trip to a museum archive. I am not alone.

Contemporary baskets were a part of the Burke's exhibition *In the Spirit of the Ancestors.* These baskets demonstrate the same techniques that have been used since basketry was created. One example I saw of reaching into the past and reclaiming techniques was with the weaver Karen Reed's ancient-style hat (fig. 5.8a-b). Her hat illustrates that although the technique is the same one that has been used in past generations, today the shape is different. Most contemporary weavers don't weave a double hat. It is called a double hat because it is two hats woven together, with inner and outer hats sharing the same warp, joined at the hatband. I asked Karen Reed about the fragment she studied to reconstruct the hat. She said she felt a strong connection to the hat fragment found at Wapato Creek (in Puyallup, Washington) near her grandmother's land. She said she felt like "the person who made the hat was guiding her" in the creation of the new one (fig. 5.9).

Many techniques have remained the same over the generations, but new materials have led to surprising innovations in design. Pat Courtney Gold is one such trailblazer: weaving Wasco sally bags using both traditional and innovative materials—commercial hemp, chenille, commercial wool, faux deer hide—and incorporating new designs combined with traditional ones. Her bag was made using Hungarian hemp and chenille to weave motifs inspired by a Wasco basket collected by Lewis and Clark in 1805 (fig. 5.10). Using the same full-turn twining her ancestors used, Gold's creation will be the basket that the future generations will marvel at when they visit a collection. Her designs are thought provoking—like weavers long ago, Gold includes in her weaving what surrounds her today.

I cannot end this essay without discussing hats, the very thing that compelled me to start weaving. Creating a twined hat could take months for a weaver. The process includes going out to select the perfect spruce tree, digging, cooking and splitting the roots again and again, deciding on a design, and then of course actual weaving. In writing, that process doesn't sound too difficult, but in reality gathering enough roots for a hat could mean working from six in the morning to midnight for seven days. Once weaving is complete, you could have someone paint a design on the hat or just present it as it is: a beautiful piece of art. After all that work, would you think to cover it entirely with paint, not a design, just paint? In the Burke collection I have seen at least three painted hats, but my two favorites are the green hat (Burke catalog # 1–1278) and blue-green hat (fig. 5.11).

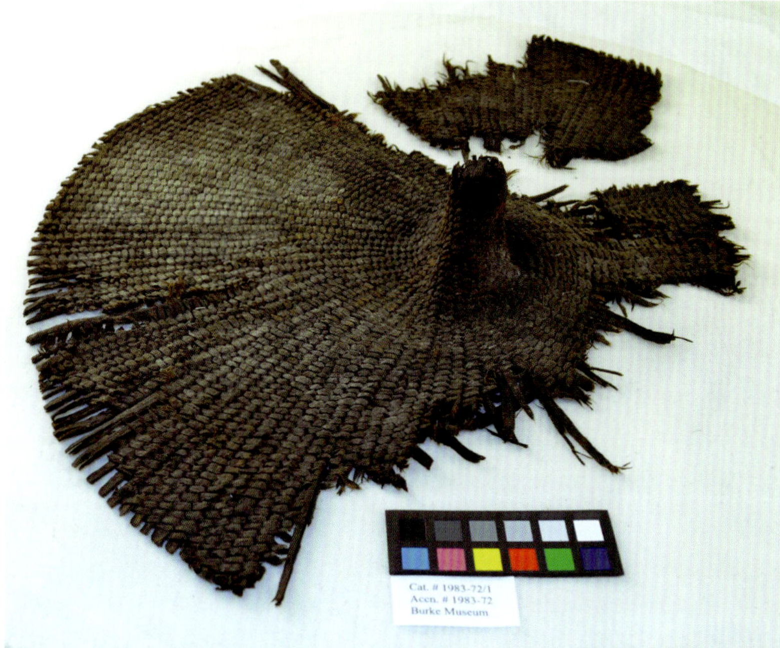

FIGURE 5.9 *Wapato Creek Hat.* Coast Salish—Puyallup, 1450–1620 CE. Red cedar. Burke Museum #1983–72/1.

Someone once asked if it was okay to paint a design on a twined hat she had bought from me. I replied that the hat is now hers to do with what she pleases. If I were to keep a hat for myself, though, I could not hide all my months of work with one thick coat of paint. I have seen many collection notes that state hats were painted to waterproof them. There must be another reason for the paint, however, because spruce root hats would already be waterproof. Spruce roots can even be watertight—they were used to make drinking cups. We may never know why the hats were painted, but these hats captivate me. I cannot explain why, but I always feel it has been a good trip when I return from a museum archive and have viewed one of these painted hats.

Fortunately the Burke Museum, long known for its integrity in representing Native artifacts

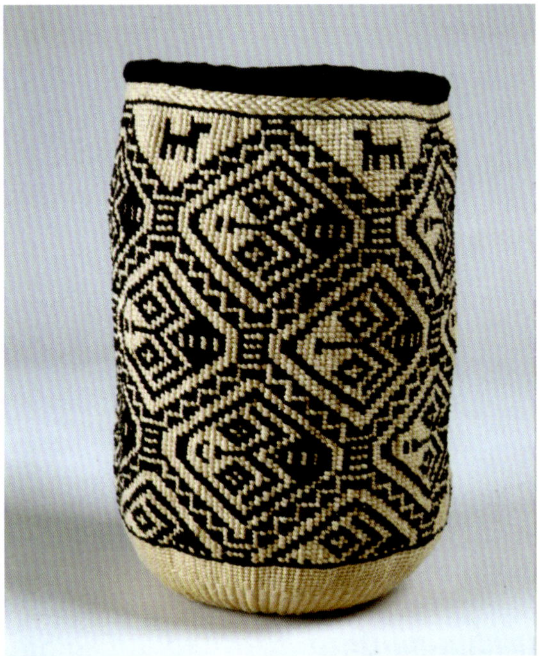

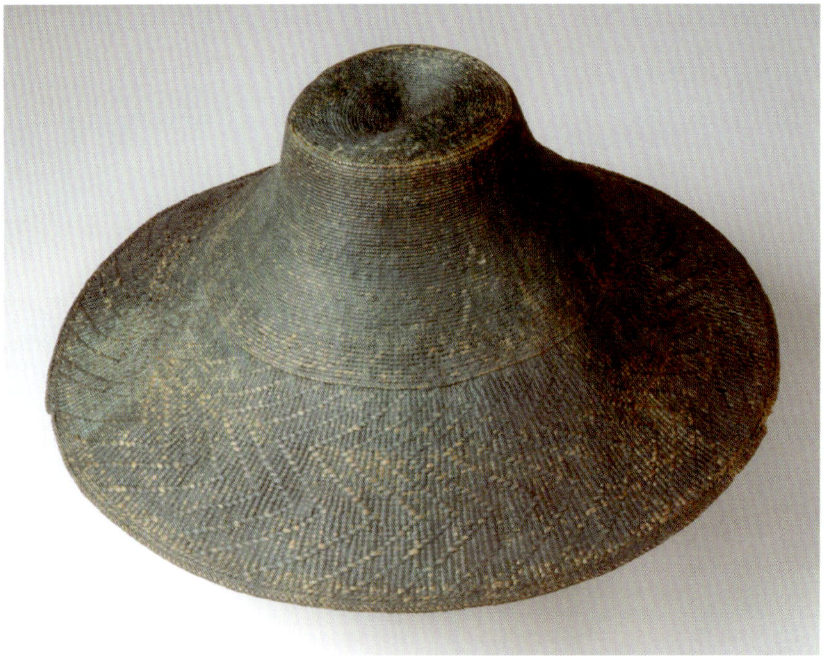

FIGURE 5.10 Pat Courtney Gold (Wasco—Warm Springs). *Sally Bag*, 2000. Hungarian hemp warps, cotton wefts, chenille wefts, suede, 11.5 × 7 in. Purchased with funds given by Lawrence Christian, Burke Museum #2000–122/1.

FIGURE 5.11 *Basketry Hat*. Haida, nineteenth century. Twined spruce root, paint, 16.5 × 6.3 in. Gift of John Putnam Estate, Burke Museum #2005–21/6.

and preserving culture, has many amazing baskets in its collection. The Burke collection holds novelty and traditional baskets as well as tools and other items needed for weaving. During my study I felt welcome and was assisted in any need. I am happy to say the objects I have studied will be available to teach and reconnect with when my granddaughter is ready. She is now thirteen but learned to thigh-spin at age two and harvest-bark at seven. The Burke is a house of knowledge waiting for her to open the door.

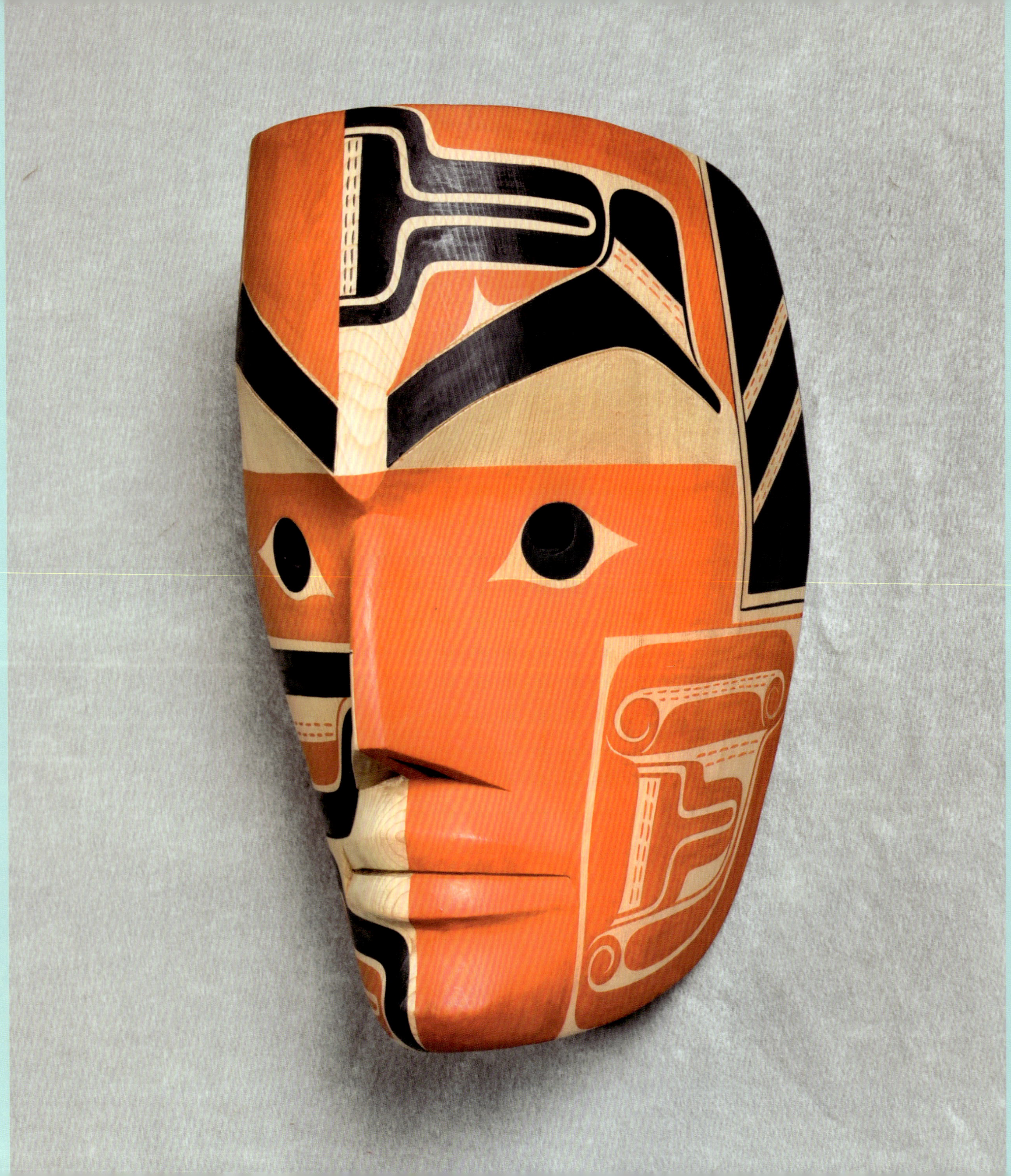

SIX

NOTES ON MASKS

JOE DAVID

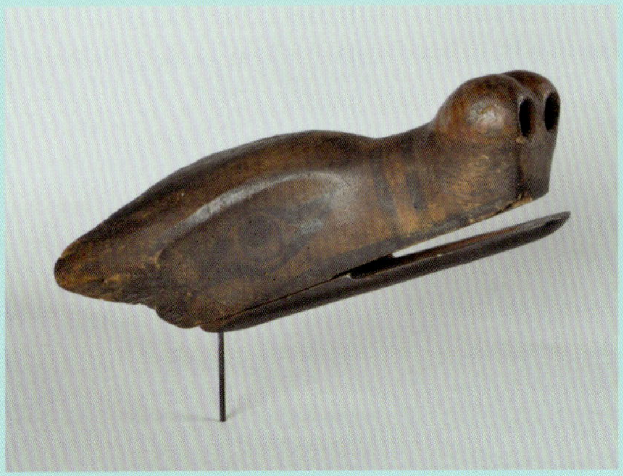

FIGURE 6.1 *Wolf Mask.* Nuu-chah-nulth. Red cedar, paint, nails, 13 × 6.6 × 4.3 in. Gift of Jim Bergstrom, collection of Mrs. Paul Smits, Burke Museum #2.5E1668.

All my life I've been fascinated with faces. I think most people are, to some degree. Some of my first drawings were of people, and most of my first attempts at fine drawing were portraiture. And of course most of my first attempts at fine carving were masks. I've carved more masks than anything else. I don't know if the numbers go into the thousands, but they are certainly in the hundreds. My first powerful experiences with masks happened at a young age at the village of Opitsaht (among the Tla-o-qui-aht people of Vancouver Island), where I was born and raised. Masks were used in ceremonial dances performed by family and tribal members, accompanied by beautiful and powerful songs. When performed by an experienced and graceful dancer, masked dancing is a captivating experience (figs. 6.1 and 6.11).

Several times when I was a child, I experienced hearing the sounds of the Tlookwana bull horn. These bull horns are carved of cedar; hollow and horn-like at one end and like a flat reed at the opposite end. When blown, they vibrate and make an eerie sound. It's a sound related to Tlookwana—the wolf people ceremonies—supernatural people ceremonies. In the dead of night the bull horns would start sounding at the far end of the village. As they neared, they would of course grow louder and have a powerful effect in our imaginations. I would imagine wolves growing in size in proportion to the sounds and darkness. Added to all this would be the serious mood of our parents—the adults, our protectors.

As the sounds neared, the terror at some point would shift to silent pauses, until during the most potent of these there would come a thundering knock on our door. Our father would silently, reverently, and bravely open the door, connecting the two worlds of natural and supernatural, light and dark. Following would be a loud declaration of ancient words. Words not understandable to the ears of children, as the language of the ancients and the supernatural differed greatly from the usual day-to-day of our home and village. But our father would in the end respond. With his response accepted, the door would close and the supernatural visitors would back into the darkness and their trumpeting powers would move on.

Not a word would be exchanged between anyone in the house. All were as silent as a pack of wolves, accessing information that touched nerve endings seldom awakened.

At this early age I witnessed my father carving masks as well as other objects. But for some wonderful, mysterious reason the masks possessed an extra-strong special energy and life for me. Of all the art forms I practice, mask-making is my life's passion (fig. 6.2). And although I may have already made my ultimate masterpiece, I choose to believe that the best mask is still in my future. I live and search for this mask in me as well as for that masterpiece in other carvers—past, present, and future. In my intense study I surmise that past generations produced countless masterpieces and the present generations hardly any in comparison—for the apparent and obvious reason of the artists' personal power, power accumulated from experience and participation in a cosmos and community that saturated a person with the force.

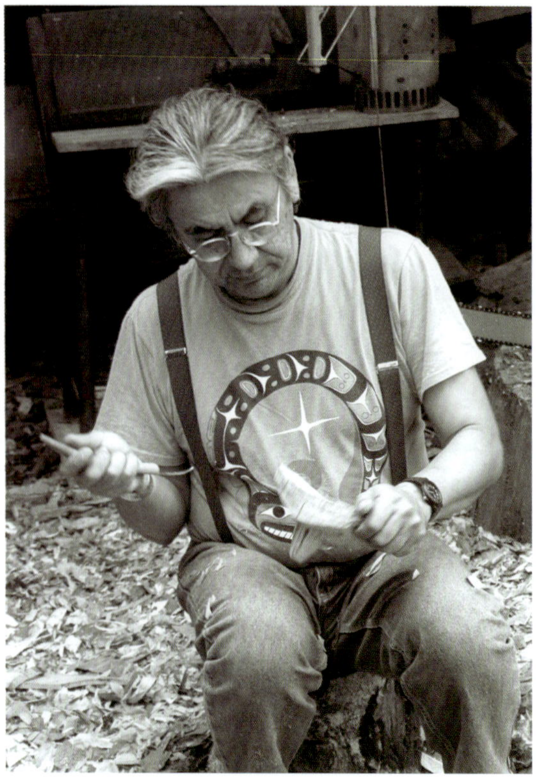

FIGURE 6.2 Joe David carving a mask, 2000. Photograph by Greg Blomberg.

TEACHINGS

Carla Holm, personal friend and daughter of Bill and Marty Holm, once had a frog speak to her in a dream and it said, "What is, is!" So I carved her an ivory frog and named it IS.

As a young and eager man in 1970, I met the artist Duane Pasco, who in turn introduced me to Bill Holm, curator of Native art at the Burke Museum. A year before I had met the work of Bill Holm in the form of a museum display of Northwest Coast art and culture at the Burke Museum. I'd also been seeing some carvings by Duane around Seattle in a few select places. This coming together of people, this IS was the beginning of some great friendships and my formal education in the arts and cultures of the Pacific Northwest Coast. In my educated and professional opinion, I consider Bill Holm and Duane Pasco to be the Grandmasters in Northwest Coast art. In addition to my personal endeavors and passions and work ethics, these two men are the sound foundation of my knowledge and expertise in "the art" (fig. 6.3).

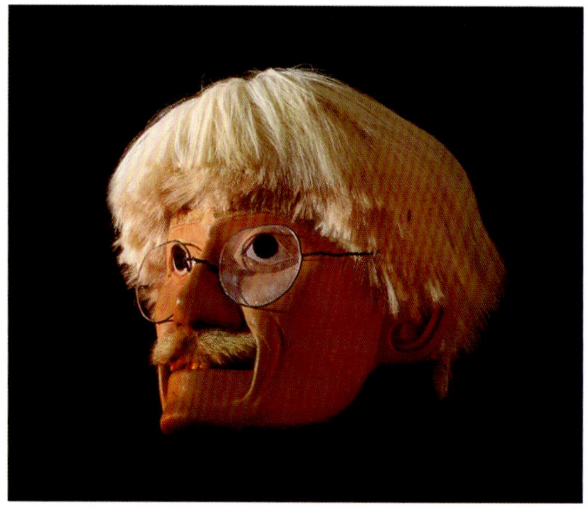

FIGURE 6.3 Duane Pasco. *Portrait Mask of Bill Holm*, 1982. Red alder with mountain goat hair, coyote fur, copper, acrylic paint. 12 × 9 in. Collection of Charlie and Gayle Pancerzewski.

Both Holm and Pasco are master mask carvers and formidable teachers. I have had the great fortune of bearing witness to this during my time sitting in on Bill Holm's classes at the University of Washington in the early 1970s. I have been a beneficiary during my time carving beside Duane Pasco. Holm's classes were basically lecture series backed with slides of mostly historical pieces. The first quarter he taught two-dimensional art, the second quarter three-dimensional art, and the third quarter ceremonial use of the art objects. In his classes Bill's slides showed the characteristics

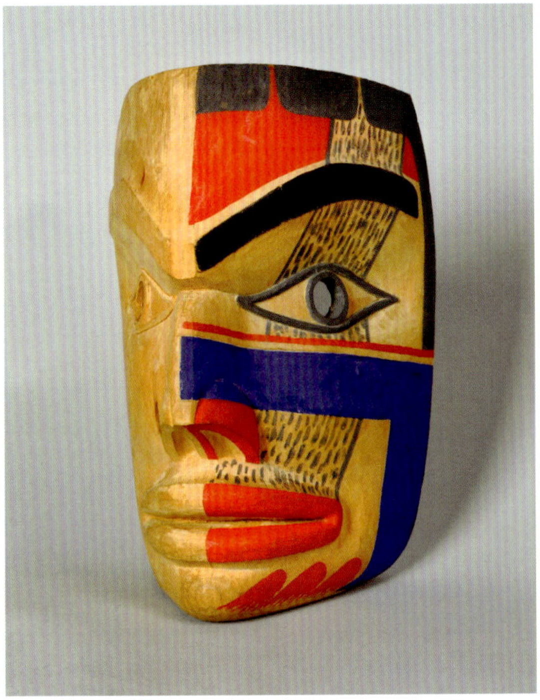

FIGURE 6.4 Bill Holm. Partially painted mask illustrating Nuu-chah-nulth tribal style, 1973. Wood, paint, 11.9 × 8.2 in. Burke Museum #2.5E655C.

of each tribal style, their uniqueness, how they differed from the other tribal styles (fig. 6.4). With the Northwest tribes it took a good eye to see and learn. And learn I did. Thank you, Bill Holm and Duane Pasco!

A great many people didn't have Holm and Pasco as teachers. I suppose a great many people do not have the eye, or have not learned from people actually involved in Northwest Coast art. These include so-called artist-carvers, especially the art dealers, and too many of the academics. This has resulted in the evolution of the today's "generic" form of Northwest Coast art. But this is not a fair or honest assessment in all respects. People are sometimes misinformed and mislead: students, collectors, amateurs, and professionals. There are, of course, a good many artist-carvers who are learned and practiced in specific tribal styles.

THE FOREST

I have read that the Iroquois carve some of their masks right on the living tree in the forest. I imagine the idea being that the spirit of the tree remains an integral part of the wood of the mask. Traditional people were respectful and spiritual in relation to the materials of daily and ceremonial life. They asked, begged even, for anything taken from the natural world, like cedar bark from the tree or even the entire tree from its surrounding relatives in the forest. I have done this on occasion. Almost always I am very grateful and respectful, as are most carvers, for a good piece of wood for a project.

I have plans to some day go into the forest in my traditional territory and carve a Wildman of the Forest (Ulth-ma-koke) mask, camping there until it is completed. Maybe leaving it there as a tribute to the trees and beings of the forest with the hope that I am able to access some of the energy of the deep for my carving. Ulth-ma-koke is the name for the so-called Wildman character and translates as Yellow Cedar Face/Yellow Cedar Man (fig. 6.5). *Ulth-mupt* means "yellow cedar" and *ko-us* means "human being." The Wildman of the Woods has long been my life's goal, to carve a truly wild one, and it has not been an easy undertaking. I have made a few masks that have hit the mark, and I have made many that have failed to portray the character, the man, the spirit.

The mask in figure 6.6 represents Ulth-ma-koke. When I set out carving this all-red mask, I attempted to represent my father and uncle's generation, whereas most masks represent a person from the distant past. I wanted this mask to have characteristics of a more recent period with more naturalistic features, where the old ones are often stylized or abstract. For instance, the old masks

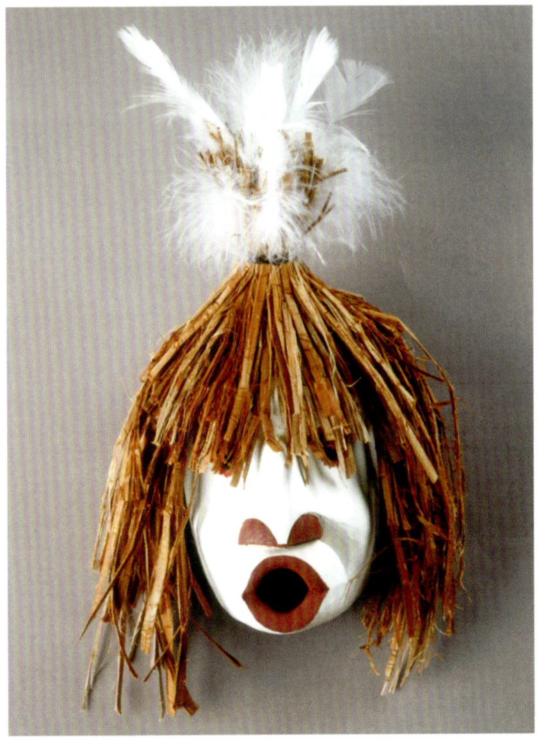

FIGURE 6.5 Douglas David (Nuu-chah-nulth). *Mask*, 1999. Wood, paint, cedar bark, feather, string, 13.3 × 4.7 in. Burke Museum #2004–2/181.

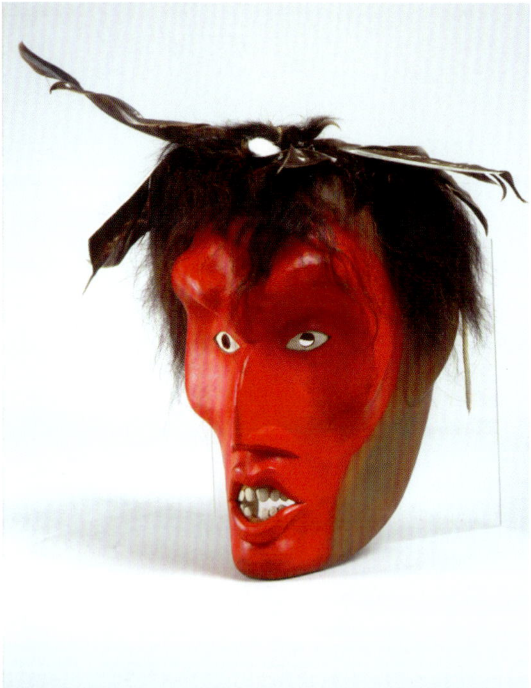

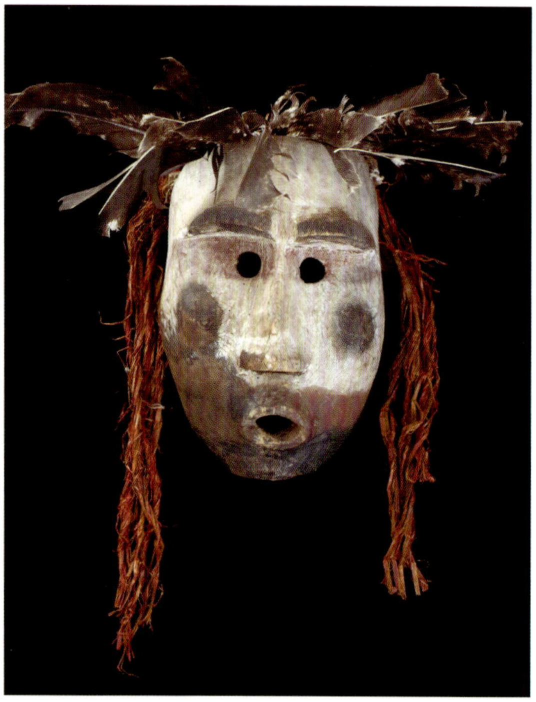

FIGURE 6.6 Joe David (Nuu-chah-nulth—Tla-o-qui-aht). *Ulth-ma-koke—Wild Man of the Woods*, 1999. Red cedar, acrylic paint, feathers, leather, 13.7 × 9 in. Gift of Arthur B. Steinman, Burke Museum #2004–2/184.

FIGURE 6.7 *Wildman type mask.* Nuu-chah-nulth—Ucleulet. University of Oregon Museum of Natural and Cultural History #2–1354.

usually have a protruding roundish hole for a mouth and simple round holes for eyes (fig. 6.7). I gave this guy more naturalistic eye and mouth features, and it worked. I'd even say the mask resembles one of my uncles.

I know from experiences (sixteen years on the small island of Echachisht, off the west coast of Vancouver Island) that living with and on the land, the Northwest Pacific Coast—with the forest to my back and the vast cosmos my canopy—my art, heart, soul, and mind is much more inspired and imbued with power than when I have lived in an urban environment. I won't say so it goes for anyone else, but I can see the power differences in the works of others with these varying lifestyles. Power comes from life experience!

PORTRAITS

Over time and with experience I have noticed that some masks resemble in features and expressions the carvers-artists or someone close to him or her. I choose the term "artist" rather than "carver" because I believe when things like this happen, art is happening; simply carving is not necessarily art, no matter how well made the object may be. My observations have lead me to believe that there are many portrait masks from the past (and the distant past) that not only represent a specific person but actually resemble that person. In the end, of course, I believe all art is self-portraiture in one way or another (fig. 6.8). Across the board, man, woman, animal, bird, the mythical, and the supernatural. "We are one!" "All is one!" Our ancestors knew this and lived it and portrayed it.

TLA-O-QUI-AHT STYLE

There are also styles within styles, period styles, village styles, which might say more about the creators rather than their communities. All the same, there are distinct styles. In some cases,

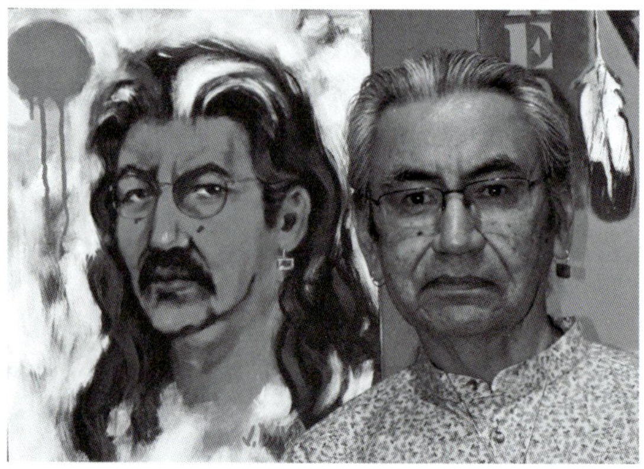

FIGURE 6.8 Joe David with self-portrait, 2007. Collection of Nancy Davenport. Photograph by Greg Blomberg.

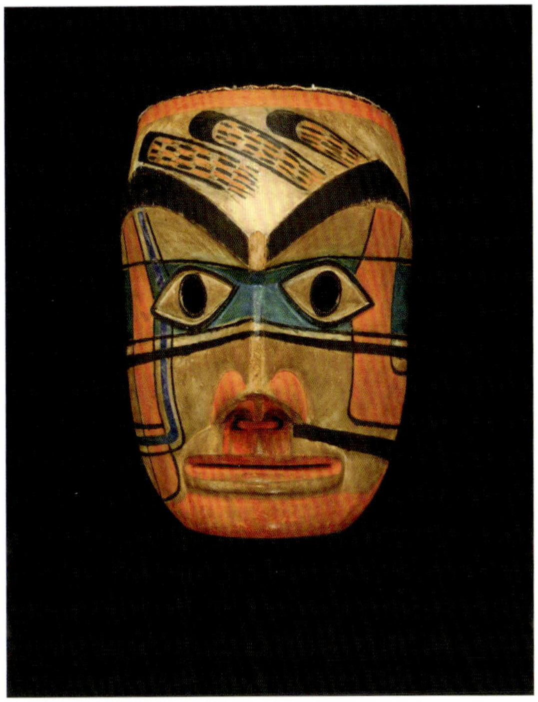

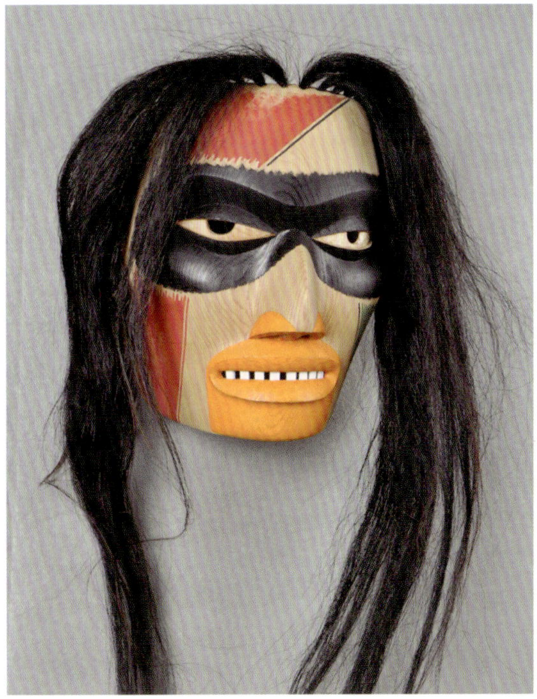

FIGURE 6.9 *Changer Mask.* Tla-o-qui-aht, attributed to Chief Atlieu, collected in 1935. Wood, paint, 7.4 × 10.8 in. Royal British Columbia Museum #18275.

FIGURE 6.10 Douglas David (Nuu-chah-nulth—Tla-o-qui-aht/Dakota). *Shaman's Mask,* 2000. Wood, paint, horsehair, string, 11.4 × 10.4 in. Burke Museum #2004–2/179.

the evolution of a style can be recognized in collected objects. A great number of cultural artifacts were collected on the western coast of Vancouver Island, and many of these things have been documented as having been collected at Tla-o-qui-aht (Clayoquot) (fig. 6.9).

Because I am from there, I have studied at great lengths many of these objects, especially the masks. This has allowed me to believe I can now easily recognize what I would call the "Tla-o-qui-aht style." I have gone to great lengths to create my masks in that style. Because it is basically self-portraiture, and thank goodness I have developed into a good artist and carver, by nature this style now comes easily to me. On occasion, I have noticed that my carvings and masks actually resemble my father and uncles and grandfathers. I accept the honor, however humble, to be a link in this so-far-unbroken chain in my people and family's history. I am proud to say I have a son, Douglas, who has become an active and accomplished carver as well (of masks especially) (figs. 6.5 and 6.10).

THE ART MARKET

The modern-day Northwest Coast art market has been by and large a mask market. Mass appeal (mask appeal) has dictated. What does this say about the old culture and the new art market culture and the carvers' culture? Who knows! But it is worth noting that this vast market has been dominated by male buyers. A personal guess would be that these men are identifying or attempting to identify with these masks, these characters, these faces. Whether they be beast or noble, there is an alliance that is wanted and perhaps needed. I believe some buyers actually develop a companionship with the masks. The art market is mostly responsible for the development of a generic Northwest Coast style and representation.

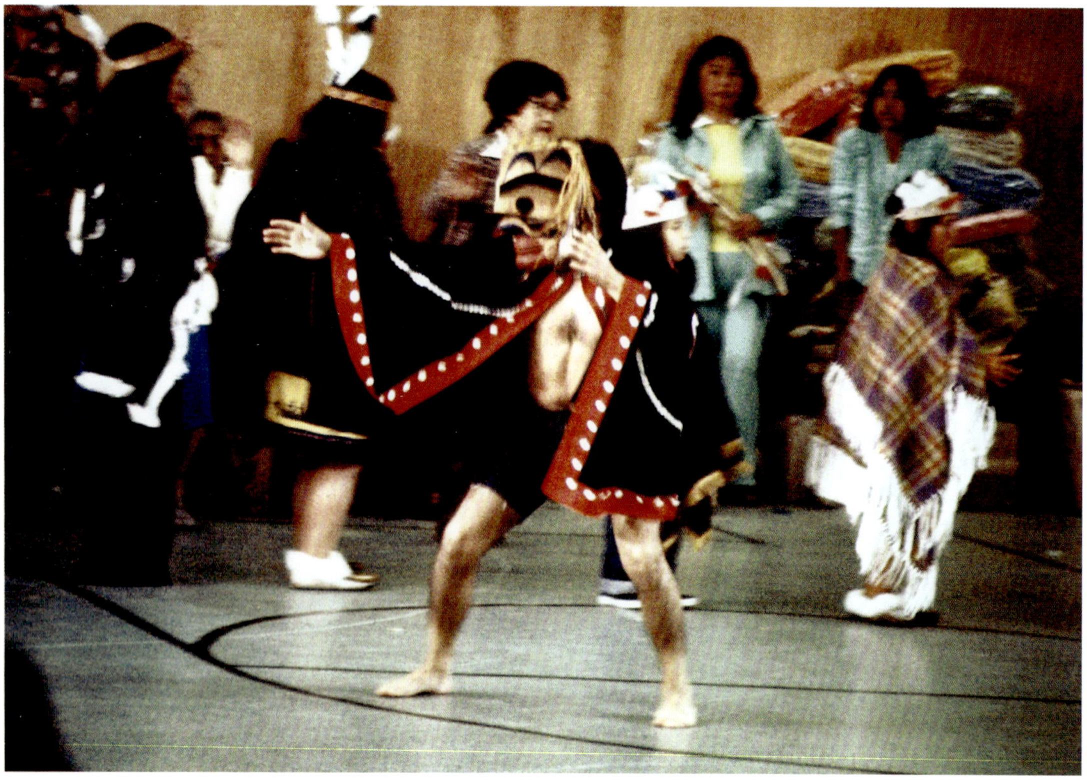

FIGURE 6.11 George David performing masked dance, Tofino, 1977. Photograph by Bill Holm.

WANNABES

I admit when I make a mask and wear it, I occasionally to some degree wannabe that character. It's fun and it satisfies something, somewhere, somehow. In the old days an accomplished dancer could easily become one with the mask/headdress character, as easily as an accomplished artist-carver could execute his duty (fig. 6.11).

THE ARTIST

The mask titled *The Artist* is one of about a half dozen I have carved over the years with that name (fig. 6.12). The first one basically dictated its own name—it was beautifully carved and colorfully painted with sweet, gentle features. It was only when it was finished when I realized its title—that it represented an artist. Others I've made in varying period styles, from the distant past to the recent past. The distant-past mask was carved in a very stylized manner, painted in the two old colors black and ocher-red. This mask is in the style of the early twentieth century. I will from time to time make more of these guys, which I suppose are basically self-portraits.

My son Douglas's mask is a copy of a mask I carved and represents a shaman (see fig. 6.10). In my mask the all-white left eye is representative of a person who has seen a very strong spirit. This actually happens to some people. For this reason I have always referred to the left eye as the spirit's eyes or the shaman's eye. Lately I tend to paint black around or near the left eye and red around or near the right eye: black for the spirit world and red for life and the earth plane.

MASKS

I have many favorite mask stories and favorite masks. As a child, I remember seeing masks and headdresses stored in shadowed places in homes. Though silent and motionless, they evoked power and motion. The wood, cedar bark, and paint breathed and had its own life smells. Even though the eyes were open, there was a strange sense of rest and otherworld placement.

I also remember, when I was very small, there was one remaining old longhouse, belonging to one of our head chiefs. A house no longer used for living in, but for ceremony. This memory is my favorite because it could come from a dream or a parallel reality experience. When I was a child, I had some powerful "world crossover" dreams and experiences. I believe it was all possible because some powerful elders were still alive and present. Elders born and raised in those powerful times of "Before." The land was fertile from countless centuries of cultural practice now unimaginable and undreamable.

Now to the memory of this very old, open-doored longhouse: We were never told not to enter uninvited, but nonetheless the big old place seemed to stand empty of village sound and motion. I remember entering, probably led in by an older brother or cousin, on a safe and sunny day into that old-world place: a world belonging to people mostly long gone. I remember the challenge of the length of the earth floor and the strength of that floor and how the power grew as we ventured farther to its end. Until finally, deep enough and empowered enough, masks, headdresses, and related mysterious objects could be

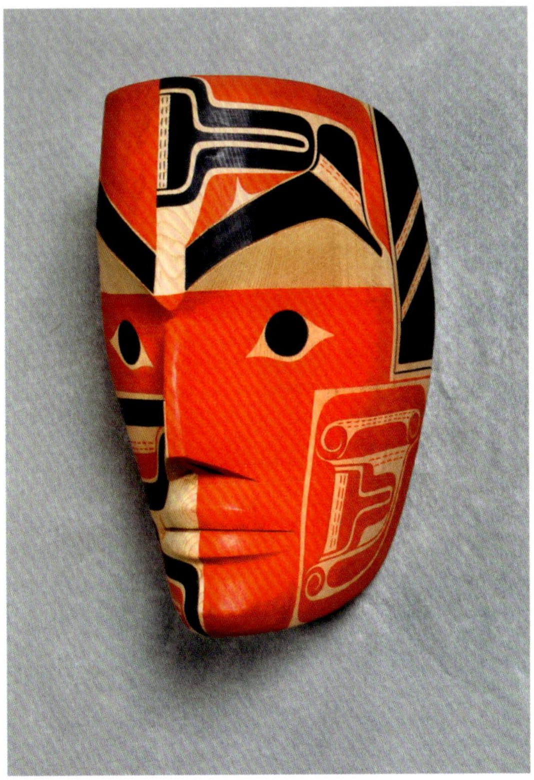

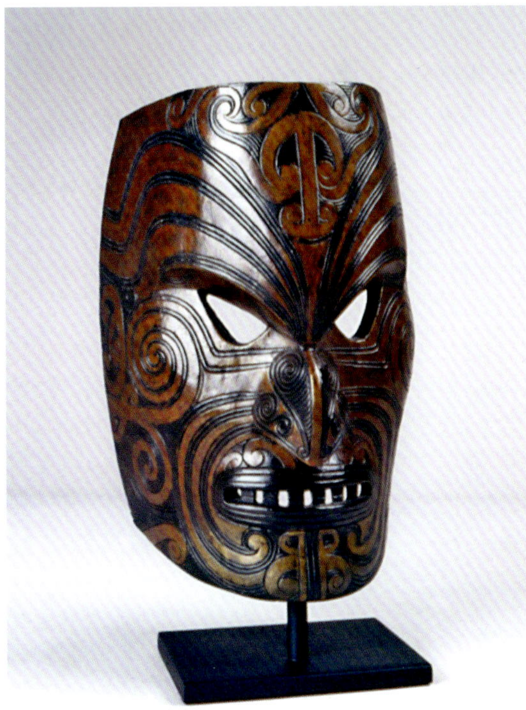

FIGURE 6.12 Joe David (Nuu-chah-nulth—Tla-o-qui-aht). *The Artist*, 1999. Red cedar, acrylic, 11.2 × 5.1 in. Burke Museum #2004–2/186.

FIGURE 6.13 Joe David (Nuu-chah-nulth—Tla-o-qui-aht). *Maori Warrior*, 1996. Bronze. 12.5 × 8.3 × 6 in. Burke Museum #2004–2/185.

seen lurking in the smoke-drenched shadows. A part of me was familiar with these creatures, but they held such immense power that soon my mind and body was cautioned from the house and back into the sun of day.

I could easily research our village facts, and learn the periods of these old houses, but to what use and to what reality? The reality that is my mind and body and spirit remains empowered and owned by this experience and other such experiences, and that's all I know and care about for now.

In 1983, I was visiting a museum in New Zealand and was fascinated with Maori art and carvings. While there I turned around away from a display case and saw at a distance across the way what appeared to be a very old, dark Nuu-chah-nulth face mask. Its overall shape and features were distinctly like those of masks from the western coast of Vancouver Island in the late eighteenth century. Heart pounding, I pondered, could it possibly have been brought to these islands by Captain Cook or someone else? I approached the case that displayed the mask, and upon close viewing, it was of course Maori with full moko representation (facial tattooing). I took some photos, planning to someday carve a copy.

Twelve years later I again found myself in New Zealand, as I was invited to be part of an gathering of indigenous artists. I had not yet carved the copy of the Maori mask. I brought my photos and planned to visit the museum, to see once again the old ancestor face. The mask/face was no longer on display, so I was brought to a basement storage room by some hosting Maori friends to try to locate it. It couldn't be found, however, and my friends soon got involved with viewing other objects. I set about pacing up and down, speaking to the ancestor, asking to meet him. In my pace I stopped, turned left, walked a few more steps, stopped and bent down to find on a low shelf the old-timer. He had guided and revealed himself to me, to the surprise and delight of my Maori hosts. I cradled and thanked the old guy before taking multiple photographs of him. He was as impressive as I remembered. From that trip I successfully carved my copy, in native New Zealand wood, and later had it cast in bronze (fig. 6.13).

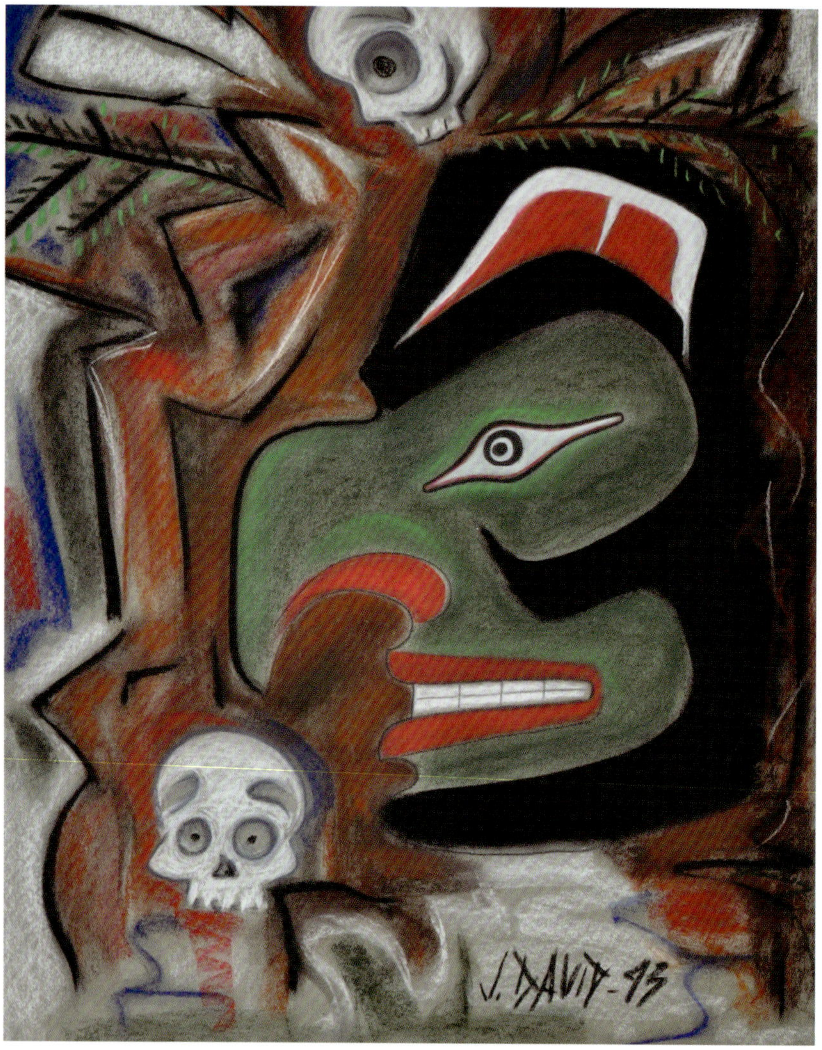

FIGURE 6.14 Joe David (Nuu-chah-nulth—Tla-o-qui-aht). *Bukwus*, 1993. Oil, pastel, paper, ink, 29.1 × 23 in. Gift of Arthur B. Steinman, Burke Museum #2004–2/382.

Once many years ago, I dreamed I was with my late cousin, the artist Arthur Thompson and we were somewhere in Nitinaht territory, preparing for some potlatch-like ceremonies. At a certain moment a great excitement shot through the gathering. Up over a rise in the distance came a parade of people in ceremonial attire, all singing. They were Tla-o-qui-aht, my people, and in the lead were our head chiefs wearing Thunderbird headdresses. Others following in order were wearing headdresses and masks and other regalia that I recognized. But at the end, the last four were wearing masks I'd never seen before. They were representations of human skulls and were very old-looking. The wood was dark and appeared to be worm-eaten, and it looked like there were remnants of cedar bark attached to the tops.

These masks had a very powerful effect on me. I have attempted a few times to carve representations of them, but feel I have not yet done justice to the dream (fig. 6.14).

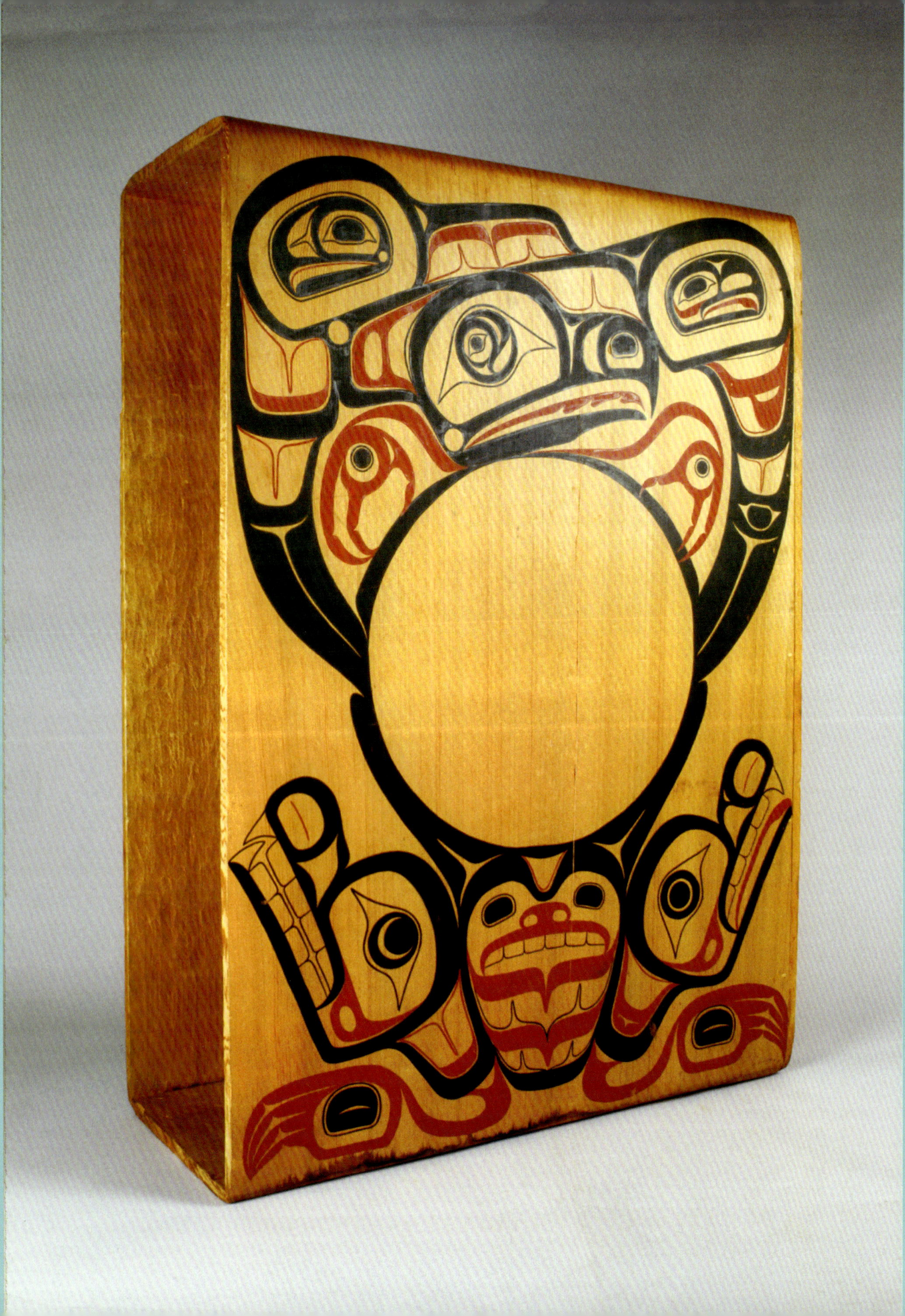

SEVEN

NORTHWEST COAST BOX DRUMS

ROBIN K. WRIGHT

References to bentwood box drums are contained in the oldest written documents on Northwest Coast art, the journals of the late-eighteenth-century explorers and fur traders. This art form has enjoyed a resurgence on the Northwest Coast in recent years. Box drums are deep bass percussion instruments, constructed with the same techniques used to make bentwood boxes and chests. The ends and the two sounding sides of the drum are made from a single cedar plank that is kerfed, steamed, and bent, with a separate piece pegged or sewn on one of the resultant openings. The proportions of box drums differ from those of boxes or chests, however, with the top, bottom, and end panels being very narrow, and the sounding sides very broad. They produce the most resonant sound when hung from a rope looped through holes in the top and suspended from a beam of the house. They can also be played by tipping them up on one lower corner and holding them from the edge so as not to dampen the sound when the sides are pounded with the fist or a wrapped drum stick (figs. 7.1a-c).

Other types of drums used on the Northwest Coast came to be better known in the twentieth century. Small round skin drums, made by stretching rawhide over one side of a bentwood frame, were used during the nineteenth century, primarily on the southern coast by Coast Salish religious dancers. On the northern coast they were used primarily by shamans in their curing work. Perhaps through their use to accompany the singing at gambling games (known as *lehal*), the use of round skin drums spread during the twentieth century. They have become today the most frequently used drum at potlatches and other social occasions. During the nineteenth century, however, the drum most frequently used on the northern Northwest Coast during the display of chiefly prerogatives was the bentwood box drum. With the introduction of the commercial bass drum, brought by missionaries to the coast during the late nineteenth century for use in church bands, the box drum was gradually replaced. This chapter presents some of the earliest evidence we have for the use of box drums on the northern Northwest Coast, ending with some information on box drums recently made.

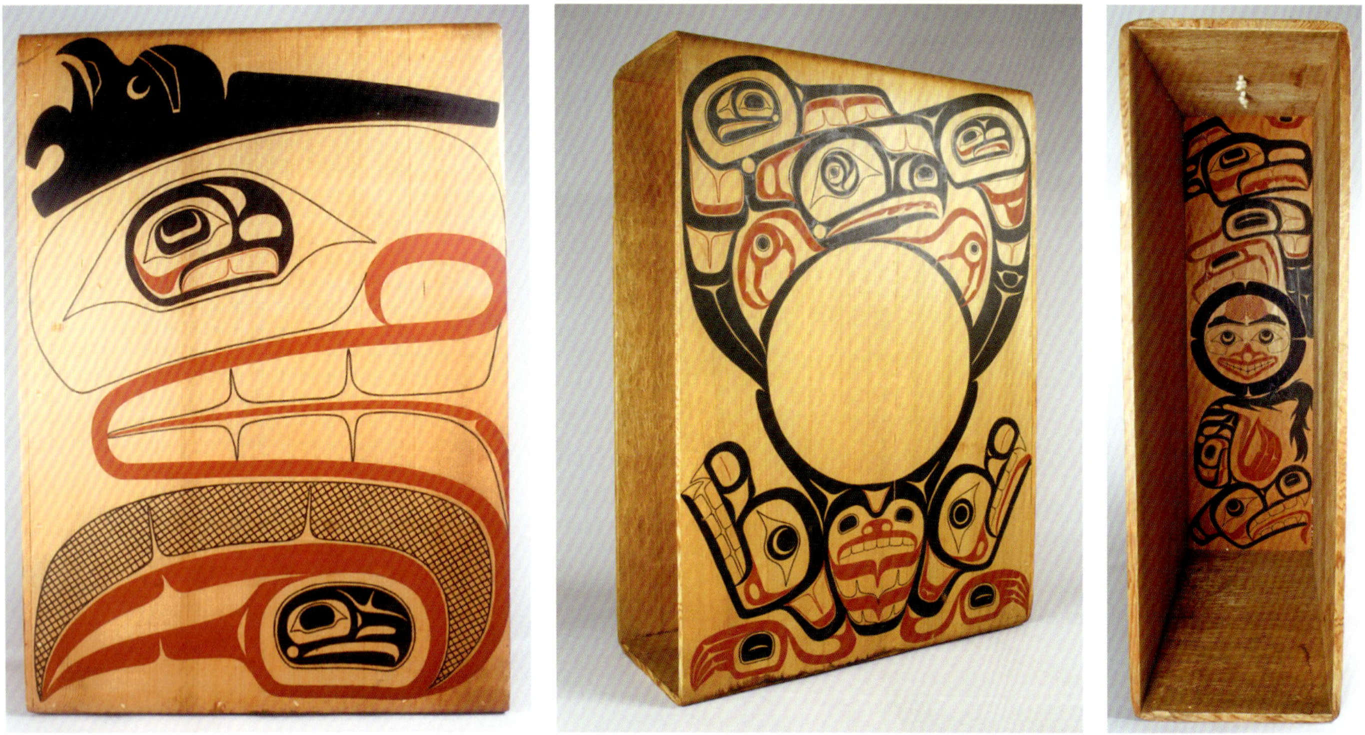

FIGURE 7.1A-C David Boxley (Tsimshian). *Box Drum*, 1997. Wood, red cedar, paint, 44.5 × 14 × 1.2 in. Gift of David Boxley, Burke Museum #2005–137/1.

The first mention of song, dance, and musical instruments on the Northwest Coast comes from the four journals kept on the Spanish voyage of Juan Pérez. They record the first encounter between the Haida people and Europeans at sea off the northwestern tip of Haida Gwaii (the Queen Charlotte Islands), near the village of K'yuusdaa on July 19 and 20, 1774: "Several canoes of Indians came into view, and seeing that we were not making any headway, they approached us and began trading with our crew. But first, they sang and danced, and cast feathers in the air. . . . The king or captain referred to above carried his tambourine, jingling it. Before arriving they danced and sang" (Beals 1989: 78). Juan Crespi, one of the priests on the voyage, described the same scene, saying: "These canoes came alongside without their occupants manifesting the least distrust, they [were] singing and playing instruments of wood fashioned like drums or timbrels, and some making movements like dancing" (Griffin 1969: 235).

Crespi mentions "drums or timbrels," while Pérez describes a "tambourine" that jingled. This may have been a circular puffin beak rattle rather than a skin or wooden drum. The first description of an instrument that is clearly a box drum comes from the journal of the French expedition led by Captain Étienne Marchand in August 1791, while exploring the fortress on Lucy Island near K'yuusdaa in Haida Gwaii: "He here remarked several boxes without a lid, the use of which the islanders explained: these perform the office of a drum from which they draw a sound, by striking with the fist against the outer sides" (Fleurieu 1801: 265).

During the next year another Spanish explorer, Jacinto Caamaño, visited the same area near K'yuusdaa and again described what is clearly a box drum, this time being played in a canoe: "Two men, in the bows of the canoe, also beat this time with the hilt of their paddles on a small thwart, placed for this purpose and for the support of a large drum, which a lusty native struck with his fists, producing sounds much the same as those of a European bass drum. This sight greatly astonished us, as did also the size of the canoe" (Wagner and Newcombe 1938: 216). Later, while surveying Napean Sound in Tsimshian territory, Caamaño exchanged names with a chief named Jammisit, signifying their esteem for each other.[1] The exchange of names between sea captains and chiefs was frequently done on the Northwest Coast during the late eighteenth and early nineteenth centuries to cement a trading relationship.

Caamaño later went on shore at the invitation of Jammisit, and his journal of this event provides the most elaborate description of masked dances and puppetry known from this period, including another description of box drums: "After two or three preliminary attempts, he started a song. This was at once taken up by everyone inside the house, man or woman, and produced a terrific volume of sound, to whose measure he then began to dance, while a specially chosen Indian beat the time on a large drum" (Wagner and Newcombe 1938: 291).[2]

We know that large box drums continued in use well into the late nineteenth century not only by the Haida and the Tsimshian but also by the Tlingit. The collector George Emmons has enumerated six—"two in the Sitka tribe, one at Hoonah, and three at Angoon." This enumeration suggests they may have been relatively rare yet important possessions (De Laguna and Emmons 1991: 294). In 1876, Reverend Collison, the first missionary to live among the Haida, described the scene when the chief Albert Edward Edenshaw and his entourage arrived at Massett:

> The following day Edenshaw, an influential chief, arrived from Virago Sound, accompanied by a large number of his tribe in several war canoes. His own canoe was manned principally by his slaves. He and his men were received with honours, and a dance of peace was accorded them. There had been a quarrel between the two tribes, and Edenshaw with his leading men had been invited for the purpose of making peace. As their large canoes approached the shore the occupants chanted the brave deeds of the past, and were answered in a similar strain by the concourse of the shore. The chanting was accompanied by regular and graceful motions of the head and body and waving of the hands. The time was kept by a large drum formed like a chest, and made of red cedar wood, painted with grotesque figures, and covered with skin. This was beaten by a drummer seated in the bow of the leading canoe. (Collison 1981: 70)

This is the only description of a box drum that includes a skin covering, and it is unclear whether the skin covered the open end or the sides of the drum.

Collison's colleague, William Duncan, had come to the Northwest Coast in 1857 and established a Christian community, first at Fort Simpson and then relocated to Old Metlakatla nearby. In 1887 he moved his followers to New Metlakatla in southeastern Alaska after splitting with the Anglican church. Duncan's establishment of a church band at Old Metlakatla was an important element in spreading the Christian message, and band uniforms and instruments, including bass drums, were sent to the aid of the missions (fig. 7.2). Rev. Collison provided an account of Duncan's introduction of instruments to the Northwest Coast, explaining that Duncan had acquired

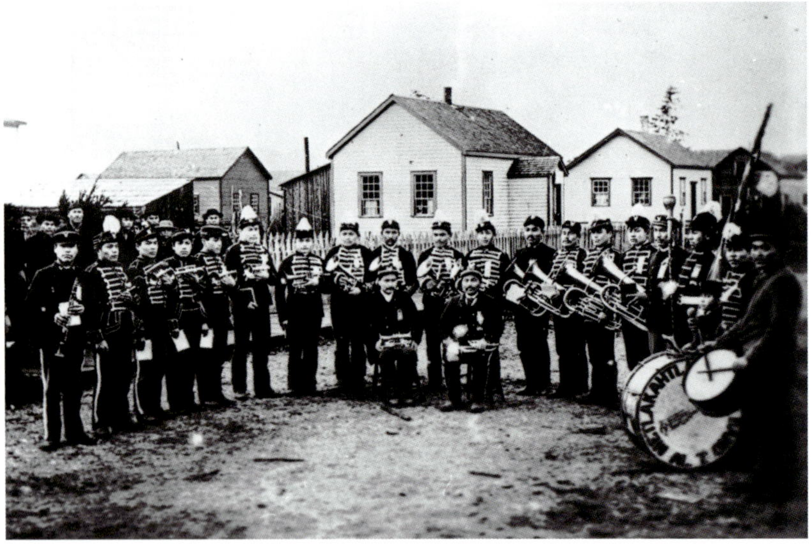

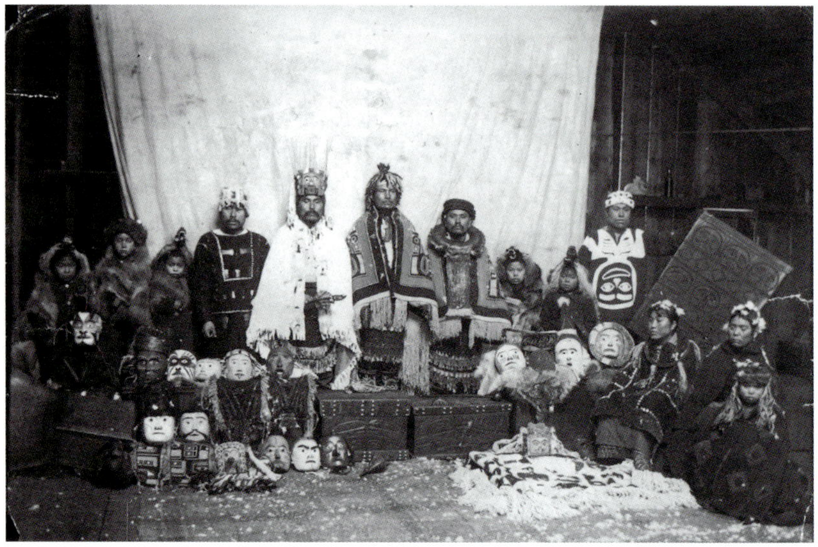

a set of instruments while in San Francisco in 1870, delayed on his return to Metlakatla from a furlough in England. He had hung them in his office in Metlakatla, where they remained unused for a number of years until Collison suggested that Duncan hire someone to teach music. A German man living in Victoria, a former bandmaster for a Prussian cavalry regiment, was brought in to teach music in 1879 (Collison 1981: 179–80). One of his talented pupils, B. A. Haldane, later became the bandmaster.[3] Many of the Native communities in this area acquired their own bands and were trained by Haldane.

Given the role of the Metlakatla community in spreading the use of bass drums in the late nineteenth century, it seems fitting that David Boxley, a Tsimshian artist who was born in Metlakatla, has been at the center of a resurgence in bentwood box drum making. In 1996, along with the Seattle Tsimshian community, Boxley hosted a Seattle Potlatch at Indian Heritage High School in Seattle. For this event he borrowed Bill Holm's box drum, which was made in the 1960s. Following the event, Boxley made several box drums for his own use and that of his dance group, the Seattle-based Tsimshian Haayuuk. At the February 1997 Seattle Potlatch three of those drums were played.

Boxley taught a box drum making class in Ketchikan in March 1997 at the Totem Heritage Center, and nine of the participants successfully built bent box drums, including Wayne Hewson, Lee Wallace, Norman Jackson, and Fred Trout. A local Ketchikan television station documented the event. This news footage showed several historical photographs of box drums, including a 1914 photo of a group of Nisga'a chiefs at Gitlakdamiks, British Columbia (fig. 7.3).[4] That photo documents the fact that box drums were still important possessions well into the twentieth century. Taken more than thirty years after European-style bass drums had been introduced for use in Christian community bands, the image suggests that ceremonial occasions when chiefs displayed their regalia still called for traditional bentwood box drums. By this time they had become important family heirlooms. Such heirlooms declared their status no doubt in defiance of the Christian missionaries, who with government agents in Canada had made the potlatch illegal in the 1880s.

FIGURE 7.2 Metlakatla Band in uniforms, 1890. B. A. Haldane is the third from the left in the band. Courtesy of the Alaska State Library, Duncan Cottage Photograph Collection, neg. #688.

FIGURE 7.3 Chief James Skean and his family, 1914. Gitlakdamiks (Aiyansh BC). Large box drum at right. Image PN4330 courtesy of Royal BC Museum. Photograph by B. A. Haldane.

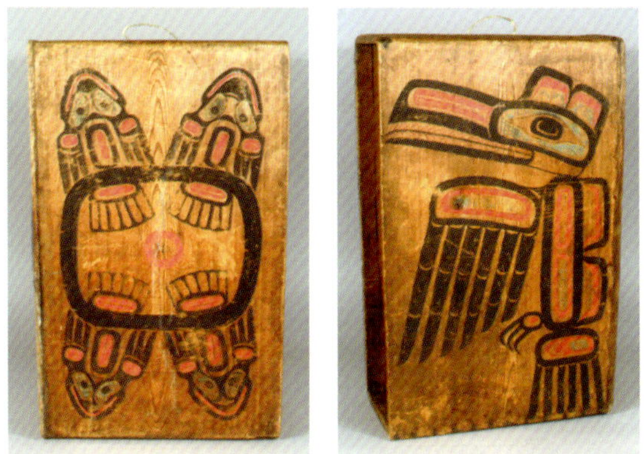

FIGURE 7.4A-B *Box Drum*. Tlingit, late nineteenth century. Red cedar, paint, 35.4 × 21.2 × 11.8. A profile raven is shown on one side, and four ravens shown from above, flying out from a nestlike rounded rectangle, are on the other side. Walter Waters Collection, Burke Museum #1–1586. Photograph by Bill Holm.

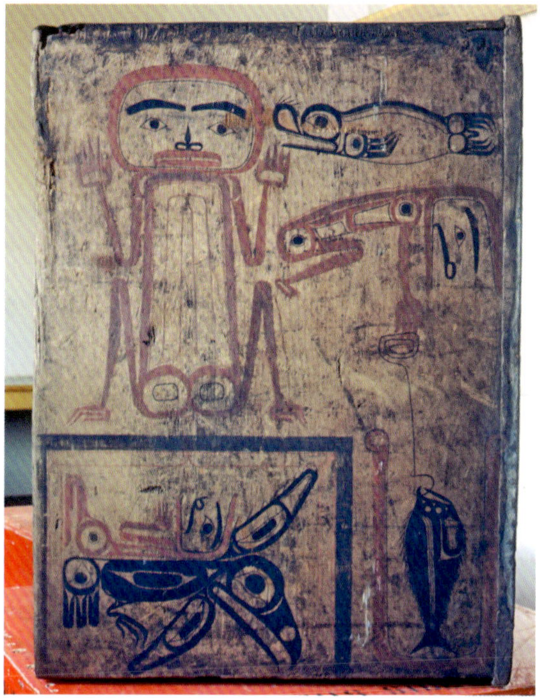

FIGURE 7.5 *Box Drum.* Haida, late nineteenth century. Red cedar, paint, 42.1 × 30.3 × 16.1 in. This image illustrates Raven and the halibut fisherman story. Courtesy of the Field Museum of Natural History #79599. Photograph by Bill Holm.

The meaning of the rows of heads and diamonds on the box drum in figure 7.3 is unknown, but it is likely that the majority of nineteenth-century box drums displayed designs that related to the family prerogatives of the owners (figs. 7.4a-b). A few Tlingit box drums are known to have been used by shamans (Holm 1987: 176–77; Wardwell 1996: 236–37). Perhaps the most narrative box drum design is on a Haida drum that illustrates the story of Raven and the halibut fishermen (fig. 7.5). This drum was collected by C. F. Newcombe at the village of Xaaayna 'llnagaay (New Gold Harbour), near Skidegate, and is said to have belonged to the chief of that village. On one side a human figure with birdlike feet sits above a box that contains Raven shown back to back with a human figure, which probably represents Raven transforming into his human form. To the right, a seal swims above another human figure with a profile face that holds a coiled fishing line with a halibut on the end. In this Haida story Raven steals the bait from the hooks of halibut fishermen, who eventually hook his beak and break it off. Raven then goes to the fishermen's village searching for his beak.[5]

In the early twentieth century, a Kwakwa̱ka̱'wakw box drum appeared in the 1914 Edward S. Curtis film *In the Land of the Head Hunters* (fig. 7.6). It is unknown whether this drum was an old one or was made by a Fort Rupert artist as one of the many props made for the movie (Holm and Quimby 1980: 49, 54, 60, 82, 83). The next Northwest Coast box drums known to have been made in the twentieth century were made after the antipotlatch law was dropped in Canada. Bill Holm made a Kwakwa̱ka̱'wakw-style box drum in 1956 for use at Camp Nor'wester at the urging of the artist Mungo Martin, who told him that this was the proper type of drum to have.[6] Mungo Martin's advice suggests that although no early journals document its use among the Kwakwa̱ka̱'wakw, this instrument was ceremonially important there as well. This drum, as well as a second drum made by Holm in the 1960s, were not bentwood but were joined at the corners. Holm also remembers a box drum, probably made by the Kwakwa̱ka̱'wakw artist Doug Cranmer, being used at the Alert Bay big house in the 1960s. Other artists—such as Duane Pasco, Jay Haavik, and Dennis Katzeek—have made bentwood box drums in recent years. The first known box drum with a Coast Salish–style design is one that was made for the Snoqualmie Tribe in 1989. This box drum was also not bentwood but was joined at the corners. It was painted by David Horsley and used on the beach at Golden Gardens Park to welcome the canoes at the Paddle to Seattle event in 1989.

The record for the most box drums ever assembled at one event may go to the Fourth Generation Ten Year Potlatch, which celebrated ten years of dancing in Metlakatla from August 7 to 9, 1997. The name refers to the participants' being the fourth generation of Tsimshian people in Metlakatla after the move to Alaska from Old Metlakatla. The ten-year celebration marked the anniversary of their first potlatch held in Metlakatla in 1987. During July 1997, I had the opportunity to visit Metlakatla on the research vessel the *Snow Goose.* When we arrived at Metlakatla, we found David Boxley there assisting Wayne Hewson, who was teaching his own box drum class. Hewson had been one of Boxley's box drum students in Ketchikan earlier in the year.

The design on his drum represents the four Tsimshian clans—Eagle, Wolf, Raven, and Killer Whale—on the corners. A circle in the middle is surrounded with ten male and female faces, representing the ten years of the Fourth Generation Dancers. Eleven box drums were made at that time in preparation for the Fourth Generation Ten Year Potlatch. These eleven box drums were

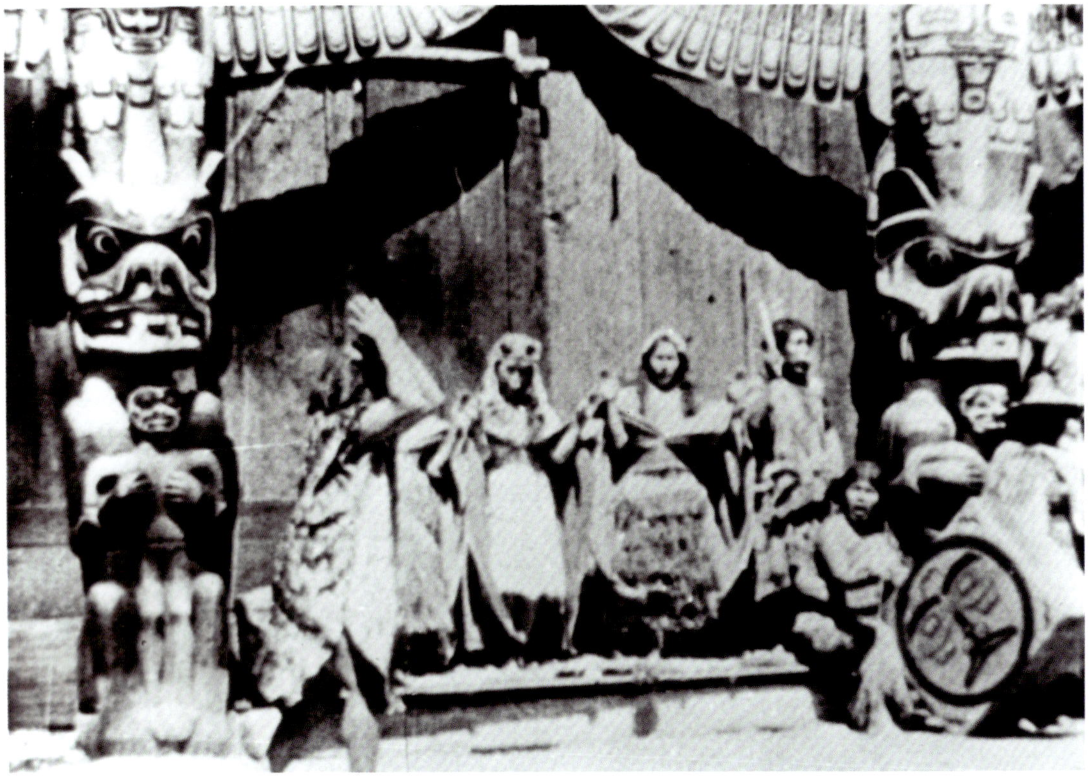

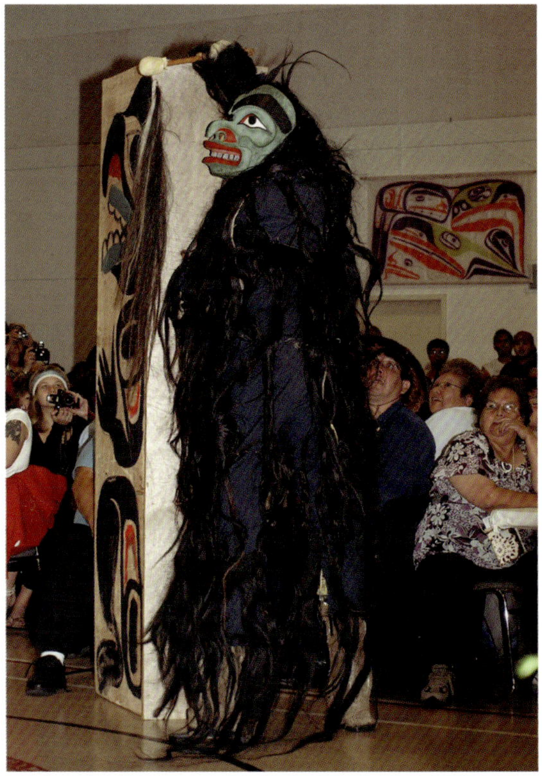

joined by several from the earlier Ketchikan box drum class, and Boxley's box drums, for a total of eighteen all playing at the same time. According to those who where there, the deep booming sound that was generated could be heard and felt throughout the village.

In 2009 the Haida artist Robert Davidson hosted a celebration in Old Massett on the occasion of the fortieth anniversary of the raising of his pole in front of the Anglican church in 1969. Fifteen box drums were played on that occasion and several were given as gifts (fig. 7.7). It is interesting that at a potlatch hosted by Davidson in 1980 in Old Massett, in honor of the living Haida, a number of round skin drums were given as gifts to the leaders of dance groups (Steltzer 1984: 68–70). Skin drums had also been given as gifts by the artist Joe David at the 1976 memorial potlatch held for his father, Hyacinth, at Tofino on Vancouver Island. They both urged the recipients to learn songs from their elders and teach them to the youth. Thirty years later, the ceremonial importance of the bentwood box drum has returned to its previous prominence, as documented a hundred years ago in the Haldane photograph of Chief James Skean and his family. The resurgence of this art form sounds as a loud celebration of the vitality of Native art on the Northwest Coast.

FIGURE 7.6 Box drum appearing in a dance scene from *In the Land of the Head-Hunters*, 1914. Photograph by Edmund Schwinke. Burke Museum #1988–78/48.

FIGURE 7.7 Reg Davidson. Gagiid box drum and Gagiid dancer leading the drummers, brought out on the occasion of Robert Davidson's fortieth anniversary of his Massett pole raising, August 2009. Photograph by Robert Leece.

NOTES

This essay has been revised from one written in response to the question "What have been the most exciting recent developments in Northwest Coast art and art history?" for a Northwest Coast Symposium at the Otsego Institute for Native American Art History, New York State Historical Society Association in Cooperstown, New York in 1998.

1 This name, if pronounced according to the Spanish spelling, would not have the English "J" sound but rather an "H" sound. In fact, the name *Hamtsid*, meaning "eating owner" or "owner of eating," is a widely known and used name among both the Heiltsuk and Kwakwaka'wakw people. It is probable that the name written in the Spanish journal as *Jammisit*, is in fact the name *Hamtsid* (Bill Holm, personal communication, August 1998).

2 For the full detailed description of this amazing performance, see Wagner and Newcomb 1938: 291–92.

3 B. A. Haldane, a Tsimshian photographer from Metlakatla, played piano, pipe organ, coronet, trombone, and violin. He was a composer as well as the director of the band in Metlakatla (Askren 2007: 45).

4 The subjects of this photo were identified as Andrew Nass, John Nass, James Skean, and Philip Nass, photographed at Gitlaxdamiks circa 1903, Royal British Columbia Museum, neg. no. PN4330 in 1998 (Brown 1998: 19, fig. 2.5). Thanks to the research done by Mique'l Askren Dangeli, we can now identify this photograph as one taken by B. A. Haldane in 1914 (Dangeli in press).

5 For the full Raven epic, see Swanton 1905b: 110–50.

6 *M<u>a</u>nat'si* is the word for box drum in Kwakwala, meaning a receptacle or container for rhythm. The word for the more common plank drum used by the Kwakw<u>a</u>k<u>a</u>'wakw is *tlixsd<u>a</u>ma* (William Wasden, personal communication, 2010).

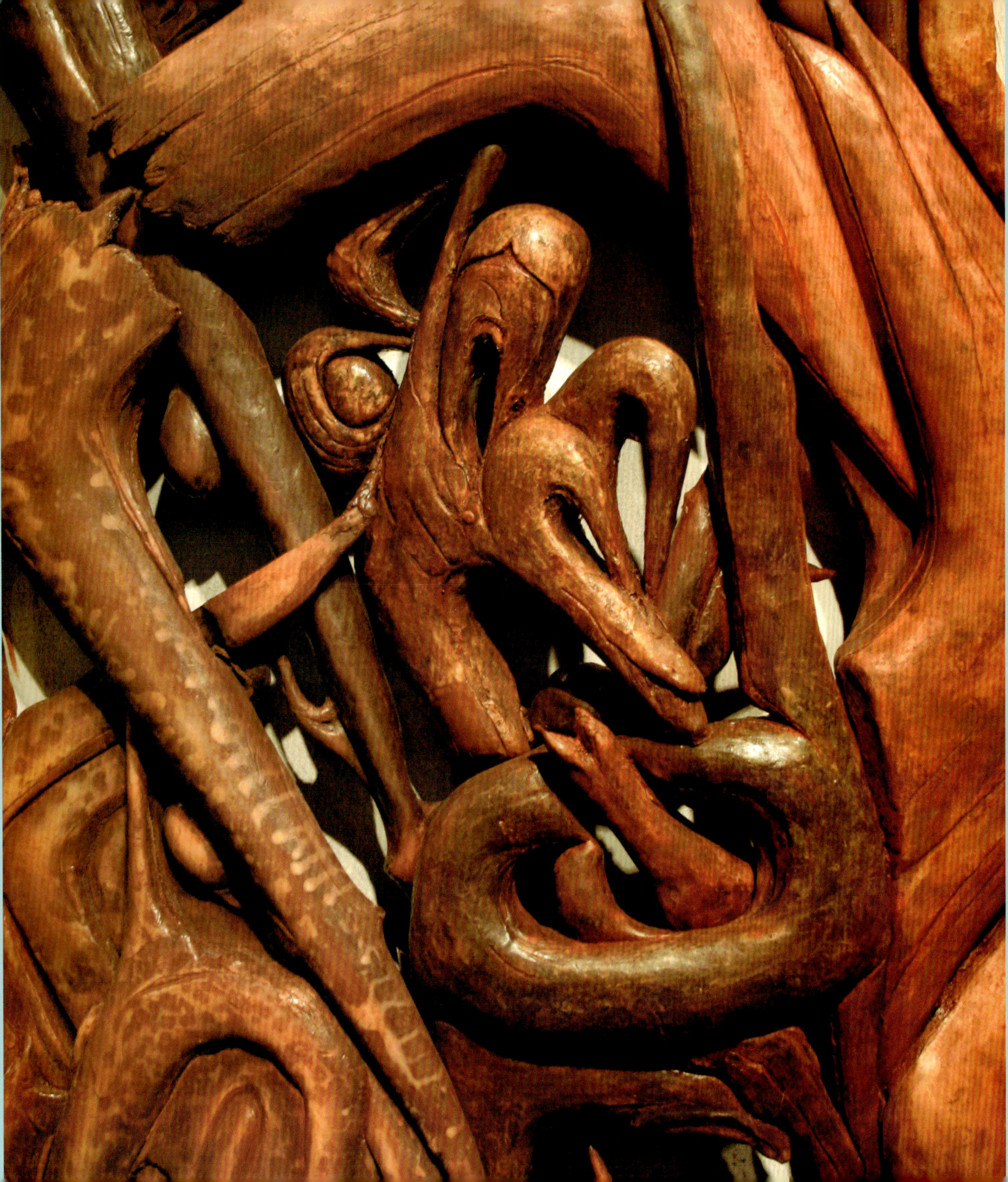

EIGHT

ACTS OF PROPATRIATION

Two Kaats' House Posts by Nathan and Stephen Jackson

EMILY MOORE

In July of 1899 the SS *George W. Elder* anchored off the beach of the Tlingit village of Gaash, located near Cape Fox in southern southeast Alaska. The last stop on a two-month expedition to Alaska sponsored by the railroad tycoon Edward H. Harriman, Gaash appeared to expedition members as a "deserted village," the very title that expedition photographer Edward S. Curtis had given a photograph he took from the shore (fig. 8.1). Framing the clan houses and their crest-topped poles behind the sweep of an empty beach, Curtis's photograph presaged the "vanishing Indian" theme that would become the leitmotif of his career. At the same time, the photograph's title revealed the mentality used to justify a large-scale removal of Tlingit property from Cape Fox. Believing that Gaash was permanently deserted—and legitimizing their actions in the name of "science"—members of the Harriman expedition removed from the houses dozens of items of Tlingit clan property, or *at.óow* ("owned or purchased thing"). These included four totem poles, four house posts, the entire house front of the Teikweidí Grizzly Bear house, and several box drums, bentwood boxes, and masks. These *at.óow* were later donated to museums across the United States (in addition to the Bronx Zoo), fulfilling Harriman's goal that the 1899 expedition would "gather useful information and distribute it for the benefit of others" (Litwin 2005: 11).

Among the confiscated *at.óow* were four house posts taken from the Teikweidí Kaats' house, two of which were eventually reunited in the Burke Museum of Natural History and Culture (fig. 8.2).[1] These house posts depict the Teikweidí crest of the grizzly bear, a bear who married the hunter Kaats' before her cub children killed him for having betrayed her. In some versions of the Teikweidí story, Kaats' has promised his bear wife never to look at his human spouse again; when he is tricked into doing so, his cub children tear him to pieces. The bear wife finds her husband's body and cries the mournful song of a loon (Swanton 1909: 28–229; Dauenhauer and Dauenhauer 1987: 219–43).

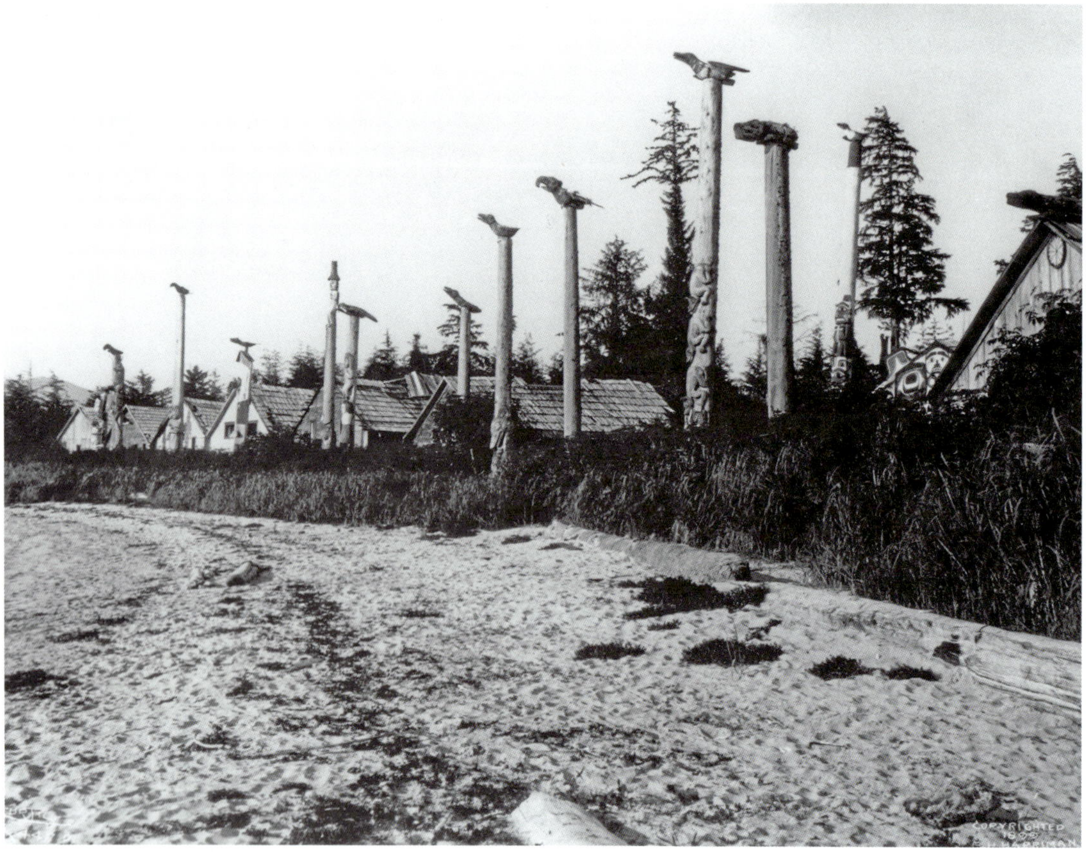

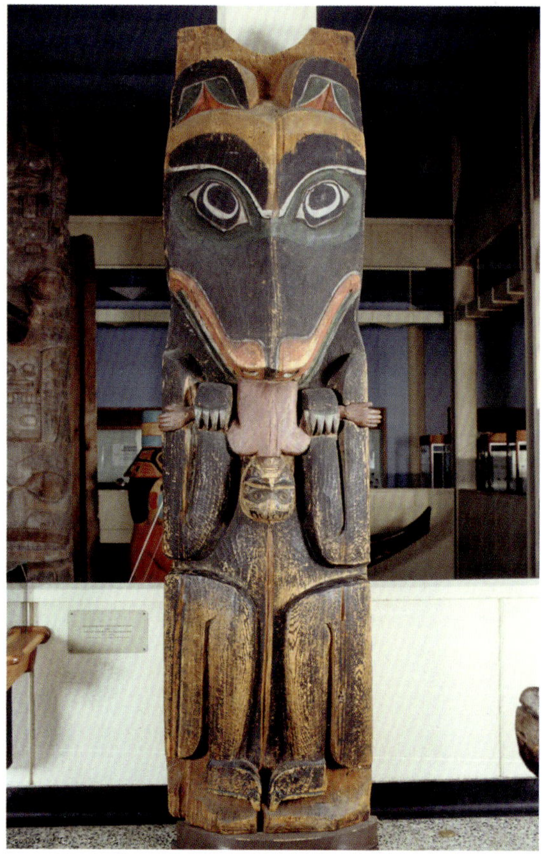

FIGURE 8.1 Edward S. Curtis. *Deserted Village*, 1899. Cape Fox, Alaska. University of Washington Libraries, Special Collections #NA 2129.

FIGURE 8.2 *Kaat's Teikweidí House Post*. Tlingit. Cedar, paint, 131.2 × 36.3 in. Burke Museum #1–10831.

The Teikweidí brown bear posts stood together for nearly seventy years at the Burke Museum; no longer proclaiming their crests in the clan house at Gaash, their role was to exemplify Tlingit carving for a museum audience (fig. 8.3). Then, in 1999, a hundred years after the Harriman Expedition had removed the posts from Alaska, Cape Fox Heritage Corporation filed a repatriation claim for the Teikweidí house posts and launched a process that would return the posts to the clan. The 1990 passage of the Native American Graves Protection and Repatriation Act (NAGPRA) had turned the tables on assumptions like Edward Harriman's—that Native property should be "distributed" in the name of science—and affirmed the right of Native peoples to protect and direct their own cultural patrimony. Reviewing Cape Fox's repatriation claim, curators at the Burke Museum recognized the Teikweidí house posts were stolen property and arranged to return them to Alaska. On July 23, 2001, the Sanyaa Kwáan finally welcomed the house posts home (fig. 8.4).[2]

As this essay details, the return of the Teikweidí brown bear posts marked a new relationship between Tlingit peoples and the Burke Museum—and it launched yet another chapter in these house posts' story. Responding to the return of their *at.óow* with an act rooted in the Northwest Coast potlatch tradition, Tlingit individuals and corporations organized to give something back to the Burke Museum—not replications of the Kaats' posts per se, but artworks that honored the crests of the posts while asserting a renewed Tlingit presence in the Burke Museum. Cape Fox Corporation, the village corporation for the Sanyaa Kwáan, offered cedar logs to the Burke to support the creation of replacement poles. In 2001, with additional funds from the National Endowment for the Arts, the Ferguson Foundation, the Sealaska Heritage Institute, and several other private donors, the Burke commissioned two new Kaats' house posts. Dr. Rosita Worl, president of the Sealaska Heritage Institute and a Tlingit woman herself, suggested the idea of a father/son team of artists, Tlingit master carver Nathan Jackson and his son, Stephen Jackson. Dedicated in August 2005, the Jackson posts represent an important new chapter in the story of Kaats' and in the relationship between Native peoples and museums in the repatriation era.

This essay examines the significance of the Jackson Kaats' posts at the Burke Museum. It also proposes to name the exchange of repatriated art for newly commissioned art as "propatriation"—an exchange that describes a growing number of museum commissions for contemporary Northwest Coast Native art.[3] Denoting the creation of an object made to acknowledge an object returned, propatriation works in dialogue with repatriation, the act which is its catalyst. Propatriation draws on a definition of the prefix "pro" meaning "forth," signaling the sending forth from the homeland or lineage. It also plays on the meaning of "pro" as "for the sake of" (as in *pro bono*), "in return for" (as in *quid pro quo*), and even "pro" as being "for" something (as in *pro-Tlingit*). (Of course, for the Tlingit and most other matrilineal groups on the Northwest Coast, propatriation should be "pro*matriation*," but for clarity's sake it seems best to keep the root word intact.) Reversing actions like those of the Harriman Expedition, propatriation works to provide museums with art endorsed by Native communities, swapping out the spoils of a colonial past for objects that Native artists design specifically for museum display. As this essay details, the Jackson posts use propatriation to assert a distinctive Tlingit narrative in the Burke Museum, one that harkens to the history of the Teikweidí house posts at Gaash at the same time that it looks to a Tlingit future.

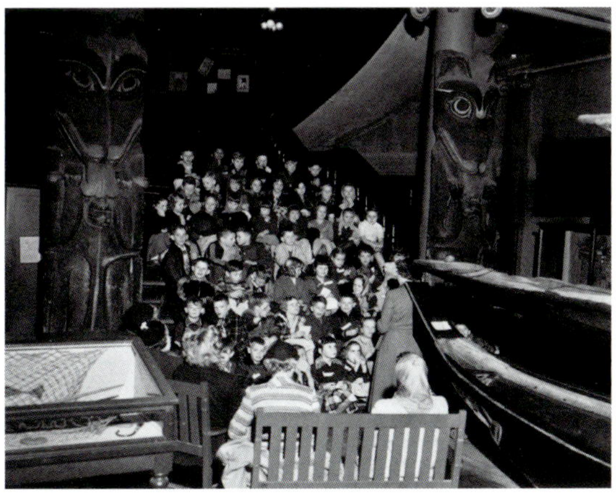

FIGURE 8.3 Third-grade students seated on a stairwell flanked by the Kaats' Teikweidí House Posts, Burke Museum, Seattle, 1950. University of Washington Libraries, Special Collections #UW19956z. Photograph by E. F. Martin.

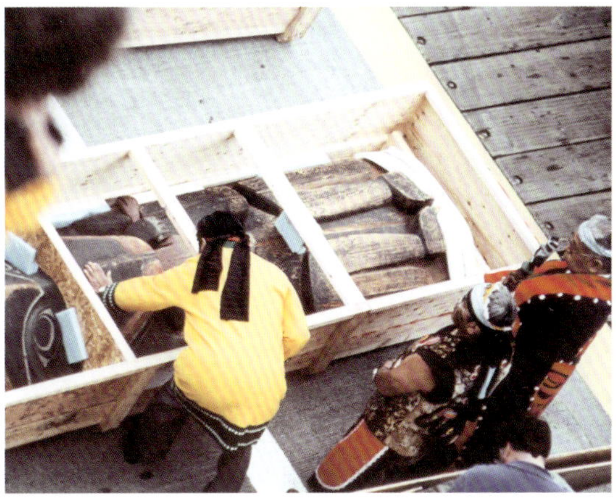

FIGURE 8.4 *Kaats' Teikweidí House Post*. Ketchikan, July 2001. Photograph by Robin K. Wright.

In designing their house posts for the Burke, neither Nathan nor Stephen chose to replicate the Gaash posts. "I felt that the original pole was the original pole," Nathan said of this decision. "I would make a rendition of my own" (personal communication 2008). Nathan's emphasis on remaining faithful to the story of Kaats' rather than to its exact physical representation honors Tlingit belief that the *right* to an origin story, crest, name, song, or other object of *at.óow* claimed by an individual or clan matters more than a physical representation of that right (Dauenhauer and Dauenhauer 1987: 28–29). It also represents a refusal to provide the Burke a copy of *at.óow* that had never been rightfully "purchased" or recognized, as required by Tlingit tradition, at a potlatch as the Burke's "owned or purchased thing."

Nathan's rendition of the Kaats' story differs from the Gaash post on several fronts (fig. 8.5). He shortened the snout of the bear, since he felt that the long nose of the Gaash post could have been mistaken for a wolf (personal communication 2008). Instead of the small, inverted human figure caught with outstretched hands in the great bear's mouth—a human figure that has been interpreted as a slave, rival, or debtor of the Teikweidí clan, or as Kaats' himself (Holm 1987: 212)—Nathan chose to depict the hunter Kaats' upright in his bear wife's embrace (compare figures 8.2 and 8.5). The man stands between her hind legs, his arms wrapped around her knees, her paws cupping his shoulders. Here the intertwining of bear and human bodies harmonizes, creating a peaceful preamble to the climax of the Kaats' story that appears in Stephen's post, displayed alongside (fig. 8.6). (Referring to his father's post, Stephen quipped that this was Kaats's "honeymoon.") Nathan also departed from the original paint scheme of the Gaash post, applying black, red, and blue-green latex paints far more sparingly to his post only for the primary and secondary formlines and the tertiary areas of the figures. With most of the cedar left bare to shine, the post showcases Nathan's signature adze technique: the meticulous stippling that delineates the contours of the figures and animates the golden surface of the post.

If Nathan departed from the Gaash post in his reinterpretation for the Burke, Stephen's house post veered in a completely new direction. In technique, form, and subject matter, the post asserts a radically different presence than the Cape Fox post that it replaces. Stephen chose to depict the Kaats' story's violent climax, when the bear children tear their father to pieces for having betrayed their mother. In a composition that Stephen has described as "multiple exposures" of Kaats' dismemberment and death (quoted in

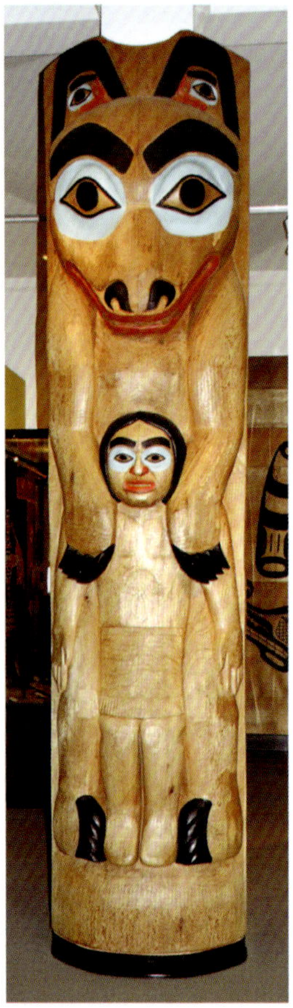

FIGURE 8.5 Nathan Jackson, *Kaats' House Post*, 2005. Cedar, paint, 11 × 2.5 ft. Funding for the Burke Museum's new house posts was provided by grants from the National Endowment for the Arts and the Sealaska Heritage Institute, as well as gifts from the Hugh and Jane Ferguson Foundation, Lawrence Christian, Betty Ewert, and John and Joyce Price, Burke Museum #2005–84/1.

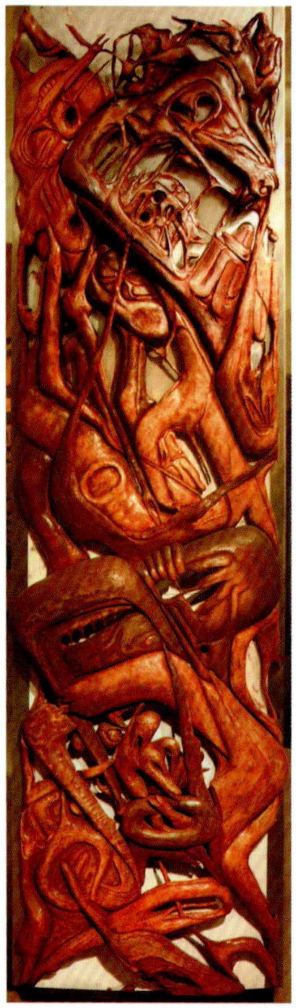

FIGURE 8.6 Stephen Jackson (Tlingit). *Nearing Completion*, 2005. Mixed media, epoxy resin, cedar, 11 × 2.5 ft. Funding for the Burke Museum's new house posts was provided by grants from the National Endowment for the Arts and the Sealaska Heritage Institute, as well as gifts from the Hugh and Jane Ferguson Foundation, Lawrence Christian, Betty Ewert, and John and Joyce Price, Burke Museum 2005–85/1.

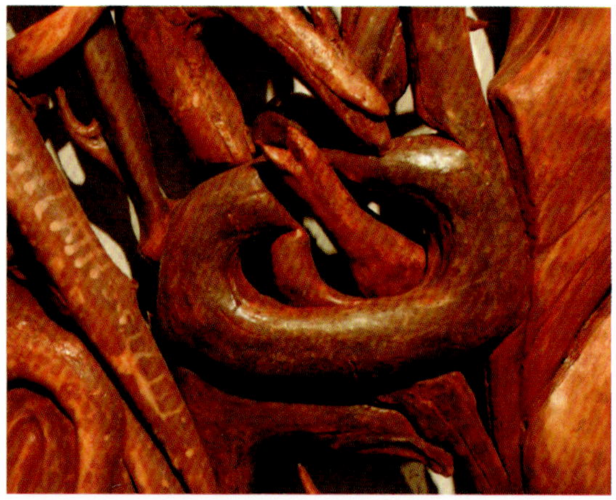

FIGURE 8.7 Ovoid form in *Nearing Completion*. Photograph by Emily Moore.

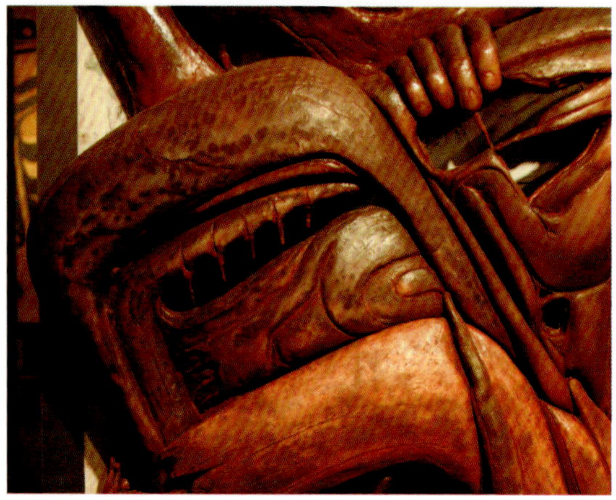

FIGURE 8.8 U-forms in *Nearing Completion*. Photograph by Emily Moore.

Jonaitis 2008: 61), fingers drip with bloody sinews, ligaments strain to hold, and intestine-like forms writhe across the surface of the post (fig. 8.7). Stephen conceived this composition in part by walking the streets of Manhattan, "imagining movement" (quoted in Jonaitis 2008: 61); significantly, his design crystallized in the months following the attacks of September 11, 2001. But if one accuses this post of abandoning Northwest Coast design completely, note first the motifs that emerge in its folds: ovoids capping the muscles of an abdomen, U-forms and trigons embedded in the guts (fig. 8.8). Even the swirl of intestine and sinew recalls the role of the primary formline, in Bill Holm's classic definition, to create a kind of "continuous flowing grid over the whole decorated area" (Holm 1965: 29).

Stephen's technique, developed specifically for the casting of this epoxy-resin piece, also pairs tradition with contemporary practice. Although he began his house post by carving in cedar, the intricate nature of the composition demanded a more flexible medium. Eventually, he developed a special casting process in which epoxy resin was poured into a silicone mold.[4] Cedar remained in the final sculpture, however: the same cedar log from which his father's post was carved made up the panels into which the resin forms were bolted. Although covered by aluminum, cedar provided the literal support for this contemporary vision of Kaats'.

FIGURE 8.9 *Kaats' Teikweidí House Post in situ,* 1899. Gaash, Alaska. University of Washington Libraries, Special Collections #NA 2136. Photograph by C. Hart Merriam.

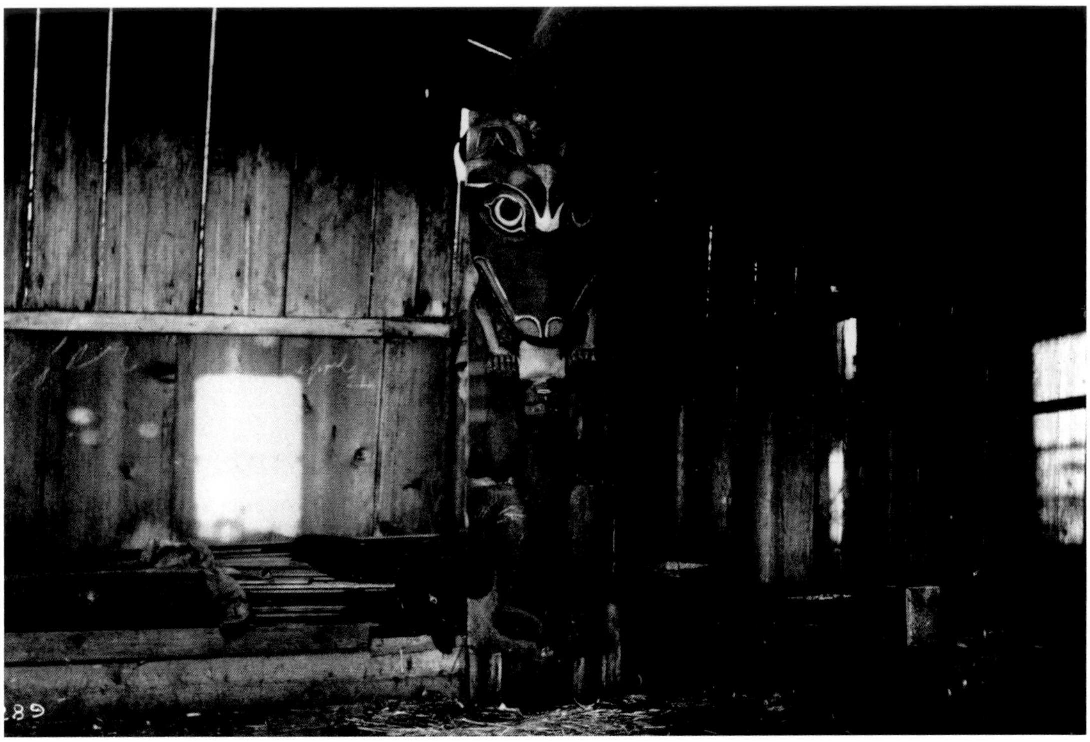

It is significant that the Jackson posts appear in the Burke Museum placed against the real structural posts that support the museum's ceiling. A photograph taken by a member of the Harriman Expedition in 1899 shows how the Gaash posts appeared in situ (fig. 8.9). Placed in the corners of the clan house, the bear posts were actually the carved outer shells of the structural posts that supported the great beams of the roof. The Jackson posts also perform this role in the Burke, covering the structural supports for the ceiling while proclaiming the crests of the Teikweidí. As several anthropologists have noted, Tlingit peoples drew a symbolic parallel between the human body and the clan house, where the eight main joints of the house were like the eight major "long, jointed" bones of the body (Kan 1989: 51; Thornton 2008: 177).[5] The grizzly bear house posts were thus an integral part of the Teikweidí house's corporeal identity and their removal by the Harriman Expedition an amputation to both the house body and the identity of its former inhabitants. The Burke Museum's decision to return the Teikweidí posts helped to heal this symbolic and physical wound; its decision to place the Jackson Kaats' posts against the structural supports of its own ceiling further honors the role of the Tlingit house posts.

In addition to recalling their traditional physical role at Cape Fox, Stephen Jackson's post recalls the violence the Harriman Expedition brought to the village. Around 1892, Gaash was struck by smallpox; in 1894, Gaash villagers, together with members of the nearby Taanta Kwáan (Tongass village), relocated to the site of Saxman near present-day Ketchikan (Worl 2005: 37). Although they had left their former village, the Sanyaa Kwáan never relinquished claim to their property at Gaash; nor would they have used the term "deserted" to describe their home village. (As Rosita Worl [2005: 37] has written, Tlingit law holds that "the ownership of clan property remains with the clan, absent or not.") But what the Tlingit saw as the ransacking of their village, the Harriman Expedition saw as philanthropy, in keeping with their directive to gather information on Alaska and to "distribute it for the benefit of others" (Harriman quoted in Sloan 2005: 11).

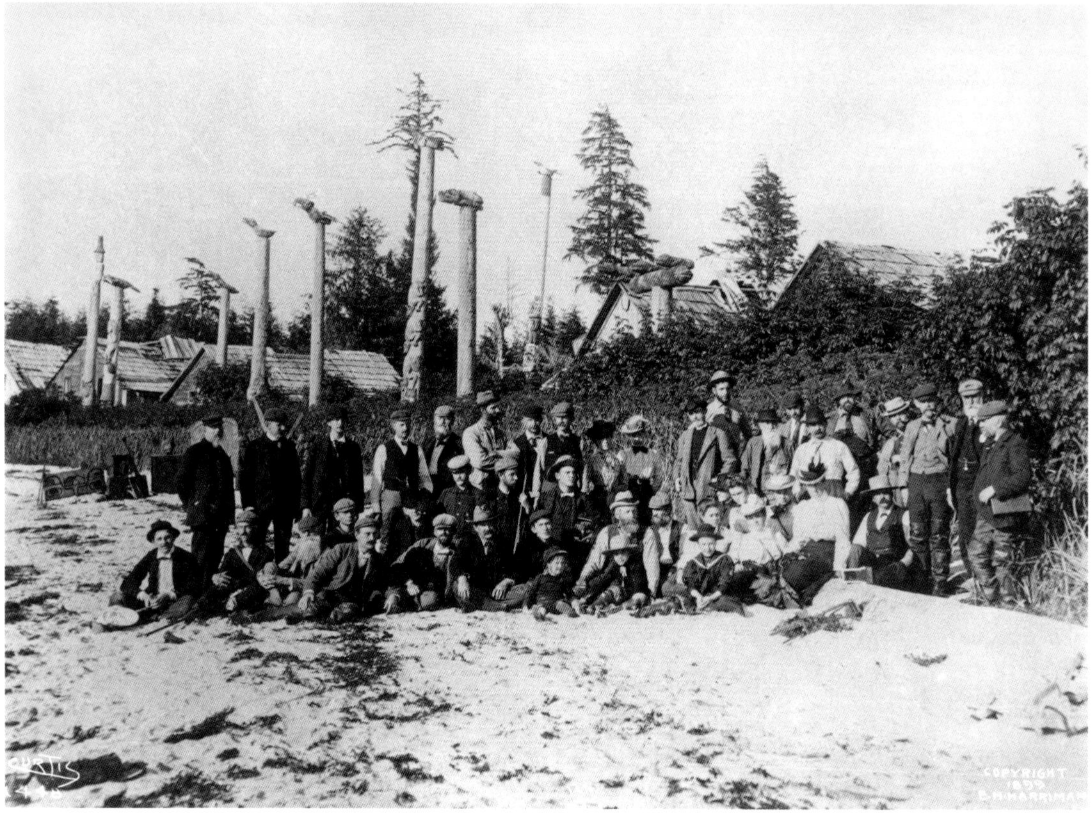

FIGURE 8.10 Harriman Alaska Expedition, 1899, Cape Fox. University of Washington Libraries, Special Collections, #NA2130. Photograph by Edward S. Curtis.

Harriman had specifically invited scholars on his 1899 expedition for research purposes, including C. Hart Merriam, William Dall, George Bird Grinnell, John Muir, and others whom Edward Curtis posed for a group photograph at Gaash (fig. 8.10). By the end of the two-month expedition, the Harriman team had gathered enough information to produce more than a dozen volumes of scholarship over the next several years (Sloan 2005: 17; Harriman Alaska Expedition 1910). The removal of the Cape Fox *at.óow*, in Harriman's eyes, was an extension of his "information gathering"—despite John Muir's protests of the "sacrilege" of removing a totem pole "to enrich some museum or other" (quoted in Sloan 2005: 19), protests that were obviously ignored.

The Jackson posts insist that this history be remembered in the Burke Museum. Referencing the dismembered subject of his post, Stephen drew a parallel to the upheaval caused by the Harriman visit, stating that he wanted to "give the cultural disruption back to the museum" (quoted in Jonaitis 2008: 61). In this sense Stephen's title, *Nearing Completion,* acts on multiple levels. At once a tongue-in-cheek play on the fact that the post was not quite finished at the time scheduled for its dedication (both posts were dedicated August 27, 2005; Stephen's post was finished later and installed December 7, 2005), the title also references the series of asymmetrical exchanges initiated by the Harriman Expedition and the inevitable incompletions of cultural translation. Stephen has emphasized that he doesn't see the act of propatriation as "closing the circle" of the Harriman Expedition. The propatriated post cannot (and purposefully does not) equalize the repatriated post, nor can the return of the Gaash posts amend for the century that the Teikweidí people endured without them. Like all acts of gift giving, propatriation introduces an asymmetrical relationship between the gifting parties. In Stephen's words, "the exchange is never complete" (personal communication 2008).

Yet what the exchange of the Kaats' house posts has provided is a space in the museum where this asymmetrical exchange can be voiced and discussed, a space where a Tlingit historical interpretation can be considered. On any given occasion when I have stood in the Burke to study the Jacksons' posts, some youngster or other has approached the tall red column of *Nearing Completion* and called out an iteration of the question, "Mom, what is *this*?" The gathering produced by the query results in a group study of the wall text for the posts which explains the history of the Harriman Expedition to Cape Fox and the wrongful removal of the posts, as well as their return in 2001 (the wall placards even include the 1950s photograph of the Gaash posts at the Burke). The biography of the Teikweidí posts is explained here, a biography that traces the diversions and destinations of objects that now include the two house posts that stand before the viewer at the Burke.[6] This is part of the power of propatriation: to open museums to histories from Native points of view, using art commissioned of Native artists who want to tell the story.

If propatriation works to acknowledge objects returned from a museum with objects made for that museum, it is not surprising that the practice has developed on the Northwest Coast. Here practices of reciprocation are fundamental to the potlatch economy, so that propatriation—a kind of "balancing" of exchanged objects—signals the vitality of Northwest Coast Native cultures in the NAGPRA era. It is a practice that behooves: while Native groups are reunited with their cultural patrimony, artists gain commissions and museums build collections they can properly call their own.

The catalyst for propatriation, repatriation, has also invigorated Native communities. Witness the repatriation process for the Sanyaa Kwáan *at.óow*, which involved nine years of research coordinated by Irene Dundas of the Cape Fox Heritage Corporation. Handed the repatriation case when she was nineteen years old, Dundas often felt overwhelmed in her attempts to establish clan ownership for *at.óow* in numerous American museums in accordance with NAGPRA requirements. Many of the elders who would have remembered Cape Fox had passed away, and for a long time, Dundas (2007) said, "we [the Sanyaa Kwáan] could not come up with the stories" that definitively linked individuals or clans with *at.óow.* Dundas dug deep, turning to snippets of recorded stories or memory; to 1900 census statistics for Tlingit names and clan membership; to BIA enrollment, Presbyterian missionary roles, cemetery plots, and death certificates; and even to tattoos in old photos that helped link crests to individual families. The outcome of this labor was extraordinary. The research generated 221 family trees with Tlingit names and house membership. Dundas said the research had resulted in a "whole lifestyle change for clans," recounting one example of a man who returned to Ketchikan from Washington state to help research his uncle's *at.óow*. Even the occasional animosities that resulted over disputes in clan ownership were positive, Dundas argued, because they rekindled Tlingit fervor for ownership and clan pride (ibid.).

The return of the Teikweidí grizzly bear posts from the Burke Museum vindicated Dundas's work and restored Tlingit *at.óow* to the Sanyaa Kwáan. It also launched the process of propatriation that resulted in the museum display of the Jackson house posts. Dundas herself was present when the Teikweidí grizzly bear posts returned to Alaska—significantly, via the Harriman Alaska

Expedition Retraced, a voyage organized by Smith College to compare the Alaska Harriman had studied in 1899 with the Alaska of 2001.[7] In a reversal of the 1899 expedition, the 2001 voyage came to return Tlingit *at.óow* to Gaash. Edward Harriman's great-great-granddaughter stood on the beach and watched as Dundas and fellow Sanyaa Kwáan member Eleanor Hadden performed a healing ceremony to restore their great-great-grandparents' *at.óow* to the clan. It was on this day that Dr. Rosita Worl and Dr. Robin K. Wright, who both participated in this event, engaged in a conversation that would launch the commission of the Jackson house posts as replacements for the Teikweidí posts. It was also on this day that the Harriman Alaska Retraced group posed for a photo on the beach at Gaash, harkening to Edward Curtis's photograph of the Harriman Expedition members over a century ago. This time, however, the photograph included their Tlingit hosts, members of the Sanyaa Kwáan (fig. 8.11).

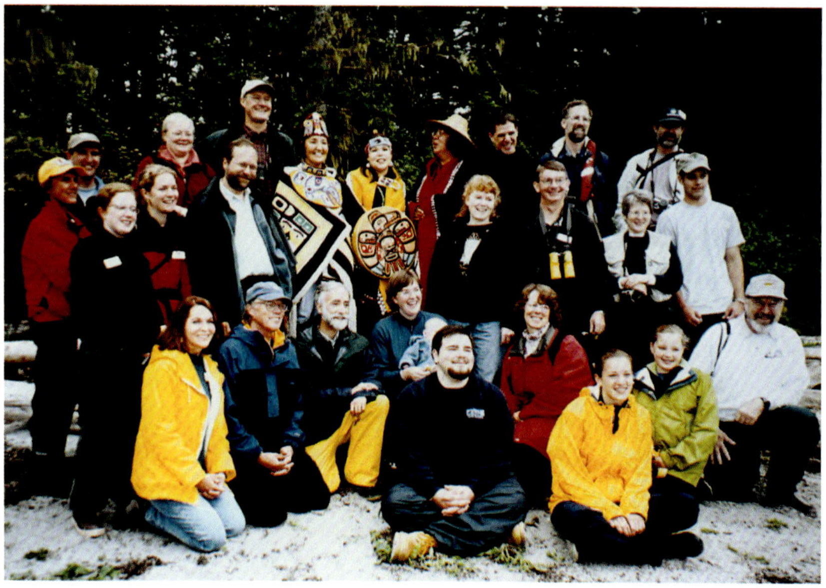

FIGURE 8.11 Participants on the Harriman Alaska Expedition Retraced trip and Tlingit hosts at Gaash, 2001. Photograph by Ellen L. Ferguson.

In part because of this history, in part because of their form, the Jackson posts embody the Tlingit concept of *shagóon*, an idea that binds heritage and destiny, past and future (Dauenhauer and Dauenhauer 1987: 28–29). The anthropologist Frederica de Laguna (1972: 2, 813) wrote that *shagóon* refers to "the destiny of a people (or individual), established in the past by the ancestors and extending to the descendants. It is one way of expressing 'the way things are.'" Rosita Worl (2005: 32) has noted that the "teachings of Haa Shagóon tell the present generation of Tlingits they are one with their ancestors, just as they—the present generation—will be united with future generations of Tlingits." In form, the Jackson posts recall the Teikweidí bear posts that preceded them but do so with new—and in Stephen's case, radically new—skins; they unite a new generation of Tlingit art with the ancestral Kaats' story.[8]

In practice, the use of the posts to cover the structural supports of the Burke Museum's ceiling fulfills both their traditional role as house posts and points to the new relationship the museum has built with the Sanyaa Kwáan—one in which Native peoples were involved in producing the museum's collections. The August 2005 dedication that accompanied the Jackson posts' debut at the Burke Museum included song, dance, and speeches, marking the event in terms of Tlingit protocol and affirmation. Unlike the Gaash posts, which had stood in the Burke as testaments to the "vanishing Indian" that the Harriman Expedition believed they had traced, the Jackson posts stand as a renewed testament to Tlingit *shagóon*, looking both ways in time.

NOTES

An earlier version of this chapter was presented at the 2007 Annual Meeting of the Native American Art Studies Association in Fairbanks, Alaska. My thanks to panel organizer Dr. Carolyn Krasner for welcoming my participation in that conference; and to Dr. Robin K. Wright for inviting me to develop my thoughts for this book. Most thanks go to Irene Dundas and Nathan and Stephen Jackson for answering countless questions.

1 Following the Harriman expedition, one Teikweidí brown bear house post was sent to the University of Washington while the other went to the University of Michigan; in 1935, Washington State (Burke) Museum curator Erna Gunther arranged a trade with Michigan for its house post and reunited the two Teikweidí posts in Seattle (Holm 1987: 212). The other two house posts from the Teikweidí brown bear house depicted eagles and were sent to the Heye Foundation Museum, now the National Museum of the American Indian.

2 It is important to note that although Cape Fox Corporation filed a repatriation claim for the Teikweidí grizzly bear house posts through NAGPRA, claiming the posts as "objects of cultural patrimony," the Burke Museum did not return the posts as such. Instead, museum curators and the state attorney general's office agreed that the posts were "stolen property" and should be returned to the Sanyaa Kwáan outside of NAGPRA law. Other museums returned *at.óow* stolen from Cape Fox as "objects of cultural patrimony," such as Harvard's Peabody Museum, Chicago's Field Museum, and the Smithsonian's National Museum of the American Indian.

3 As I have chronicled elsewhere, examples of "propatriation" are not limited to the Burke (Moore 2010). In November 2000, Harvard's Peabody Museum dedicated a new totem pole carved by Nathan Jackson to replace (but again, not to replicate) the original Cape Fox pole that had been repatriated to Alaska; in 2004 the Smithsonian's National Museum of the American Indian did the same. The Field Museum of Natural History in Chicago commissioned the Jacksons to collaborate on a pole in 2007, replacing a Neix.ádi pole repatriated to the Sanyaa Kwáan. There is also a case of propatriation that took place in Canada: in 2000, Haisla artists Barry Wilson, Derek Wilson, and Henry Robertson carved a totem pole for Sweden's Museum of Ethnography in anticipation of that museum's return of an original Haisla pole; they also carved a copy for the Haisla village of Misk'usa, since the original was too fragile to display outside (Rhyne 2009: 215).

4 Stephen experimented with several casting techniques before settling on the silicone mold. He began by carving in extruded polystyrene insulation but sought a less toxic material when he learned that polystyrene off-gassed carbon dioxide when carved. In late 2004, thanks in part to reading about the molding techniques of artist Ron Mueck, Stephen decided on resin for the body of the sculpture and a one-part wire armature with plaster and oil-based clay for the mold (personal communication 2008).

5 The anthropologist Sergei Kan has detailed the parallels the Tlingit drew between the eight major bones of the human body (that is, the forearm and upper arm on the right and left side, and the lower leg and thigh bone on the right and left side) and the eight corners of the house (that is, the places where the main beams forming the frame of the structure joined together, including the four inner corners formed by the house posts). Kan (1989: 51) notes that just as the eight places on the body were symbolically marked in a clockwise direction, following the direction of the sun, so the eight corners "of a newly-constructed winter house were marked, in a clockwise direction, with the blood of slaves or with fish oil during the rite of the dedication."

6 Here I am referencing anthropologist Arjun Appadurai's terms of "object biographies" (Appadurai 1988: 16, after Maquet 1971). In these terms, the Jackson posts are "art by destination," objects created with the *intent* that they would appear in the Burke Museum, unlike the Gaash posts, which were wrested from their clan house by the Harriman Expedition and were therefore "art by diversion."

7 The Harriman Alaska Expedition Retraced trip was organized as a Smith College alumni trip by Thomas Litwin, director of Smith College's Clark Science Center.

8 In fact, Stephen insisted on a contemporary rendering of Kaats' for his house post in part to reassert the nonlinearity of time embodied in *shagóon*. He argues that the massive draining of art from the Northwest Coast at the turn of the twentieth century through actions like Harriman's and other collectors' led to an emphasis among Northwest Coast artists on "renaissance"—a concept "that narrowed to recapturing the 'lost' 'past' as opposed to the Tlingit notion of *haa shagóon*" (personal communication 2008). Had Northwest Coast art not been so imperiled, Stephen suggests, artists might have felt more comfortable looking forward, rather than focusing on the "revival" of a classical past.

PORTFOLIO

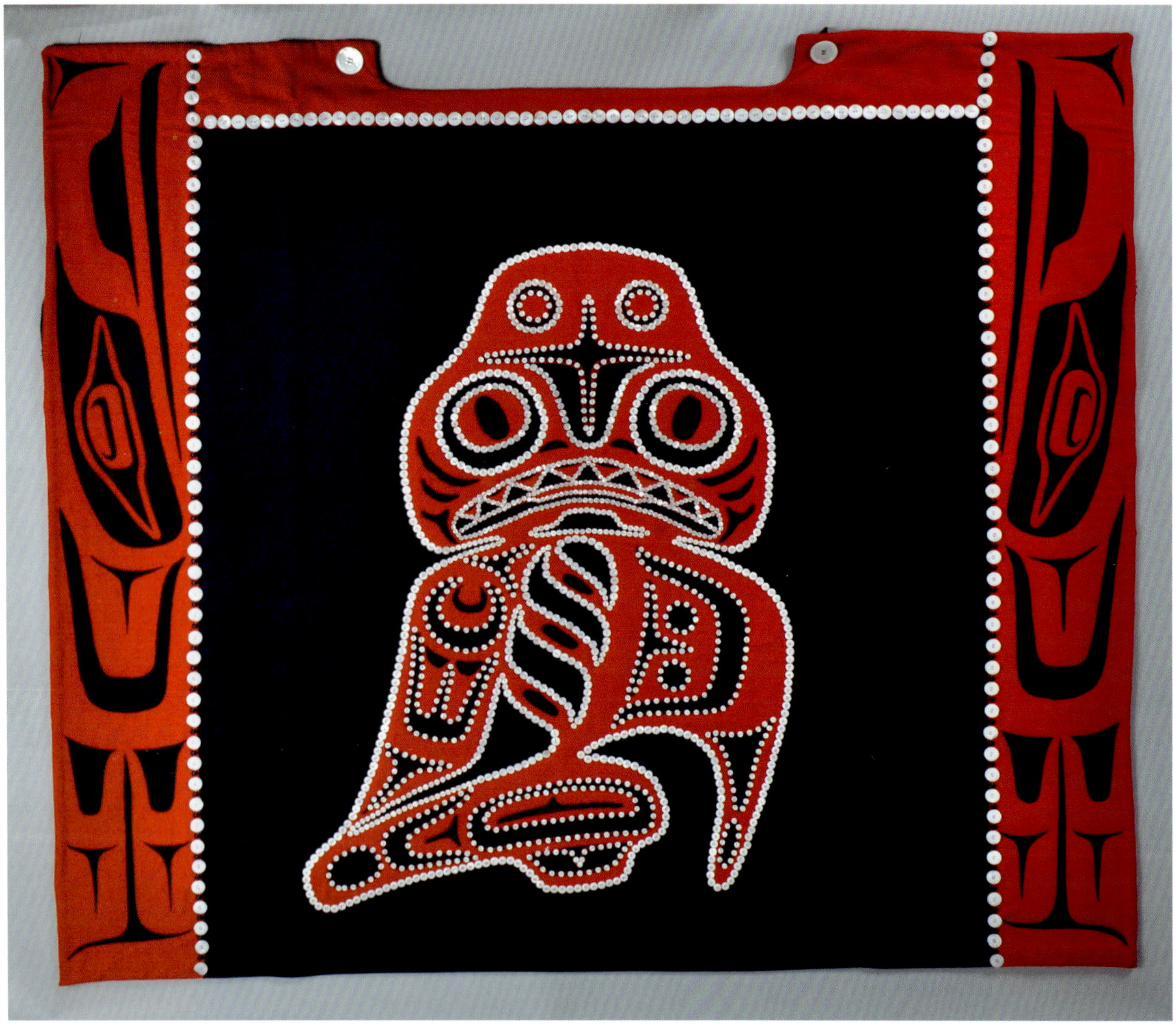

Robert Davidson (Haida) and Dorothy Grant (Haida). *Dogfish Robe*, 1985. Wool cloth, glass beads, shell buttons. 51.3 × 58.8 in. Purchased with funds donated by John Putnam and Lawrence Christian, Burke Museum #1999–23/1.

This robe is a collaborative effort between Haida artists Robert Davidson and Dorothy Grant. It was Dorothy's personal robe, worn by her on many ceremonial occasions in the 1980s and 1990s. The dogfish design appliquéd in the central panel is a crest of Grant's Yahgu'laanaas Raven clan. The appliquéd borders were an innovation in this period on Haida robes, perhaps inspired by border designs done in buttons on older Kwakwa̱ka̱'wakw robes.

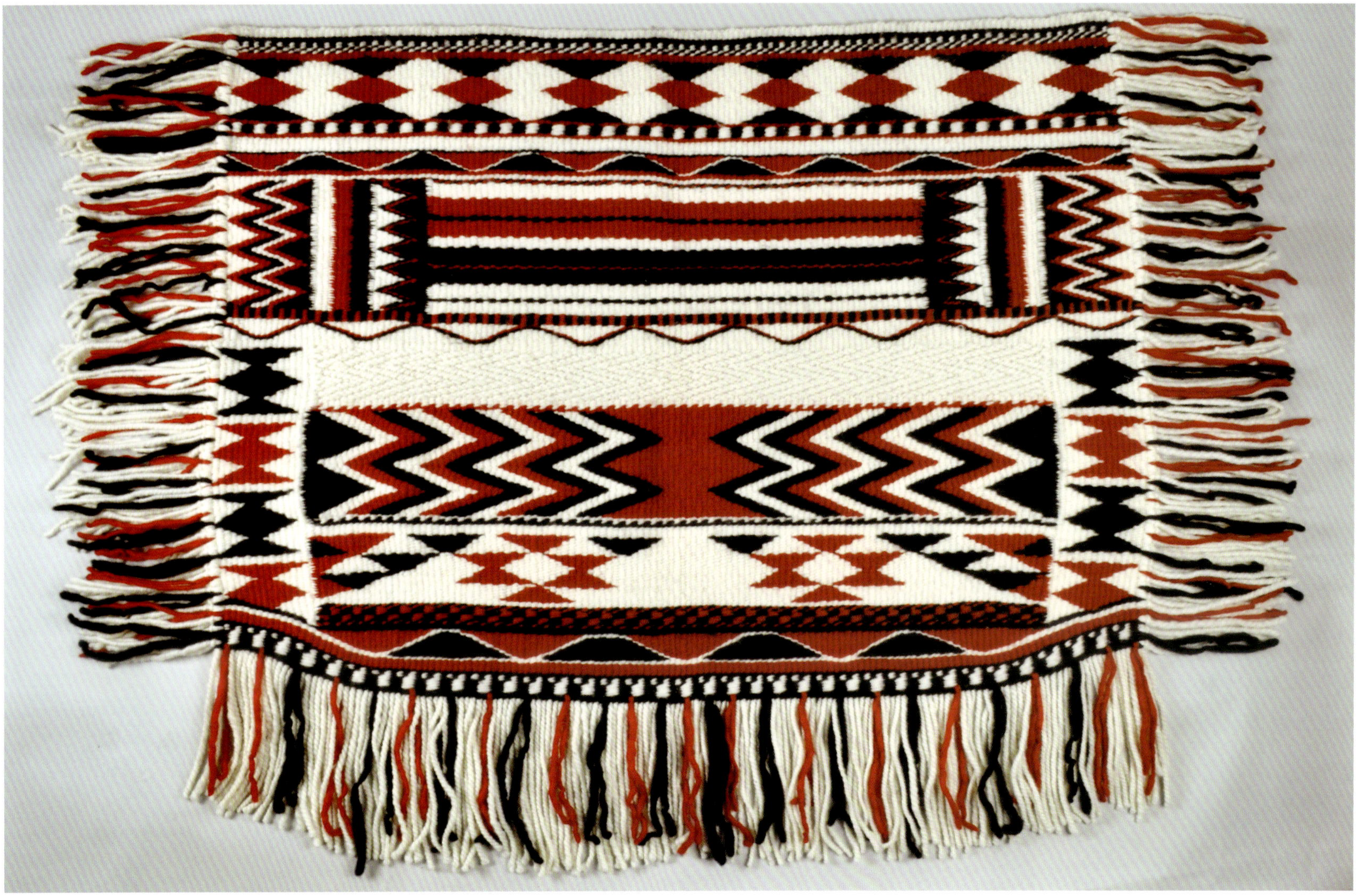

Debra and Robyn Sparrow (Coast Salish—Musqueam). *Mourning Star Robe*, 2006. Sheep wool. 84 × 58 in. Commissioned by the Burke Museum, Burke Museum #2006–13/1.

Robes like this are known as "nobility blankets" because they were worn by high-ranking Salish families who had the wealth to commission them. Sisters Debra and Robyn Sparrow have been leaders of the revival of Musqueam weaving. The robe was made for a companion exhibit of Northwest Coast weaving in conjunction with the traveling Maori weaving exhibit *Toi Maori* hosted at the Burke Museum. The artists were inspired by the colors Maori weavers used. In the course of weaving this robe, the Musqueam community and the Sparrow family suffered a number of deaths, leading Debra and Robyn to call it a mourning blanket.

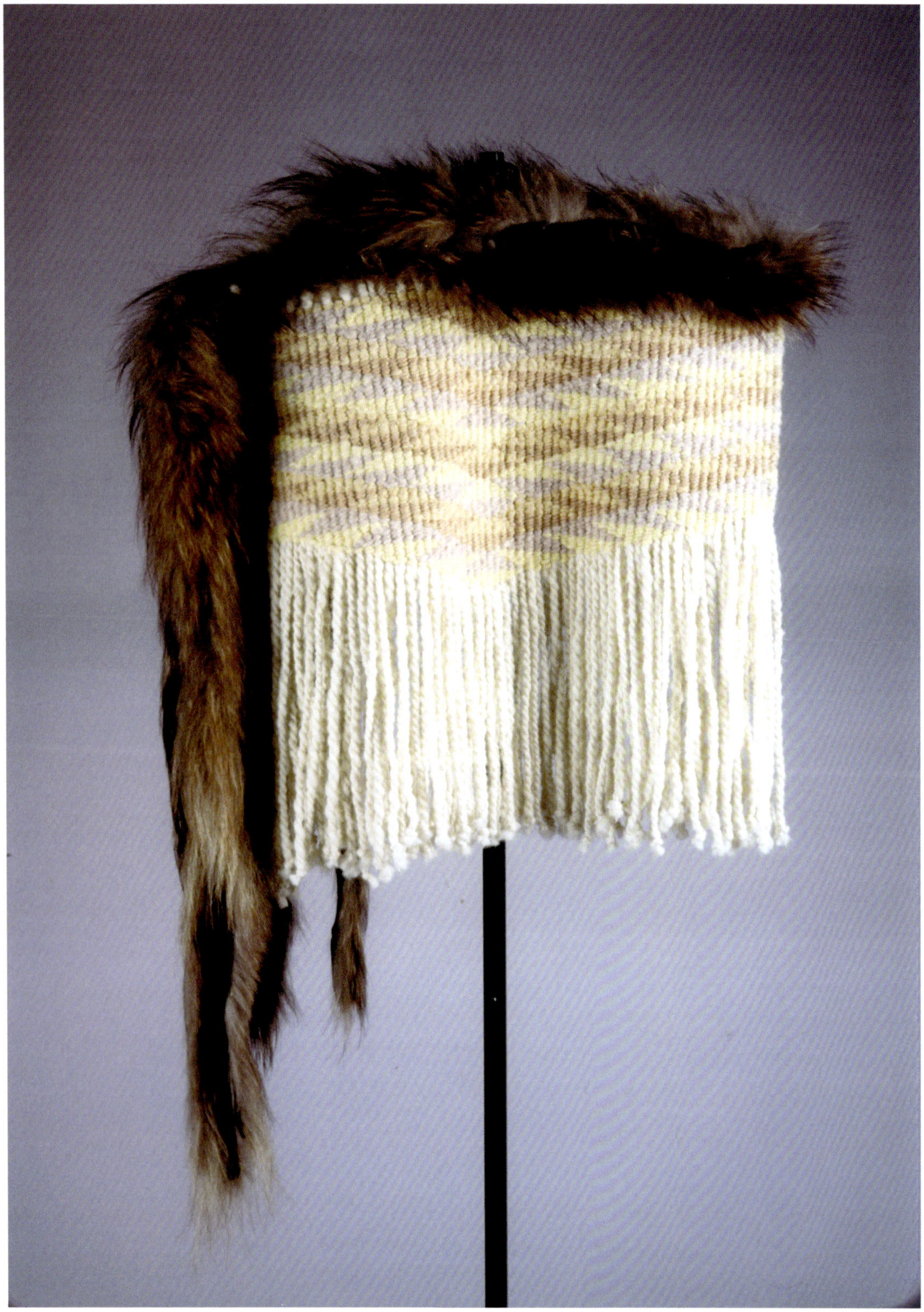

Susan Pavel—Sa'hLa mitSa. *Salish Sunrise*, 2004–6. Mountain goat wool, wolf skin. 20.5 × 19.5 in. Purchased with funds donated by Lawrence Christian, Burke Museum #2006–169/1.

This is one of the few contemporary weavings made of mountain goat wool. The wool was gathered in the Olympic Mountains and colored with evergreen huckleberries, wolf moss, yellow cedar bark, and salal berries. Susan Pavel was a student (and niece-in-law) of the late Skokomish leader, Subiyay—Bruce Miller, who founded the Northwest Native American Basketweavers Association.

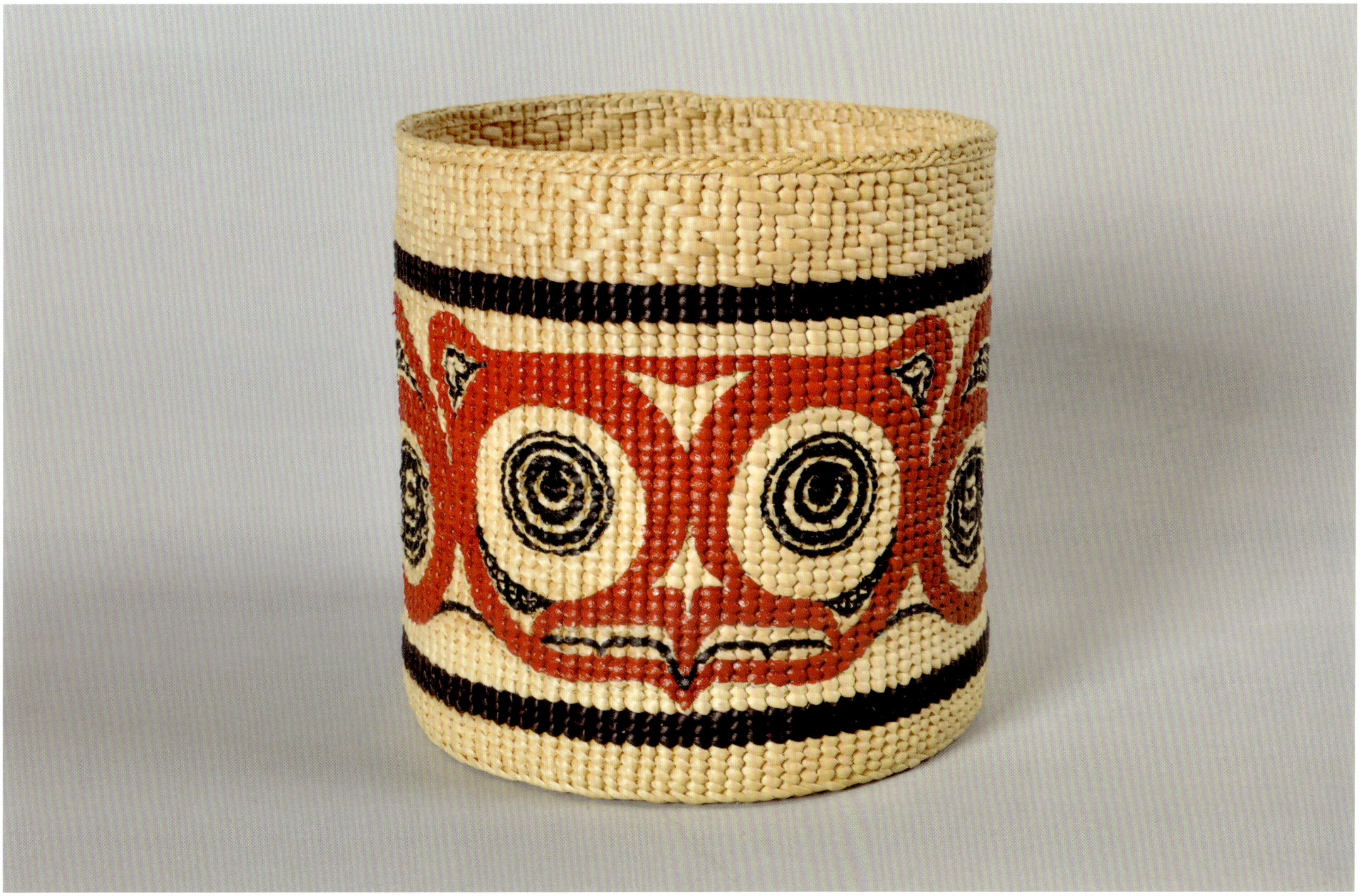

Woven by Janice Criswell (Haida/Tlingit), painted by Steve Henrikson. *Owl Basket*, 2001. Spruce roots, acrylic paint. 3.1 × 4.1 in. Purchased with funds donated by Lawrence Christian, Burke Museum #2001–26/1.

Finely twined spruce root baskets were made by both Haida and Tlingit women in ancient times, usually decorated by dying the wefts, adding false embroidery patterns, and creating a geometric pattern by skipping warps and adding wefts. In the late nineteenth century, Haida women often had their spruce root hats and baskets painted by their husbands or male relatives, a tradition that continues today. The Owl represents one of Jan Criswell's Haida crests.

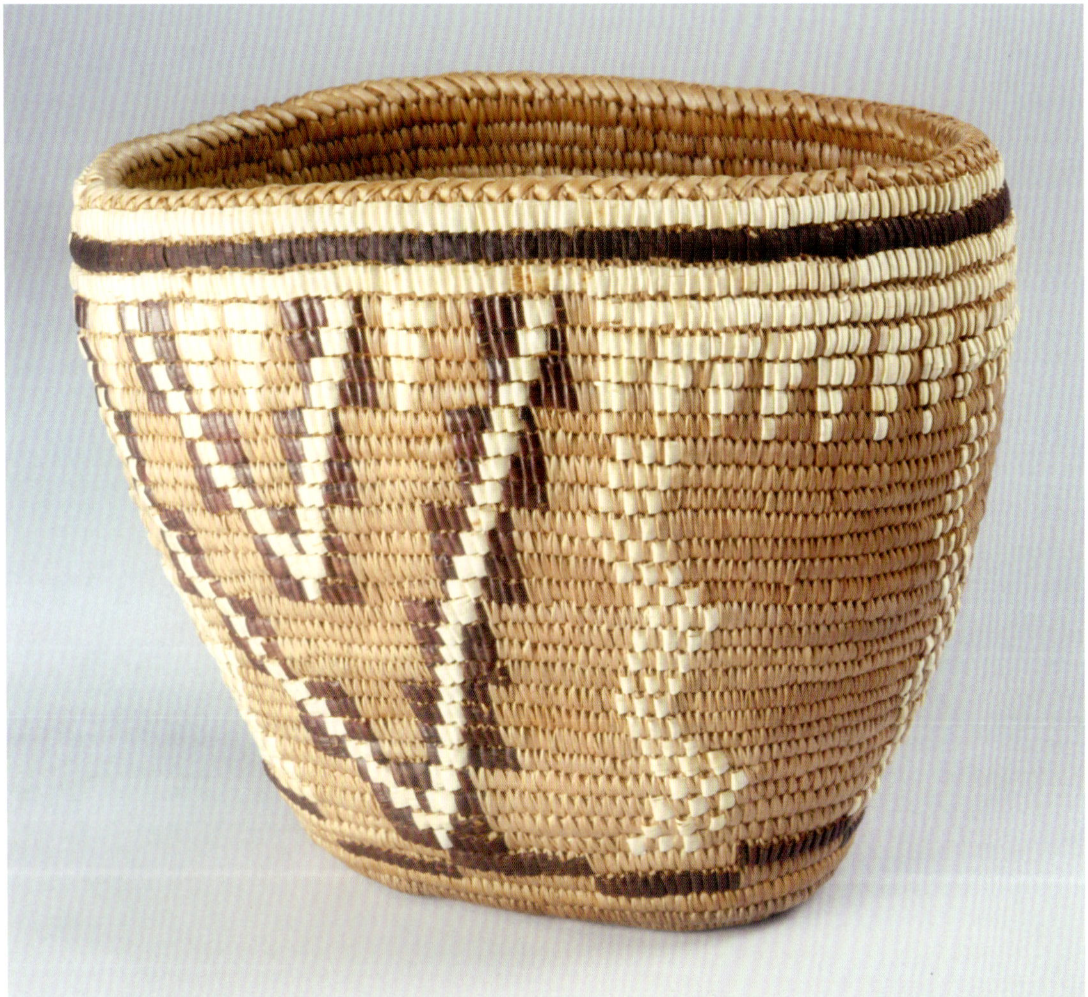

Ed Carriere (Coast Salish—Suquamish). *Mountain, Lightning, and Icicle Basket*, 1992. Cedar root, bear grass, wild cherry bark, horsetail root. 8.5 × 10 × 7.5 in. Burke Museum #2007–5/1.

This is a hard coiled cooking-style basket, inspired by an old Suquamish basket in the Burke Museum collection (2.5E528). The design is a mountain with lightning flashes and icicles. Ed Carriere learned to weave clam baskets from his great-grandmother. He was born, raised, and still lives on the Port Madison Reservation in Indianola, Washington.

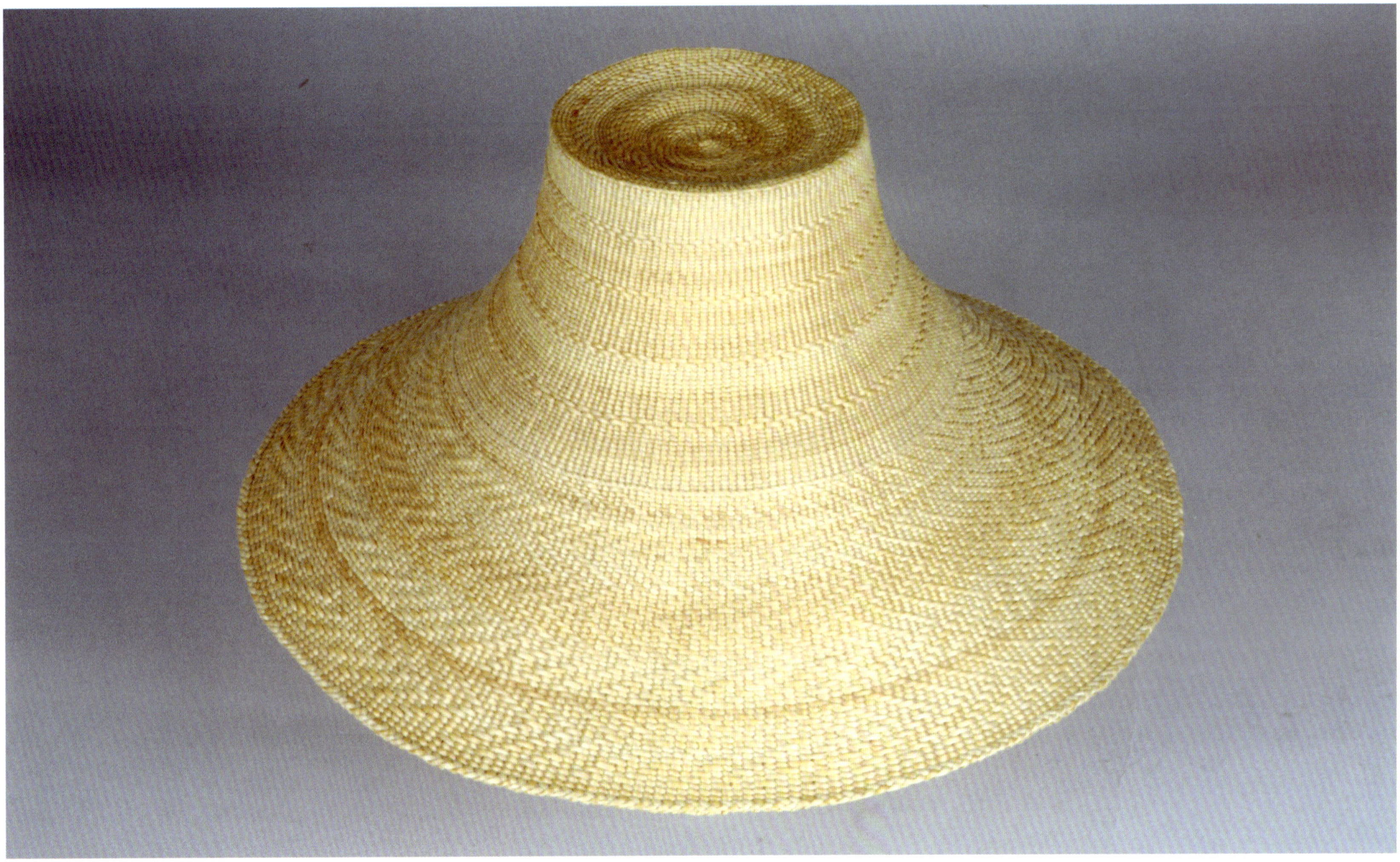

Isabel Rorick (Haida). *Basketry Hat*, 1999. Spruce roots. 15.5 × 7.1 in. Purchased with funds donated by Lawrence Christian, Burke Museum #2001–8/1.

This hat was made in the style of Mrs. Tom Price, the wife of the last chief of Sgaang Gwaii (Ninstints). The three bands of three-strand twining on the top of the hat are Isabel Rorick's signature. She has traveled to several museum collections, including the Burke Museum, to study Haida basketry.

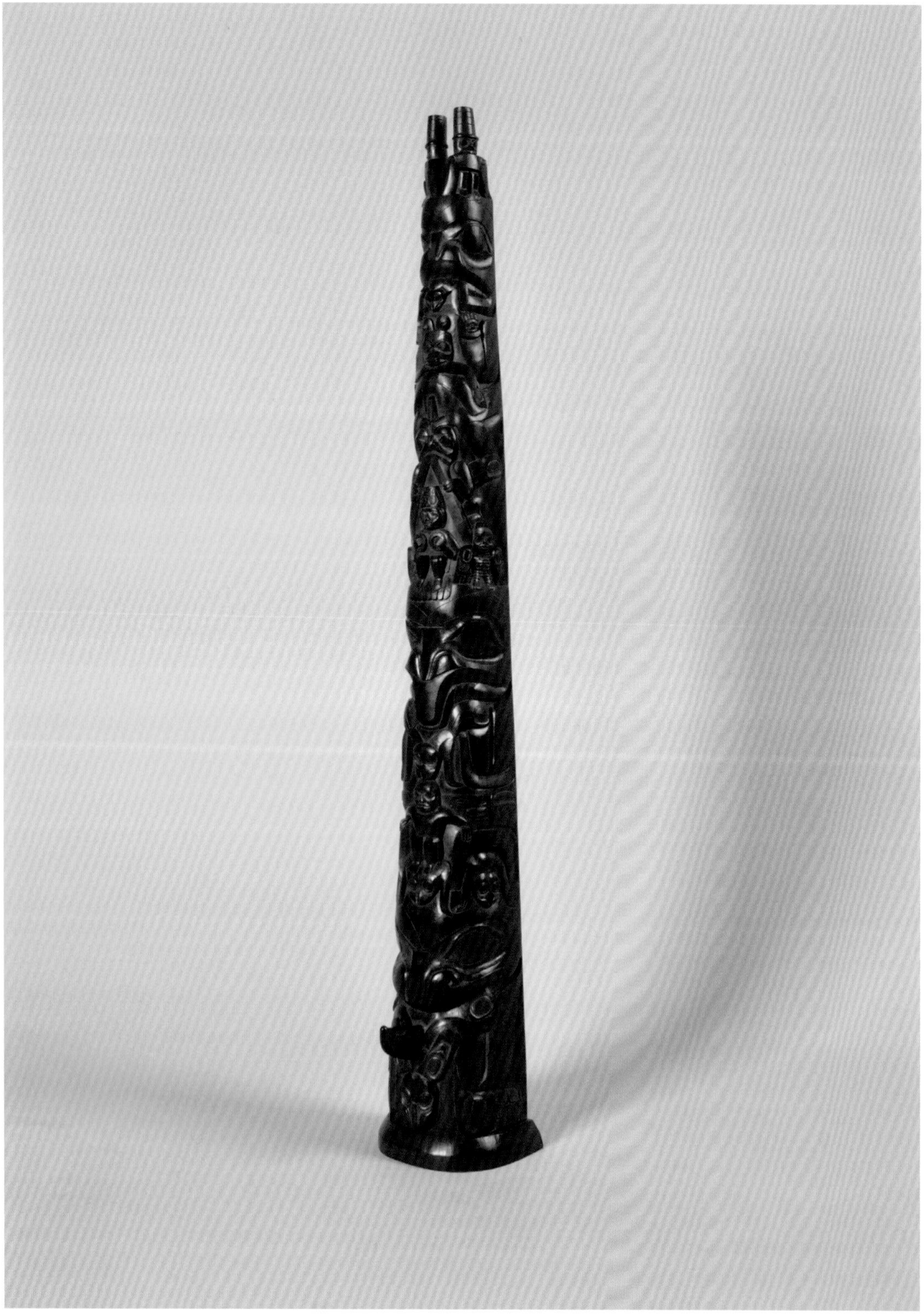

Jay Simeon (Haida). *Model Pole,* 2002. Argillite. 25.5 × 3.5 in. Gift of Arthur B. Steinman, Burke Museum #2004–2/40.

This model pole reproduces the figures from a late-nineteenth-century pole from the Haida village of Howkan in Southeast Alaska. The pole displays the *wasgo,* a supernatural sea wolf at the bottom, holding a killer whale; the bird-in-the-air assisted the hero in capturing the *wasgo*; the young man captured the *wasgo* and wore his skin; and the shaman mother-in-law of the young man took credit for his work, holding her circular puffin-beak rattles.

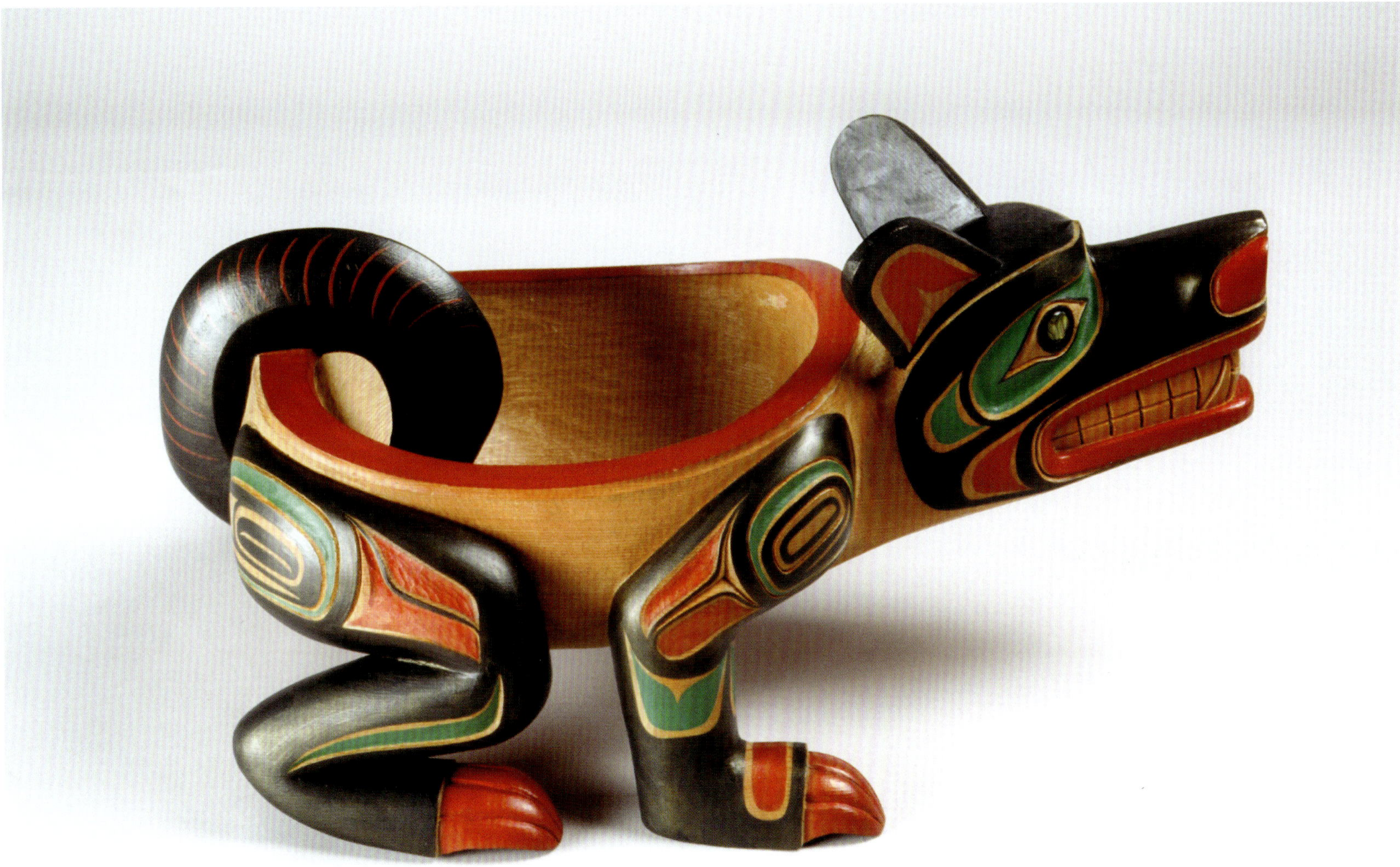

Randy Stiglitz (Coast Salish). *Wolf Feast Bowl*, ca. 2000. Red cedar, paint, abalone. 16.9 × 10.6 in. Gift of Arthur B. Steinman, Burke Museum #2004–2/114.

This wolf bowl is carved in the Kwakwaka'wakw-style typical of Randy Stiglitz's productions. Large feast dishes are used to serve food to the guests at potlatches, emphasizing the wealth of the hosts. Some dishes had imagery that suggested the proprietary rights of the host. The most famous of the large feast dishes were in the form of the *Dzoonokwa*, but many other creatures provided inspiration for feast dishes as well. Small versions of these dishes are often made for sale today.

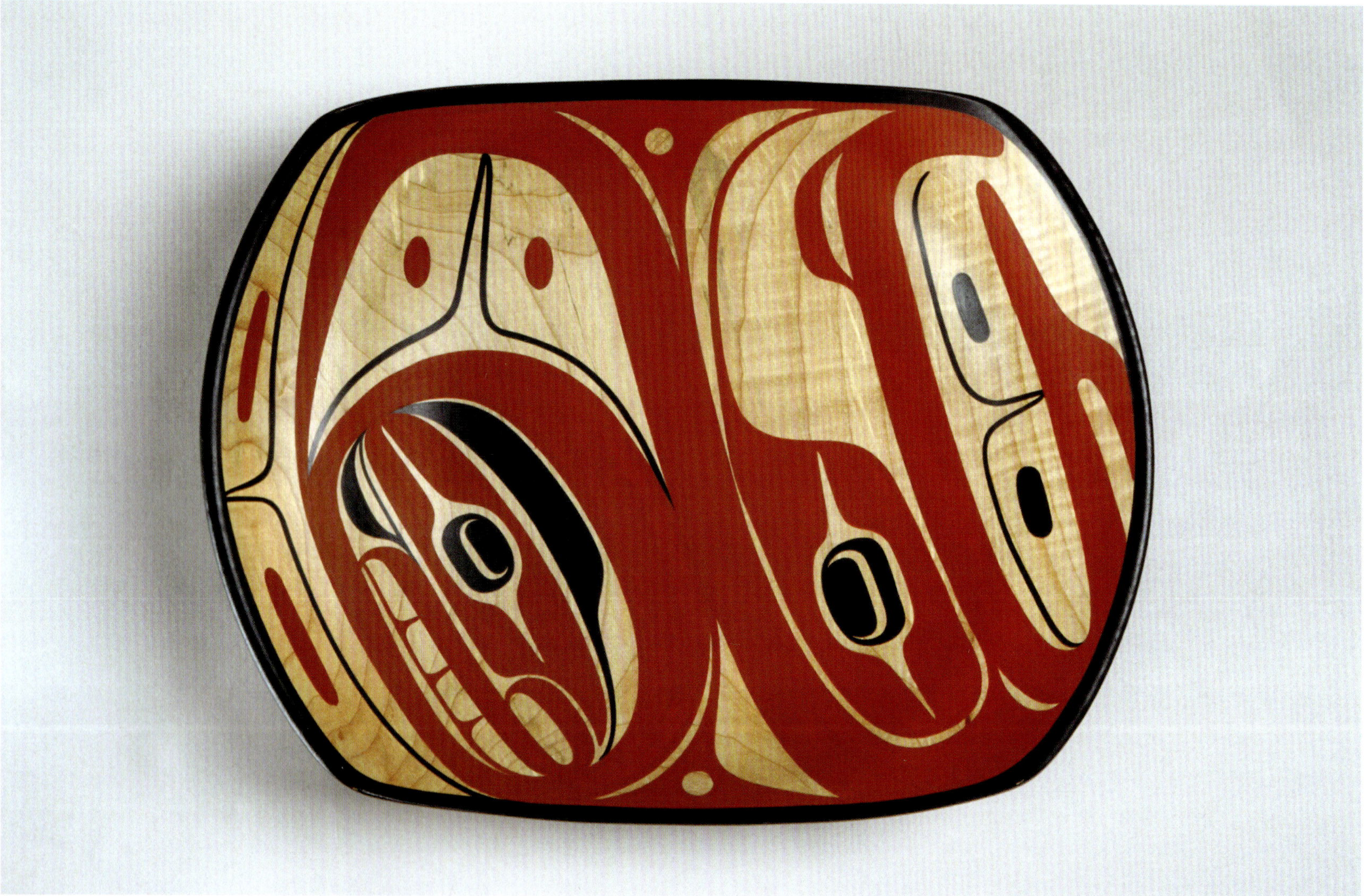

Steve Smith—Dla'kwagila (Kwakwaka'wakw). *Eagle and Man No Difference*, 2002. Maple, paint. 11.5 × 9.5 in. Gift of Arthur B. Steinman, Burke Museum #2004–2/131.

Steve Smith takes the painted forms that often appeared on the flat sides of Northern Northwest Coast chests and boxes and applies them to the curving surfaces of a new kind of container, the turned vessel. The symmetry of conventional rectangular design fields is transposed here into a new balance of positive and negative on the curved surface of the dish. Smith plays with unexpected uses of design elements and colors but maintains a proportionality and equilibrium of form. His style translates easily from the small surfaces of these vessels to the larger-than-life panels seen in his *Freedom to Move* installation at the Vancouver Airport.

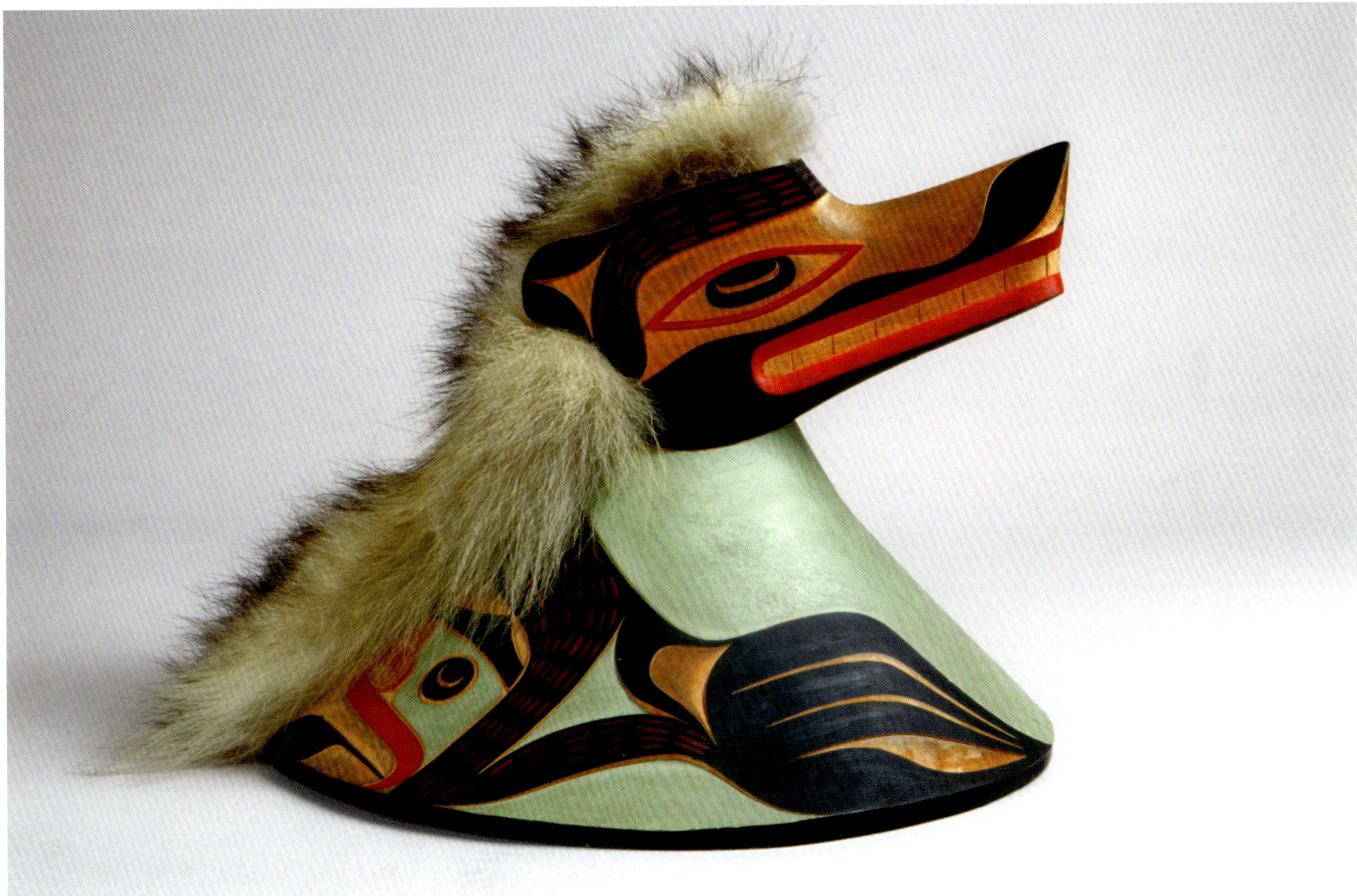

Art Thompson (Nuu-chah-nulth—Dit-i-daht). *Wolf Hat*, 1985. Alder, paint, wolf fur. 13.5 × 12 in. Gift of Arthur B. Steinman, Burke Museum #2004–2/159.

Many wolf headdresses take this raised-snout form. Here the artist has created a hat based on the form of Northern Northwest Coast crest hat, using the Nuu-chah-nulth wolf that draws on his own Dit-i-daht artistic and cultural heritage, blended with elements of the northern Northwest Coast two-dimensional style.

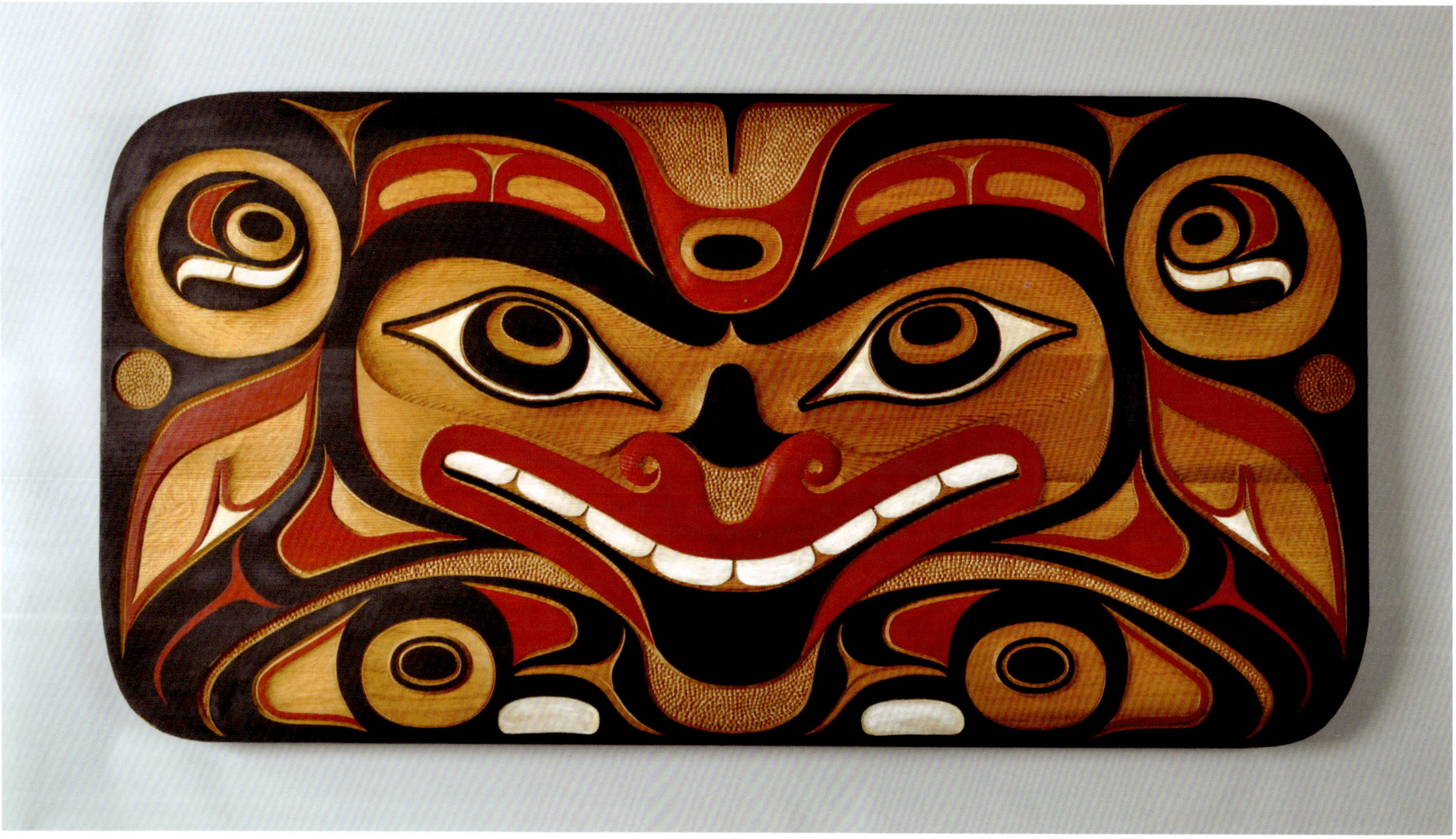

Donald Yeomans (Haida). *Grizzly Panel*, 1999. Red cedar, paint. 42 × 22 in. Gift of Arthur B. Steinman, Burke Museum #2004–2/296.

The careful placement of a few white highlights in this panel reveals the artist's selective judgment in the use of color. Yeoman's works, while rarely departing from the expected color palette of the Northwest Coast, often bring those colors into new relationships within his creations.

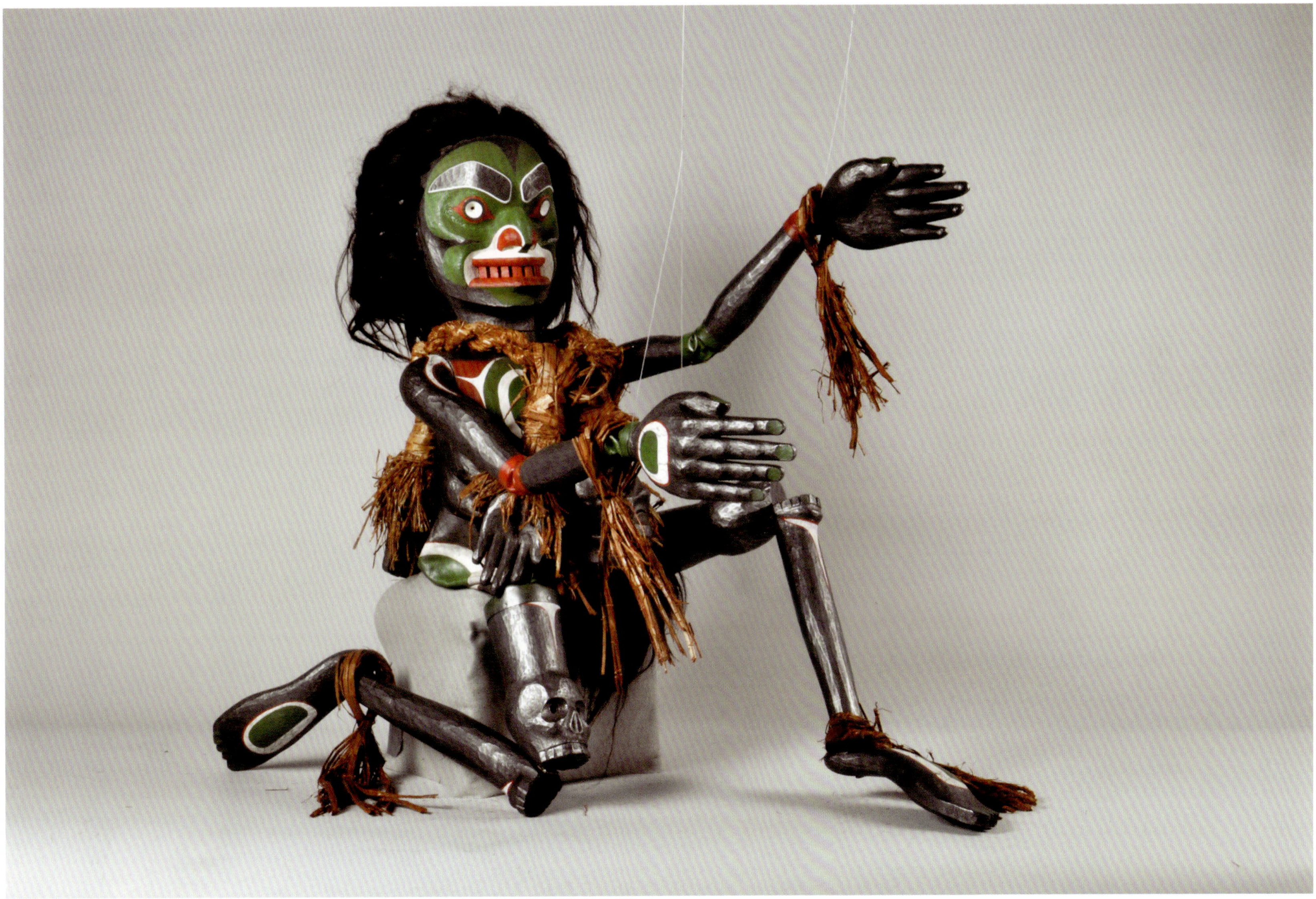

Beau Dick and Eugene Isaac (Kwakwa̱ka̱'wakw). *Towkit Puppet Headdress*, ca. 2000. Red cedar, cedar bark, fur, horsehair, leather. 59.8 × 13.8 in. Gift of Arthur B. Steinman, Burke Museum #2004–2/314.

Puppet headdresses representing a skeletal human figure are rare in museum collections. The "Towkit" (or Toogwid) dancer uses magical puppets to display her supernatural power, part of the Tseyka (or Red Cedar Bark) dances of the Kwakwa̱ka̱'wakw. This puppet wears a *bagwikila*, a cedar bark neck ring with a human corpse, as worn by the Hamat'sa (cannibal dancer), the most prestigious of the Tseyka dance privileges.

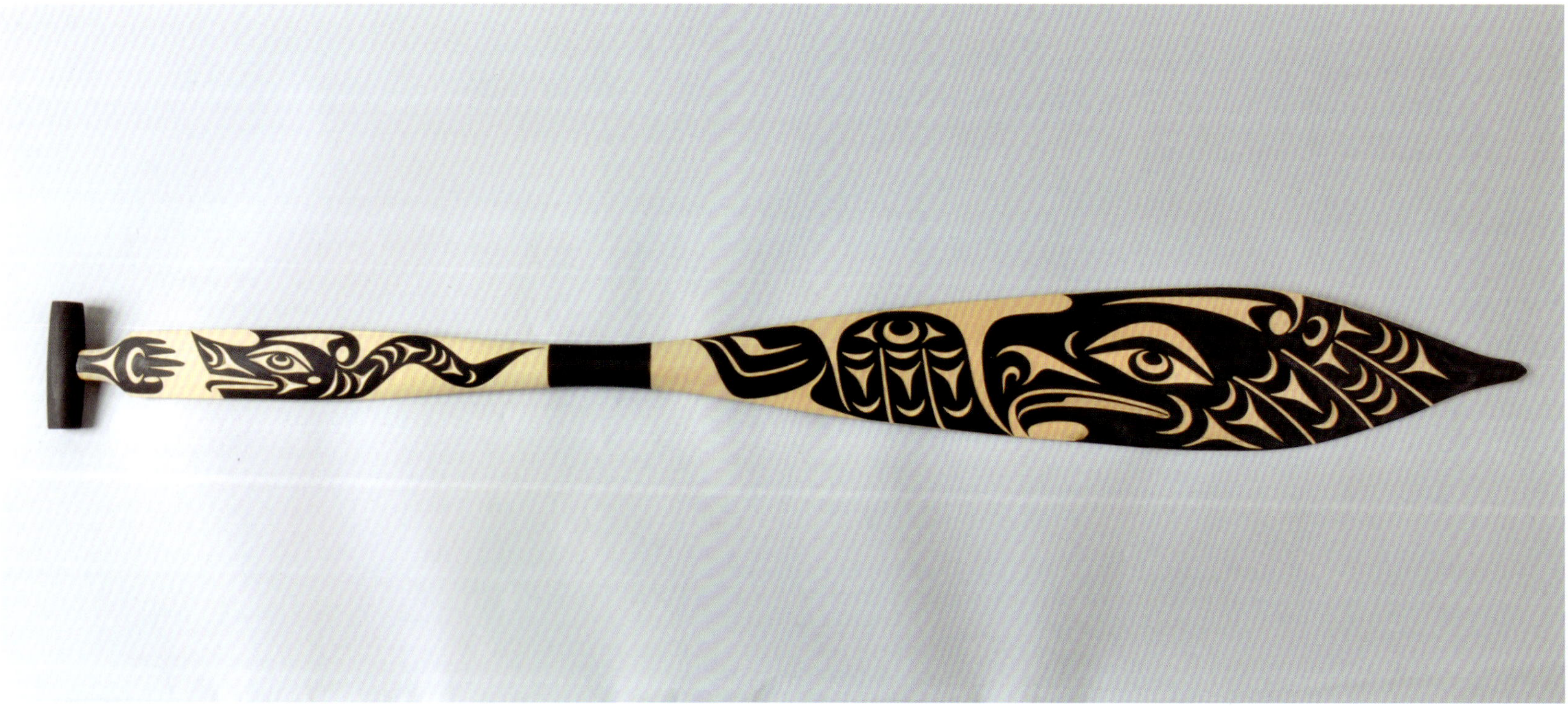

Shaun Peterson (Coast Salish—Puyallup, Tulalip). *Thunderbird and Serpent Paddle*, 2006. Yellow cedar, acrylic paint. 52.5 × 6 in. Purchased with funds donated by Lawrence Christian, Burke Museum #2006–158/1.

This paddle was acquired for the *In the Spirit of the Ancestors* exhibit and displays the Coast Salish design principles discussed by Shaun Peterson in his chapter in this book. Canoe paddles were made throughout the twentieth century for racing canoes, as dance paddles, and for sale to tourists. Canoe paddle carving today is an important adjunct to the growing importance of the canoe journeys on the Northwest Coast.

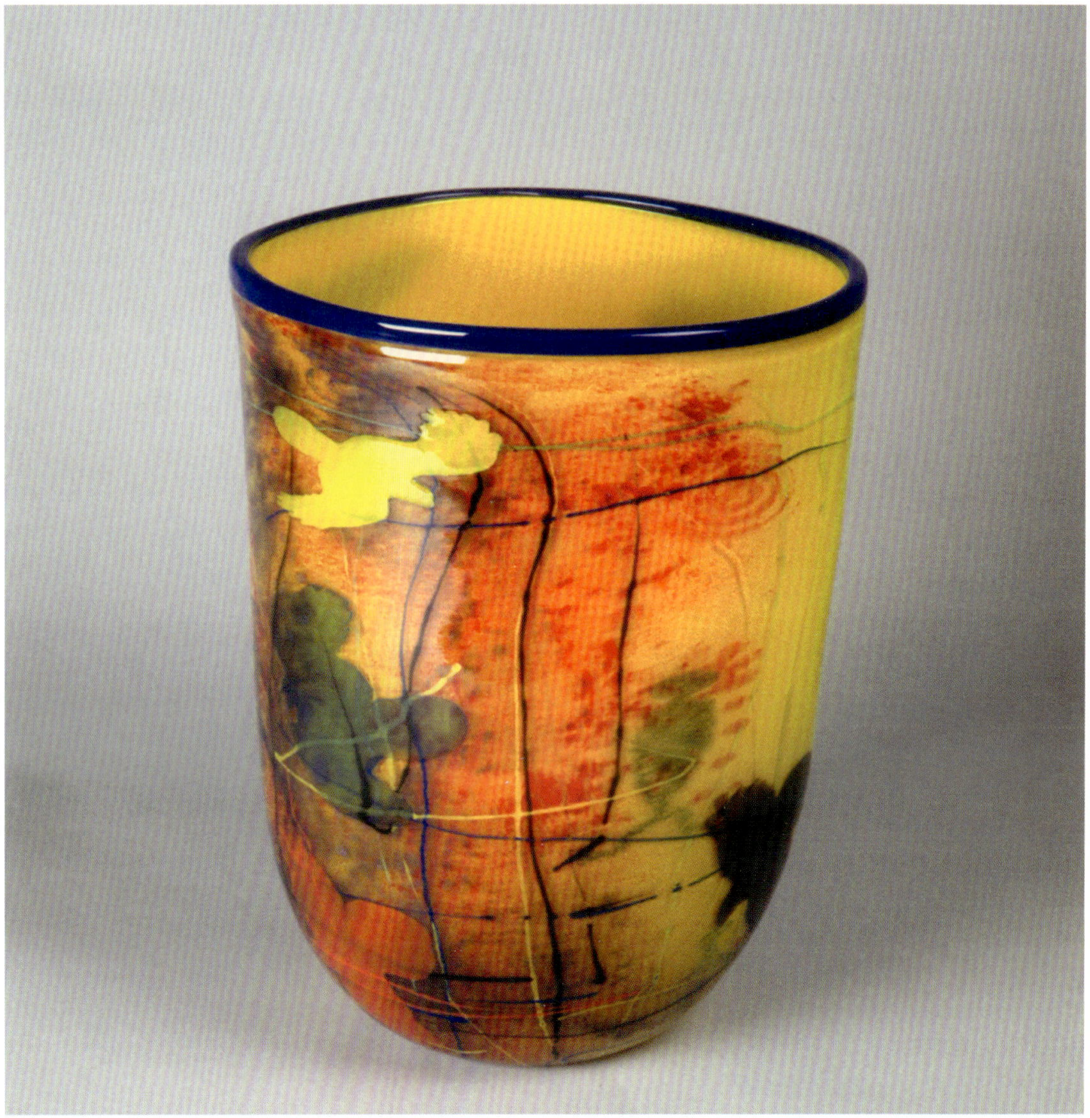

Marvin Oliver (Coast Salish—Quinault/Isleta Pueblo). *Salish Basket*, 2006. Blown glass. 16 × 12.5 in. Gift of Marvin and Brigette Oliver, Burke Museum #2007–13/1.

Seattle is a key center for the use of glass in Native American art. The work of Marvin Oliver and Preston Singletary (see fig. I.3) and the influence of the Pilchuck School has made glass an increasingly popular choice for local artists. Oliver's *Basket* series incorporates a layering of precast forms in the shape of animals and pictographic motifs into final basket form. The careful placement of forms juxtaposed with the organic saturation of color reflects both the artist's original vision and the unexpected results of the glass-making process.

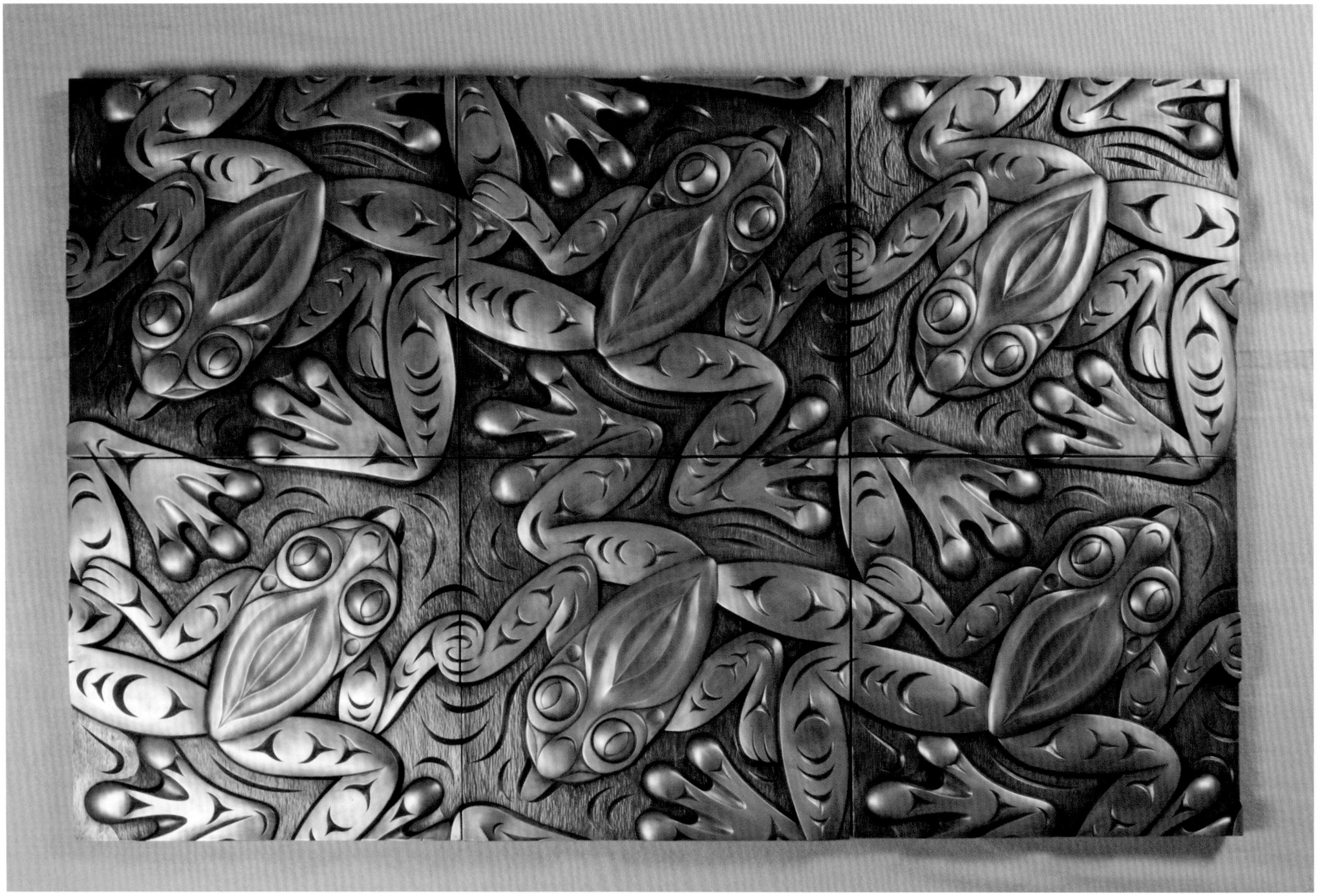

Susan Point (Coast Salish—Musqueam). *Frogs*, 2006. Cast Forton (gypsum plaster, plastics and fiberglass). 54 × 36 in. Gift of Susan Point, Burke Museum #2006–171/1.

Frogs are a recurrent theme in the work of Susan Point. Their lifecycle is a seasonal marker for the Musqueam people. Frogs are an indicator species for the health of a watershed, a concern often expressed in Point's art. Like many of her large installations, this piece is made up of a number of panels, here two repeated patterns, interlocked in an Escher-like configuration. This piece reworks the frogs created for the South Surrey Recreation Center in 2005, adding a watery background of crescent ripples for the frogs to explore.

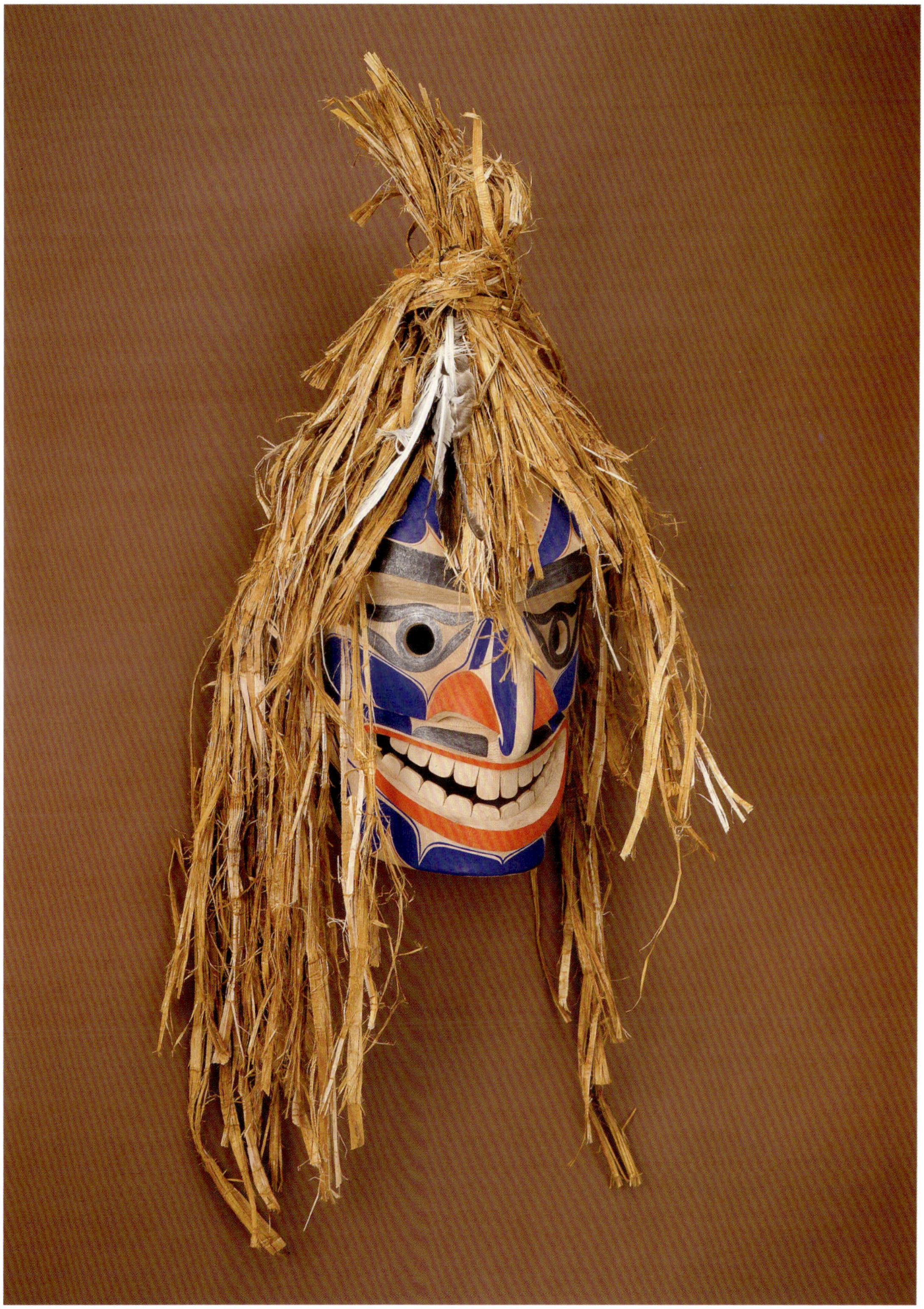

Greg Colfax (Makah). *Kwa' Laba Kuth*, 1989. Red cedar, cedar bark, feathers, paint. 29 × 12.5 in. Commissioned by the Burke Museum, Burke Museum #1989–22/1.

This Kwa' Laba Kuth, or Wildman, mask represents one of the ghostlike forest spirits that appear during the Makah Klookwalli ceremony. Similar ghostlike spirits are represented in mask forms among neighboring tribes. Their ghostly qualities are sometimes represented by skull-like heads with hooked noses and bared teeth in grimacing mouths.

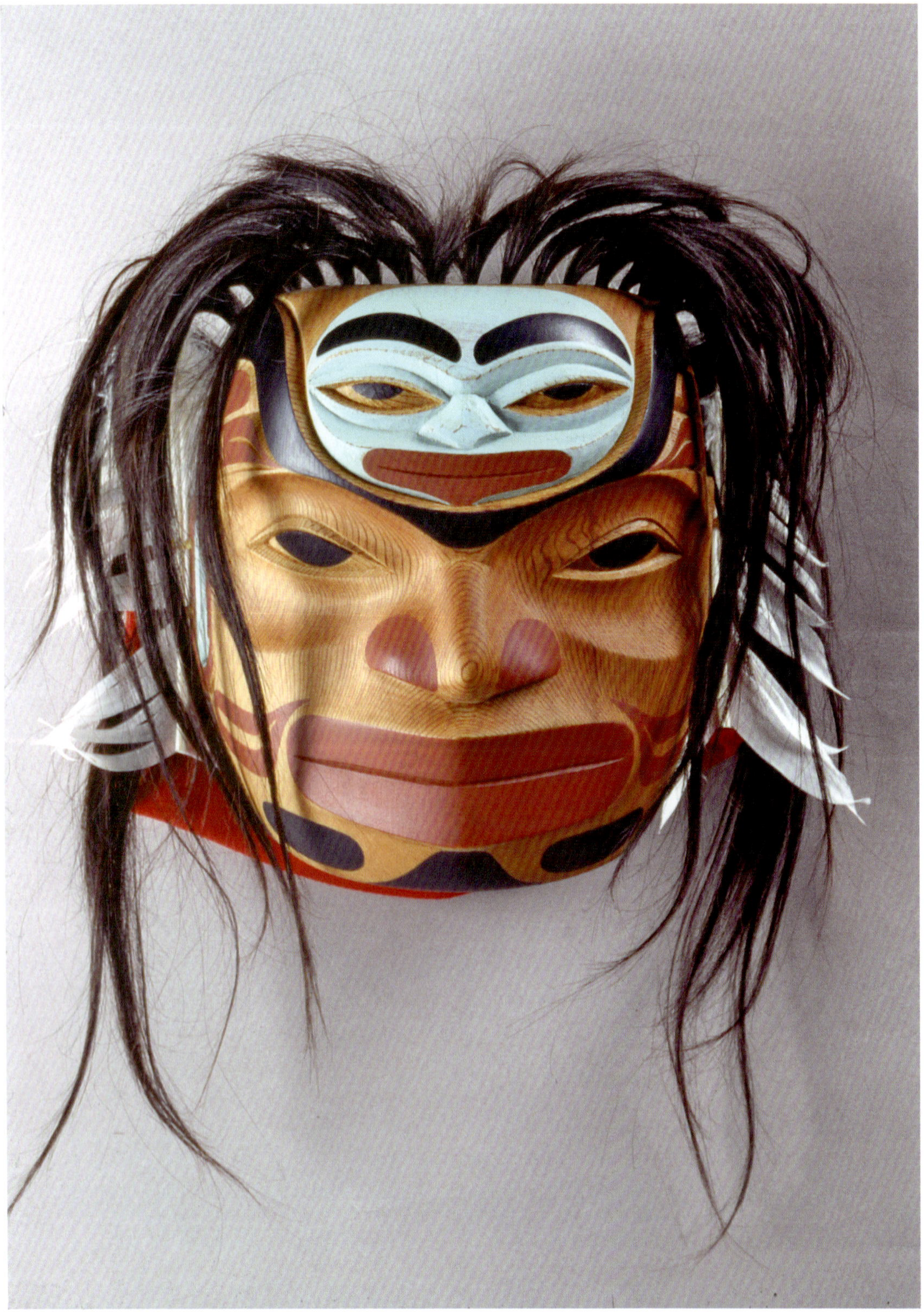

George Pennier (Coast Salish—Chehalis). *Bear and Shaman and Children*, ca. 2000. Red cedar, human hair, feathers, cloth, foam pad. 7.7 × 7.5 in. Gift of Arthur B. Steinman, Burke Museum #2004–2/153.

This maskette takes the form of a Tlingit shaman's headdress. Since the 1970s, many Northwest Coast contemporary artists have been exploring the styles of tribal traditions other than their own, drawing inspiration from both old and new objects. Themes of shamanism and transformation are foundational to many of the Northwest cultures and are embodied in the spirit face and trance-like eyes in this piece by George Pennier.

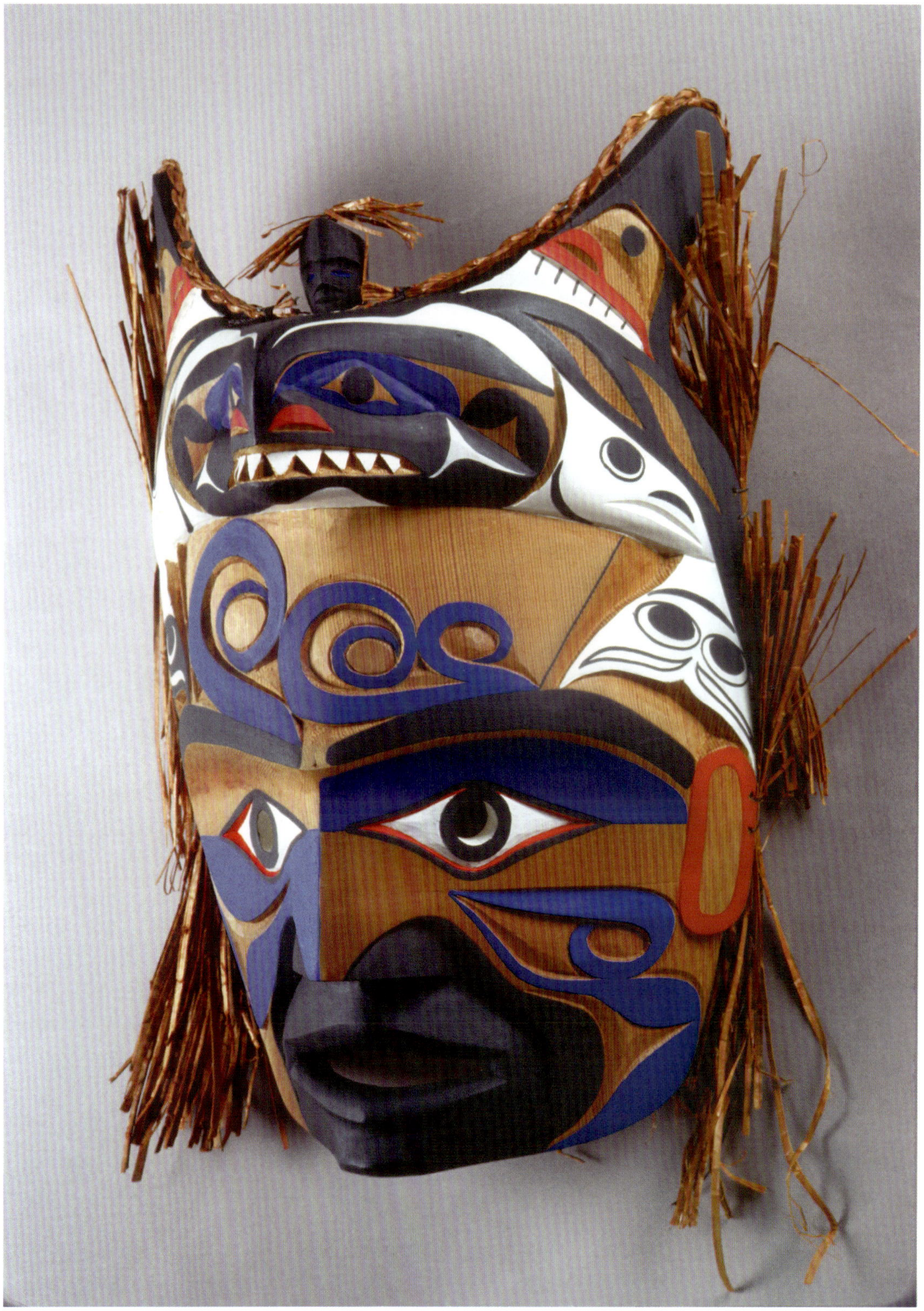

Patrick Amos (Nuu-chah-nulth—Mowachaht). *Sea Chief with Killer Whale*, 2000. Red cedar, paint, cedar bark. 18.9 × 12.2 in. Gift of Arthur B. Steinman, Burke Museum #2004–2/162.

A split image of a killer whale is worn like a headdress by this Sea Chief. The whales' tails extend down on the forehead, framing scrolling waves. A human head rises at the top, where the blowhole of the whale would be. This mask draws on the long history of whale imagery in Nuu-chah-nulth sculpture and the themes of chiefly power linked to undersea strengths.

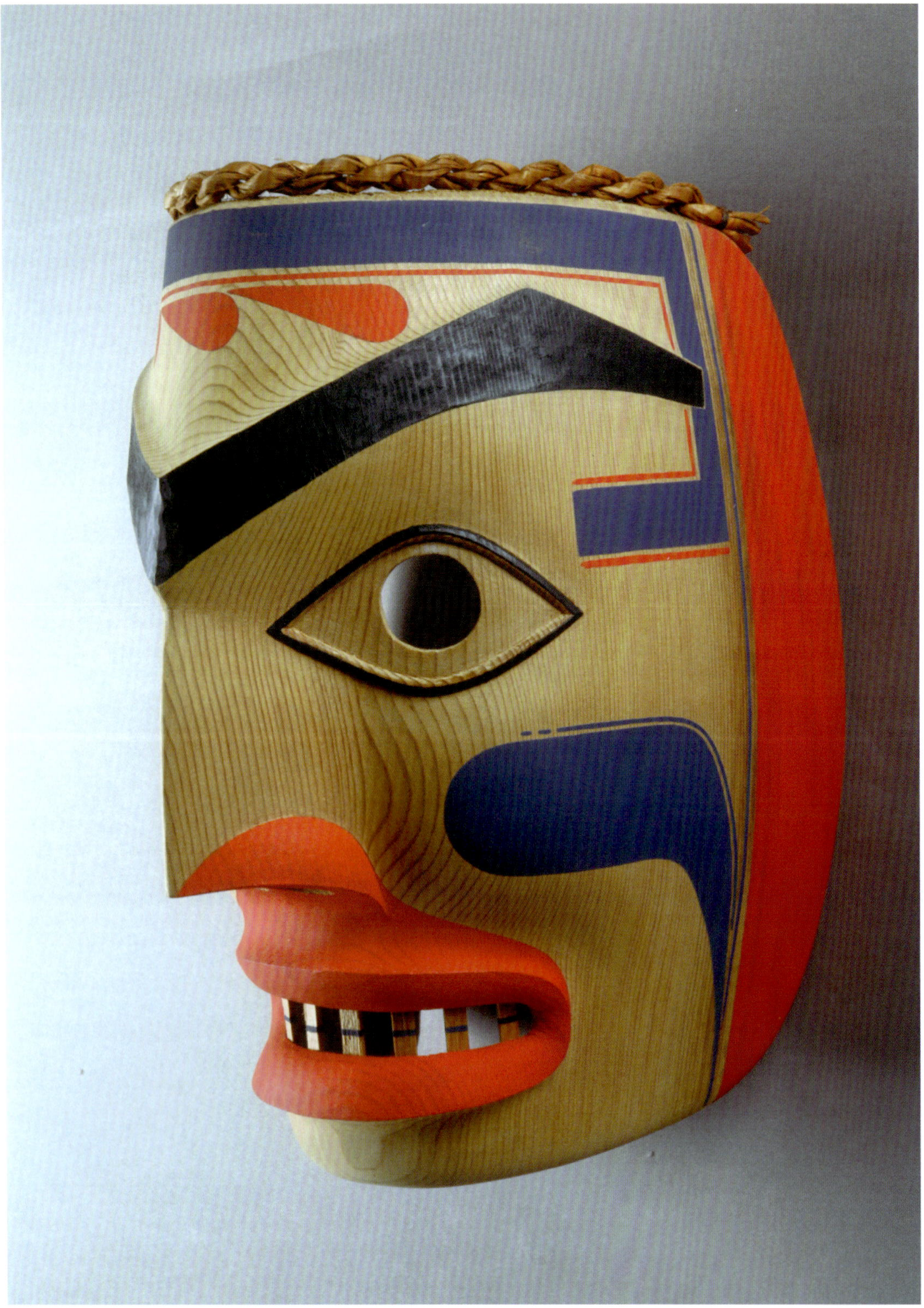

Douglas David (Nuu-chah-nulth—Tla-o-qui-aht/Dakota). *Ancestor Portrait Mask*, 2000. Red cedar, paint, cedar bark. 12.8 × 9.1 in. Gift of Arthur B. Steinman, Burke Museum #2004–2/177.

Here the artist has incorporated both the angular, geometric shapes and fluid line elements that are found in traditional Nuu-chah-nulth paintings, such as house screens and containers. The prismatic principle form seen in this and other wedge-shaped masks developed among the Nuu-chah-nulth in the nineteenth century, grows out of the more rounded forms seen in Old Wakashan–style masks collected by the Cook expedition and other early voyages to the Coast (see fig. 6.7).

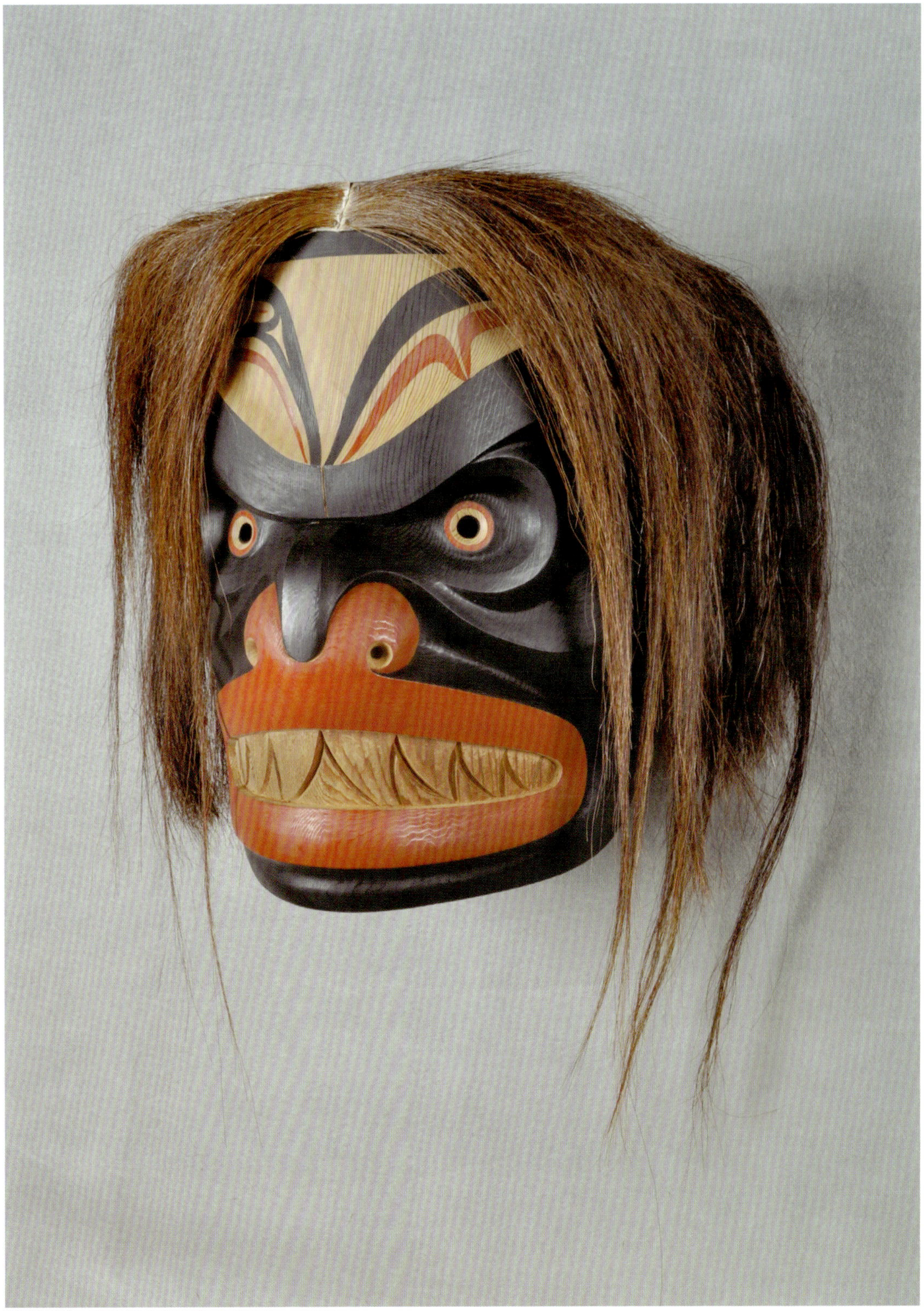

George C. David (Nuu-chah-nulth—Tla-o-qui-aht). *Bear Medicine Man Mask*, 1997. Red cedar, paint, horsehair. 14.4 × 10.6 in. Gift of Arthur B. Steinman, Burke Museum #2004–2/190.

On the southern Northwest Coast, spiritual people get their power from animal spirit helpers and other supernatural beings. According to the artist, when the spirit power comes into them, their faces can change. Here the bear and human are combined, showing the intensity of the spirit power of the bear.

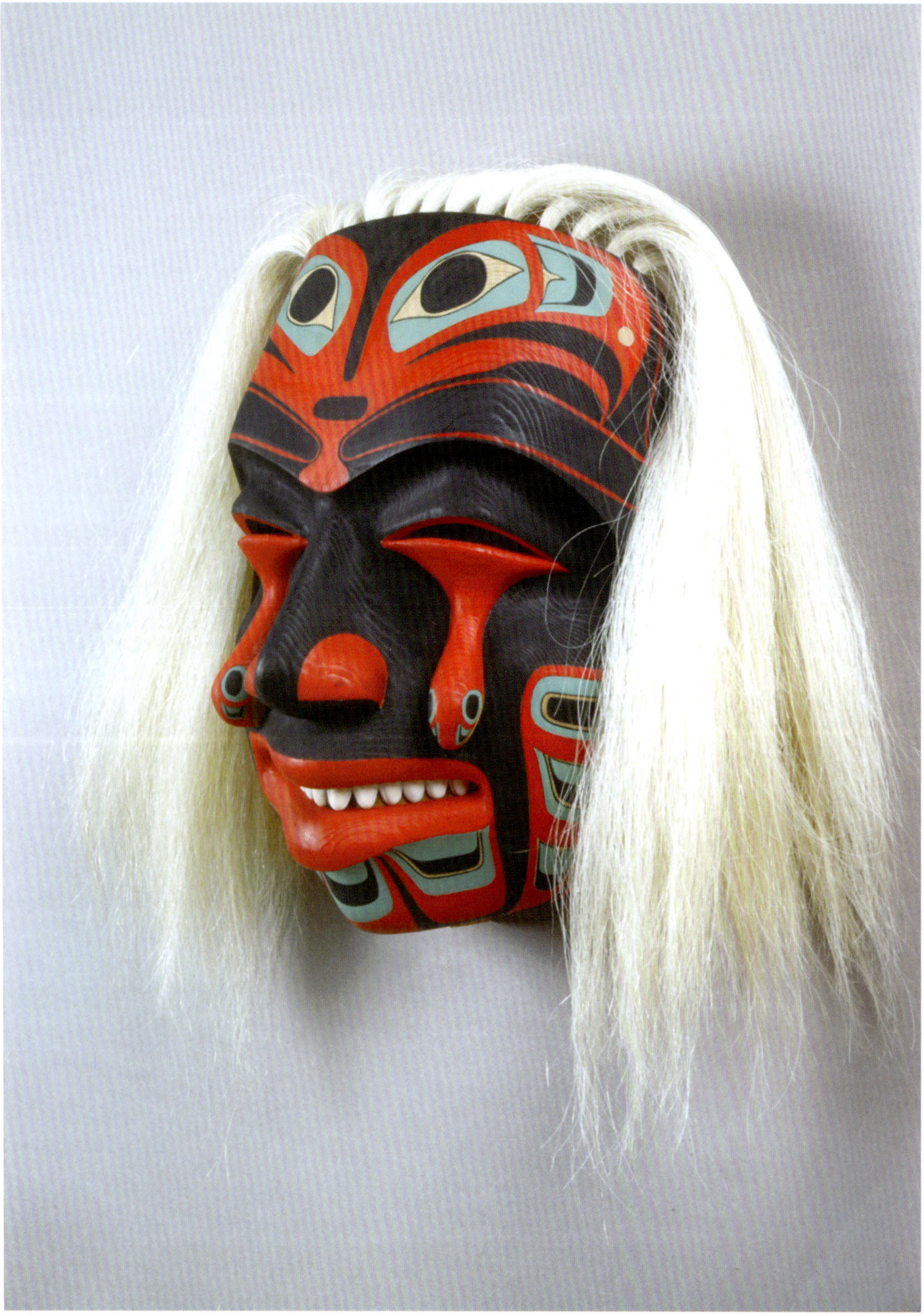

Reg Davidson (Haida). *Once Was a Fisherman*, 2000. Red cedar, paint, horsehair, operculum shells, leather. 14.2 × 11.4 in. Gift of Arthur B. Steinman, Burke Museum #2004–2/192.

"The year I made this mask, I was out fishing and there were no fish so I created that mask. The tears on the mask are the salmon that once were abundant." —Reg Davidson

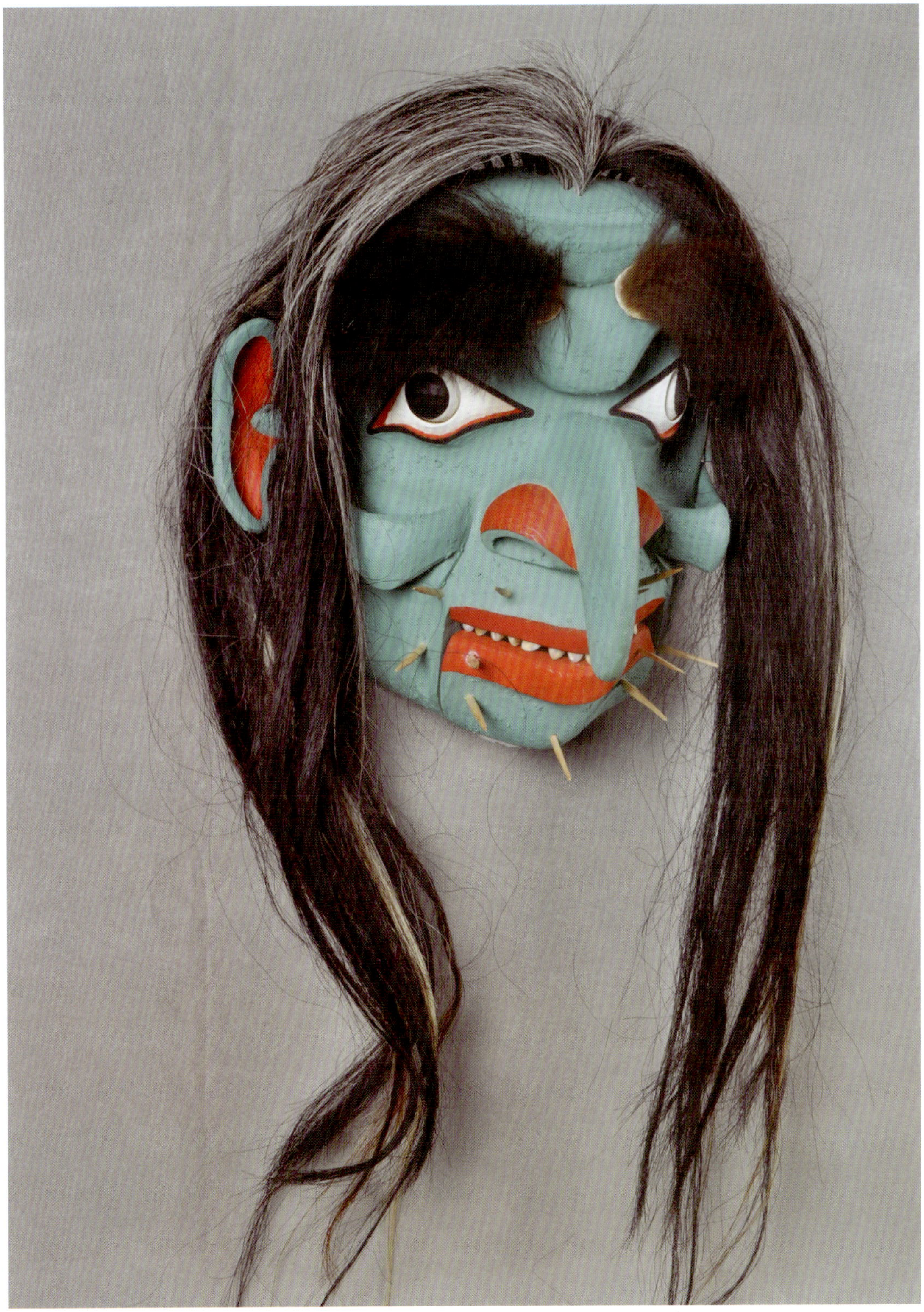

Reg Davidson (Haida). *Gagiit Mask*, 2002. Red cedar, paint, horsehair, fur, operculum shells, metal spring, sinew, foam pad. 19.7 × 18.5 in. Gift of Arthur B. Steinman, Burke Museum #2004–2/193.

"The Gagiit mask is a person that almost drowned and he was able to survive the cold waters, but it changed him into a wild man. There are stories also of changing him back to human form again." —Reg Davidson

Masks like this one are used by several Haida dance groups today as their initial performance to clear the air—the dancers screaming when the frightening supernatural being enters the hall, appearing as a giant hairy monster. By chasing him out, the air is cleared, and the performance goes on.

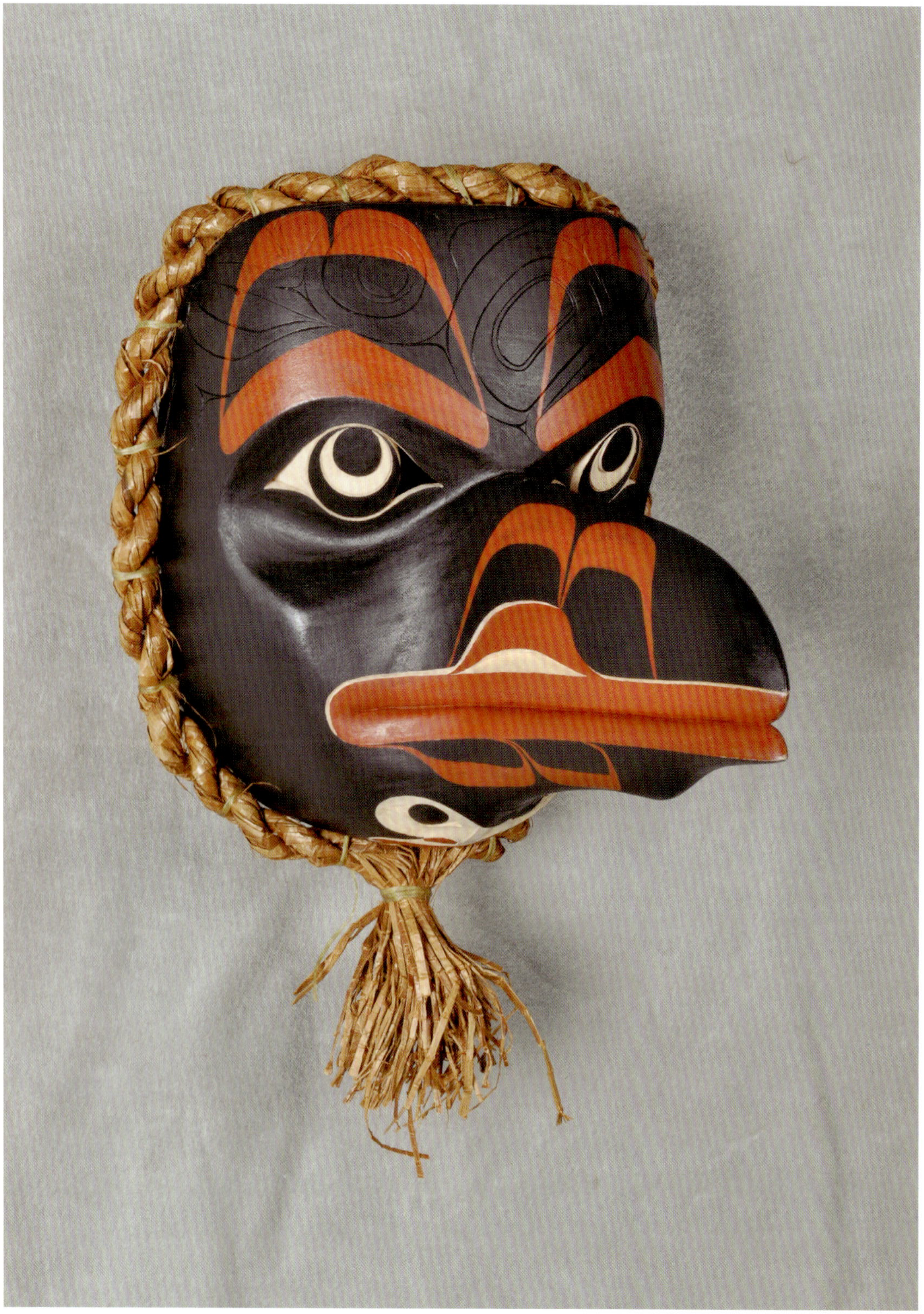

Philip Gray (Tsimshian/Cree). *Raven Mask/Triangle of Life*, 2002. Alder, paint, cedar bark. 9.8 × 8.1 in. Gift of Arthur B. Steinman, Burke Museum #2004–2/212.

This combination of a humanoid facial structure with a naturalistic bird's beak illustrates the concept of transfiguration that frequently appears in historical Northwest Coast art. This dual identity is amplified by the small face carved under the beak. A subtle two-dimensional formline design of a toothed head is carved under the lines of painting on the forehead, and the artist has embellished the hidden interior of the mask with three abstract black U-forms split by red trigon motifs.

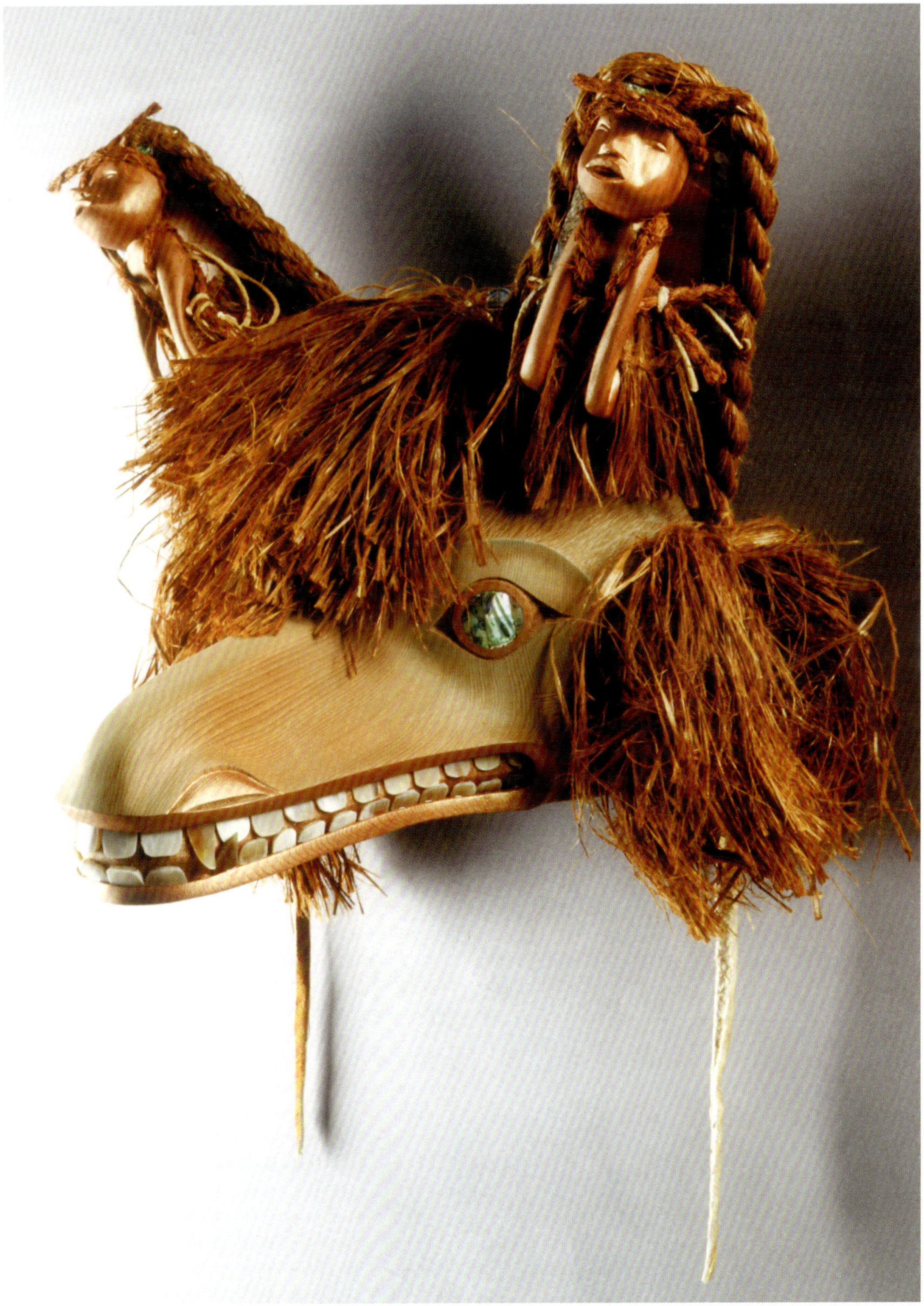

Stan Greene (Coast Salish—Semiahmoo). *Se-quam-il-tol Wolf Chief*, 2001. Wood, paint, cedar bark, abalone, rope. 11.4 × 14.9 in. Gift of Arthur B. Steinman, Burke Museum #2004–2/217.

Human figures adorn the ears of this wolf mask, indicating the close bond between wolves and human beings. According to Salish stories, long ago when humans were without a purpose in the world, some creatures poked fun at humans' inability to maneuver in the world. Wolf took pity on humans and taught them many lessons, including how to use cedar. The wolf is where humans learned the importance of the hierarchy of order.

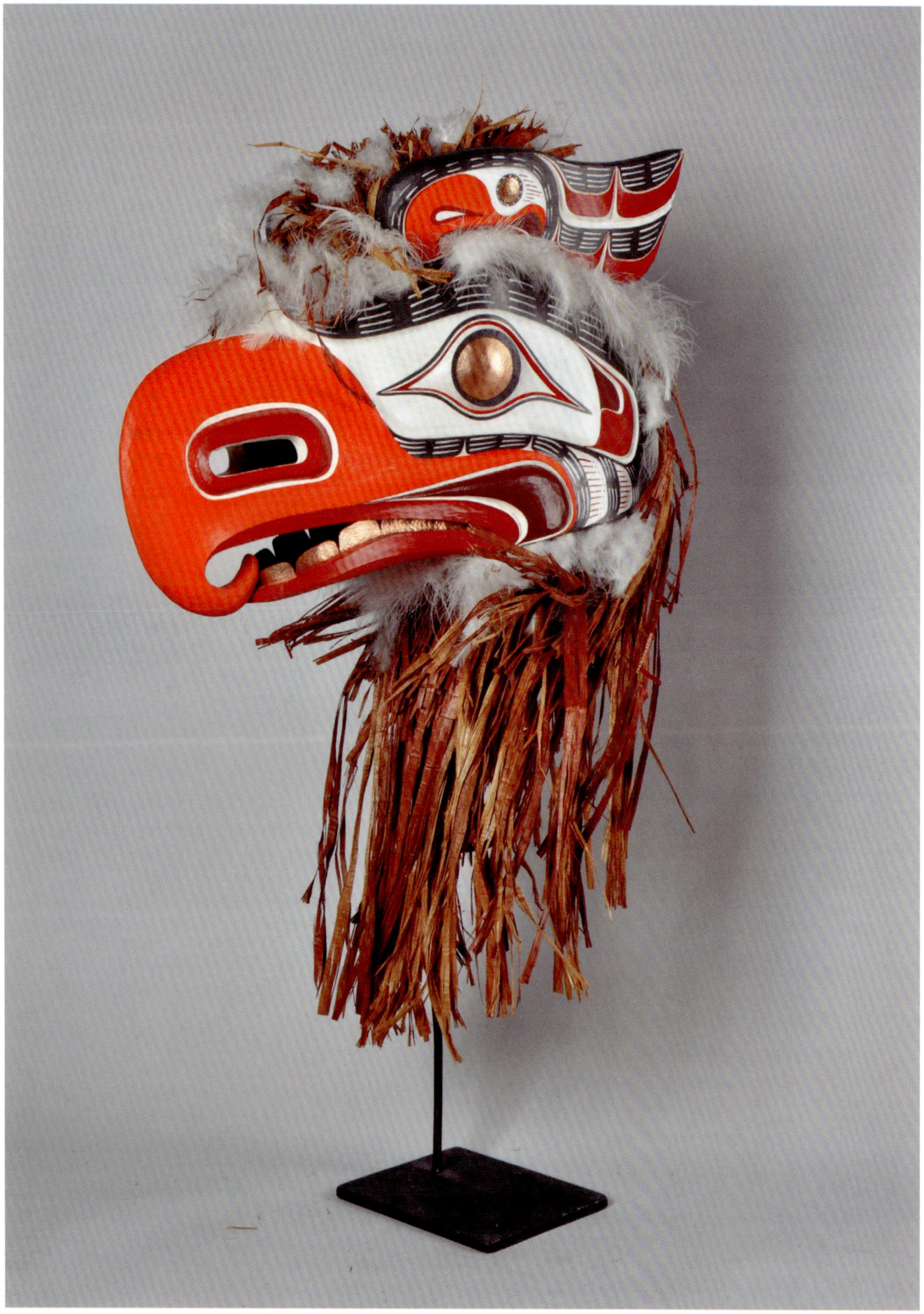

: klatle-bhi . (Kwakwa̲ka̲'wakw). *Kolus, Baby Thunderbird*, ca. 2000. Red cedar, paint, red-dyed cedar bark, feathers, copper. 19.5 × 13 in. Gift of Arthur B. Steinman, Burke Museum #2004–2/235.

"The dancer cocks the Kolus head to one side, slowly sweeping its piercing eye across the house, then tilts and reverses his swing as the song describes the Kolus, calling it 'Screecher Mask.'"—Bill Holm

: klatle-bhi . represents Kolus here as the young Thunderbird, one of the creatures that appears in the origins stories of many Kwakwa̲ka̲'wakw namima. The sweeping nature of the Kolus dance is echoed in the recurved lines of the top feathers, the white dashing creating a blurred highlight as the dancer moves.

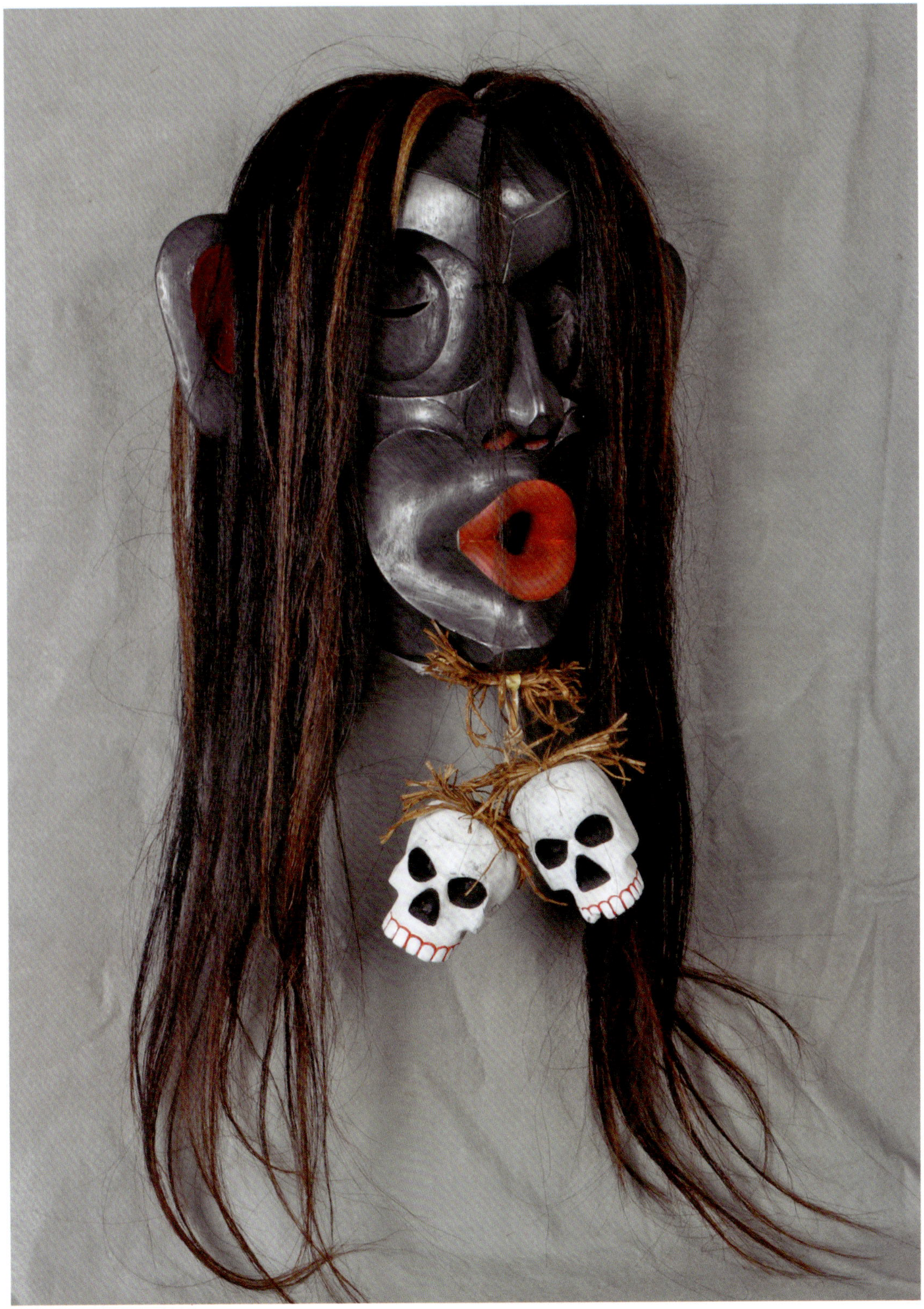

Jerry Smith (Kwakwa̱ka̱'wakw—Kwagiulth). *Tsonoqua*, 1997. Red cedar, paint, horsehair, leather, cedar bark, string. 16.5 × 16.9 in. Gift of Arthur B. Steinman, Burke Museum #2004–2/268.

"All Northwest Coast people have traditions of giant, often malevolent human-like creatures that dwell in the dark wilderness and occasionally interact with humans. The Dzoonokwa is the archetypical monster-giant of the Northwest Coast. Sometimes described as an eater of human flesh or a stealer of children, she also can be the bestower of power and wealth. For those whose ancestors have met and bested her, the privilege of representing the Dzoonokwa in carved post, mask, and dramatic performance is a prized privilege." —Bill Holm

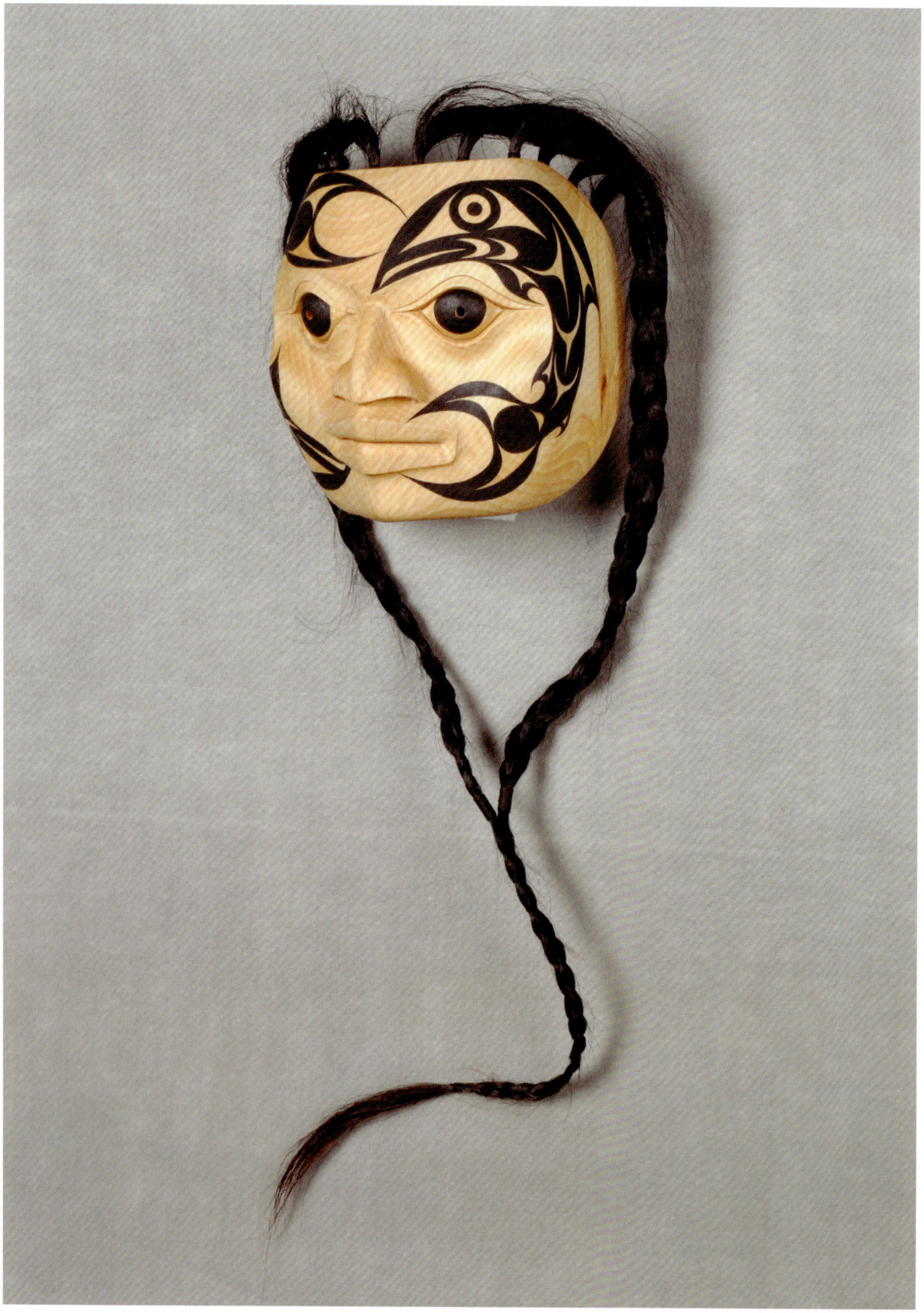

Gerry Sheena (Coast Salish). *Two Males Battle Mask*, 2003. Alder, paint, horsehair, string. 9.1 × 8.5 in. Gift of Arthur B. Steinman, Burke Museum #2004–2/274.

"Two Males battle for best spawning grounds. These battles that happen annually for thousands of years are a testament to the perseverance of the salmon spirit. It's a battle West Coast artists have engaged in to best represent an ancient artform. Striving to pay the art form the respect it deserves. The same perseverance that drives the salmon, drives me as an artist. A battle for that best spawning ground we call the art world."—Gerry Sheena

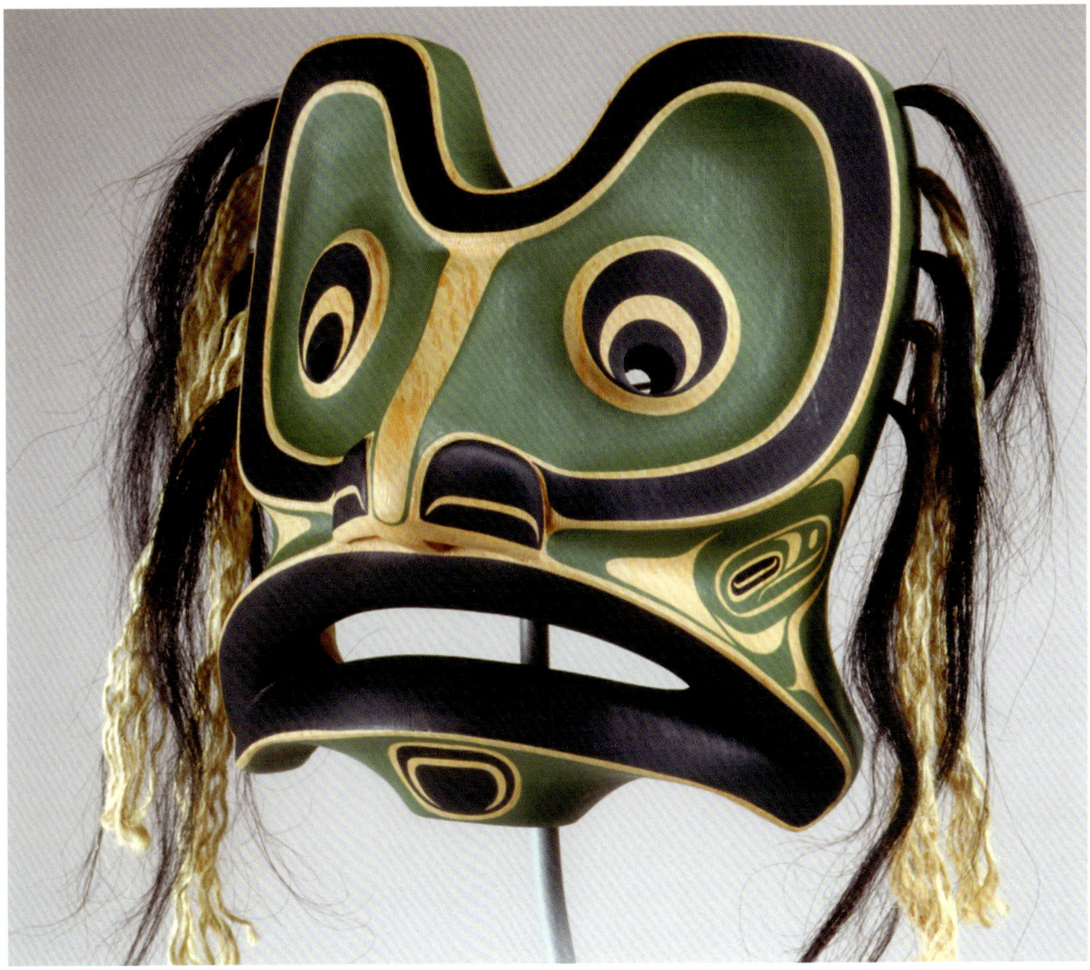

Steve Smith—Dla'wakgila (Kwakwa̱ka̱'wakw). *Man/Frog Mask*, 2000. Red cedar, paint, horsehair, rope. 10.2 × 8.3 in. Gift of Arthur B. Steinman, Burke Museum #2004–2/287.

The curved surfaces that typify the painted, turned vessels that Smith is known for can be seen in the sweeping lines in the cheek and eyes of this frog mask. The mask's overall form has been simplified to the basic outline of a frog's face, almost as if liberated from a flat design. The mixture of black horsehair and unraveled rope extend the colors of the mask's painted and natural surface down into its framing space.

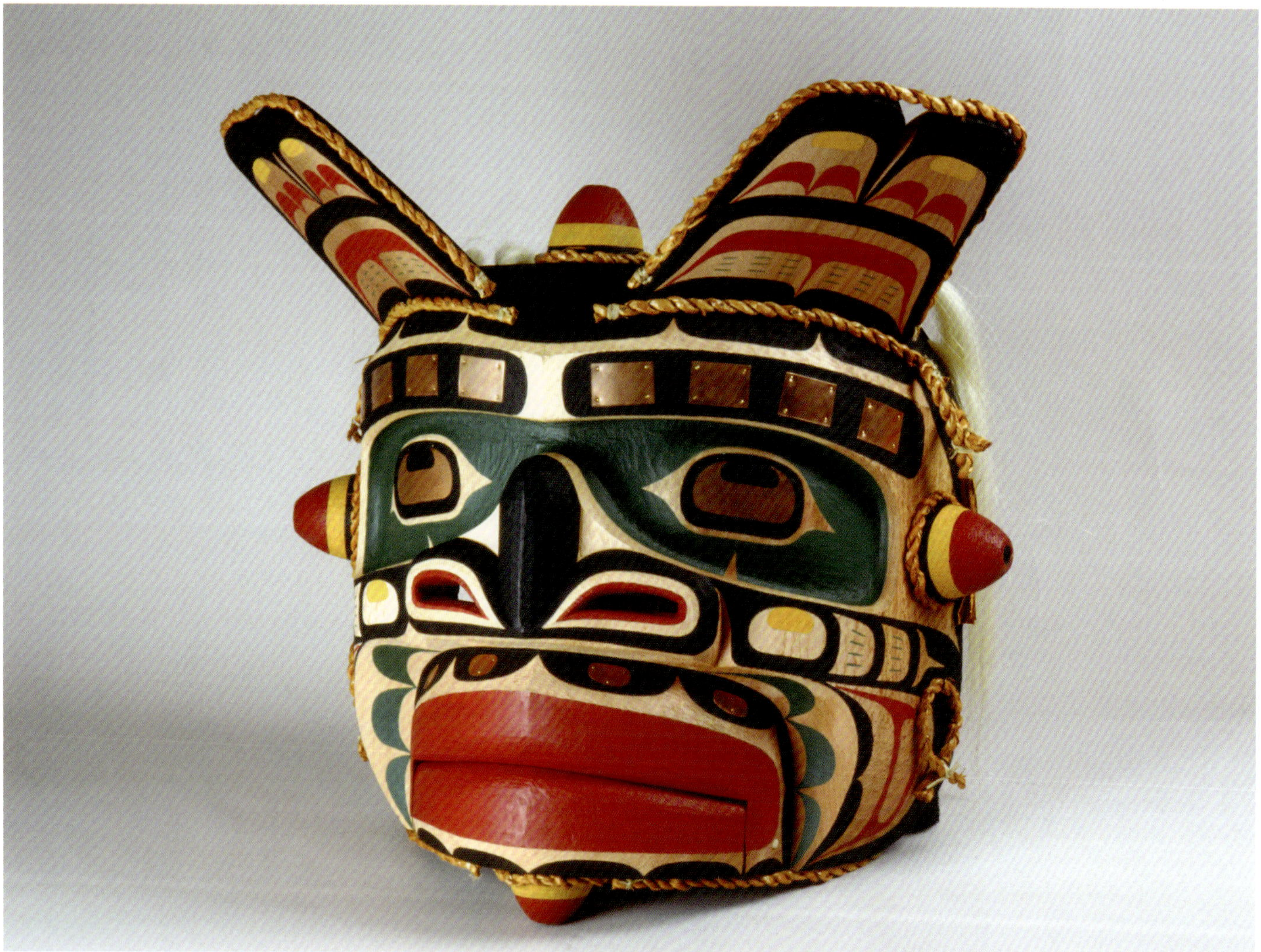

Calvin Hunt (Kwakwa̱ka̱'wakw—Kwagiulth). *Yagis, Kwagu'l Sea Monster*, 2004. Red cedar, rope, cedar bark, plastic tubing, plastic container, floats, copper, horsehair, cloth. 30 × 30 in. Gift of Charlie and Gayle Pancerzewski, Burke Museum #2004–90/3.

Spectacular sea-monster masks are part of the Kwakwa̱ka̱'wakw Tlasula ceremony. Masked dancers impersonating supernatural beings enter the big house in firelight, dramatizing an encounter and declaring the high status of the family presenting the dance. This sea monster is intended to spout feathers through the float at the top of its head by the dancer blowing on a plastic hose connected to a container concealed inside the mask.

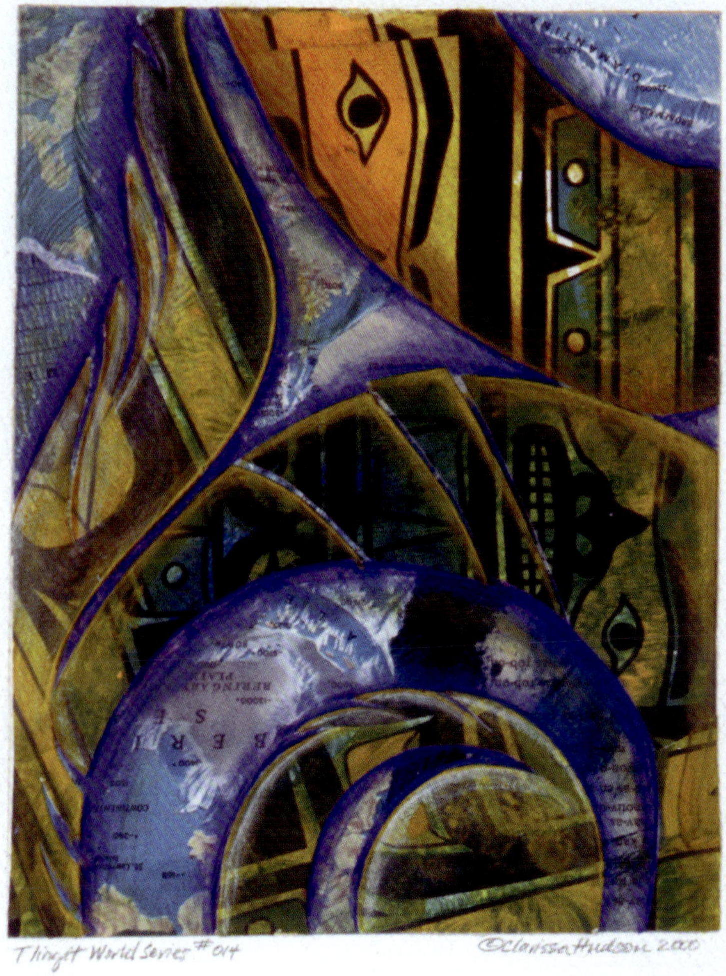

Clarissa (Hudson) Rizal (Tlingit). *Tlingit World Series #14*, 2000. Collage. 21.7 × 18.3 in. Gift of Arthur B. Steinman, Burke Museum #2004–2/394.

"I began making paper collages during the summer of 2000 and found the experience totally exhilarating. All of my previous artworks had been painstakingly pre-planned before I got down to the actual creation of them, especially my weavings and button blankets. But I found that, for me, collage making was very spontaneous . . . the pieces almost made themselves while I watched." —Clarissa Rizal

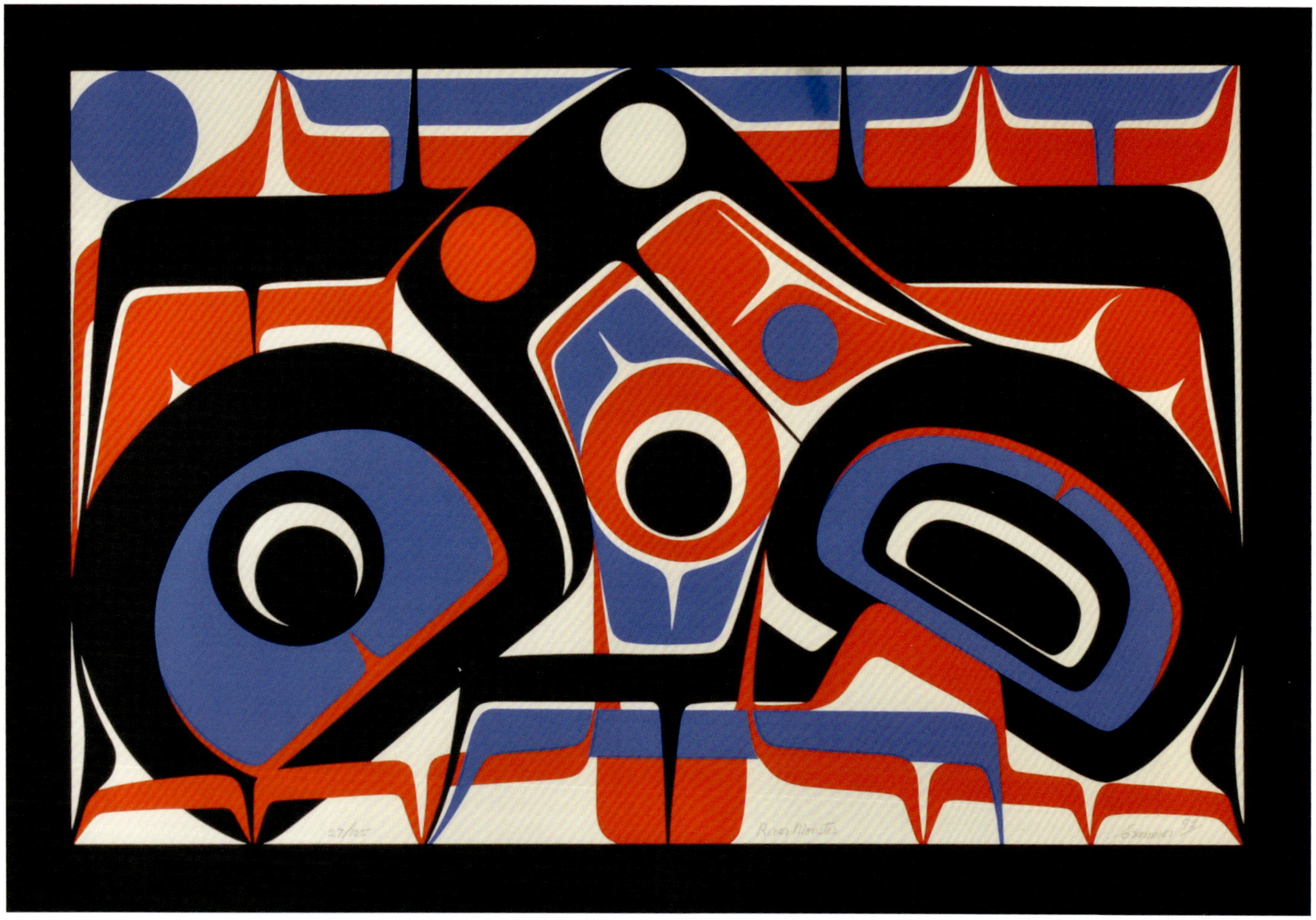

Doug Cranmer (Kwakwa̱ka̱'wakw). *River Monster*, 1992. Silkscreen print. 30 × 21.8 in. Gift of Lloyd J. Averill, Burke Museum #1996–48/1.

In the late 1970s Doug Cranmer was one of the first artists on the Northwest Coast to experiment with abstract designs based on the formal elements of the art. This design was initially untitled but received the name "River Monster" when the original painting on mahogany plywood was turned into a print in 1992. The transition from wood to paper meant the loss of the additional texture provided by the grain of the mahogany but allowed these images to be produced in multiples and gain greater exposure.

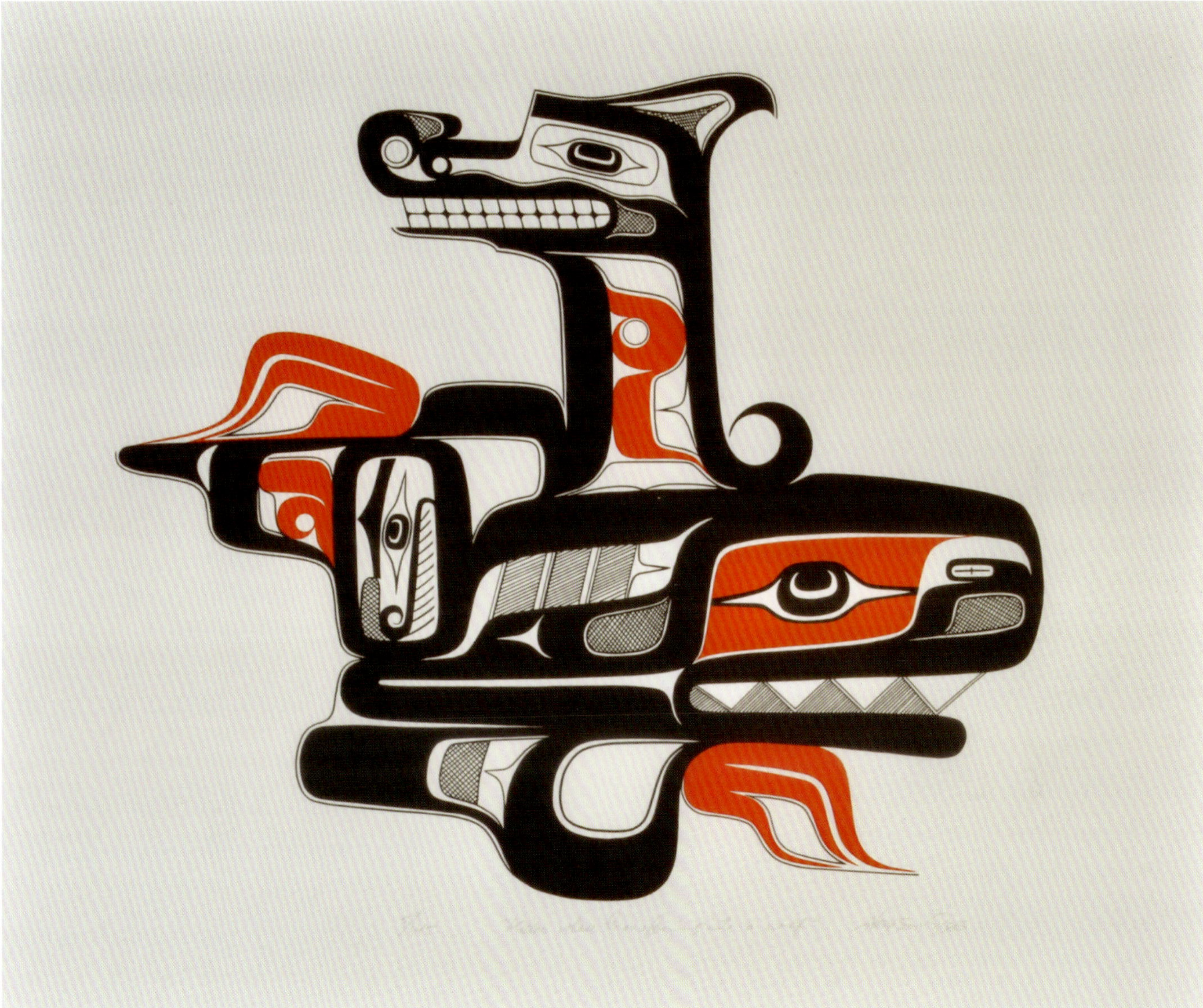

Art Thompson (Nuu-chah-nulth—Dit-i-daht). *Killer-Whale Transforming into a Wolf*, 1986. Silkscreen print. 18 × 20 in. Blackman Hall Collection, Burke Museum #1998–90/993.

"This print illustrates the transformation of a Killer Whale into a Wolf. The legend explains why killer whales travel in groups, as do wolves. This is representative of the Nuu-chah-nulth belief of inter-changeability between animals." —Art Thompson

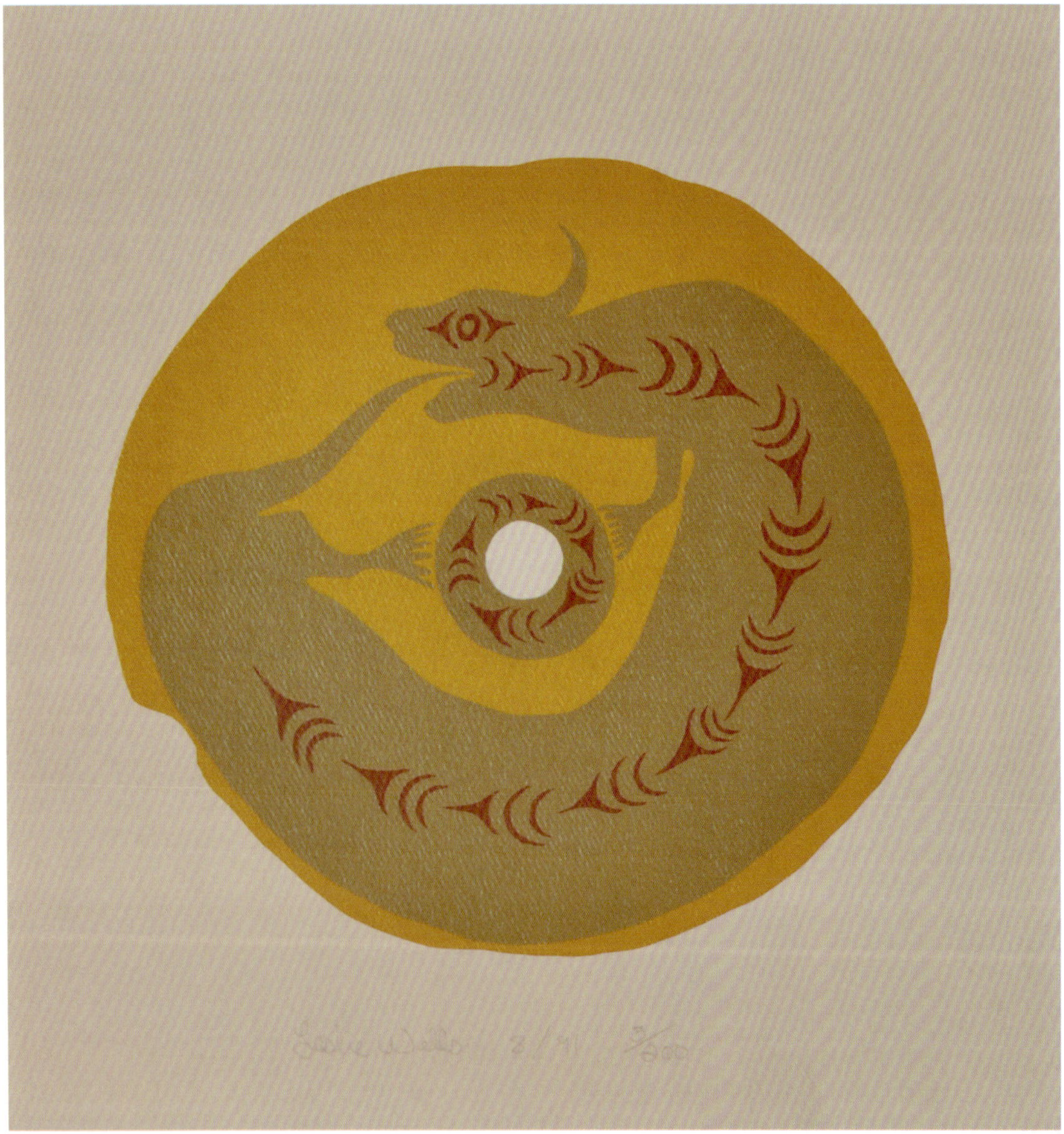

Leslie Wells (Coast Salish). *Untitled*, 1991. Silkscreen print. 11.5 × 11.5 in. Gift of Simon Ottenberg, Burke Museum #1999–151/27.

Many Coast Salish artists have been inspired by old spindle whorls in museum collections. These flat wooden disks were used as flywheels on the spindle shaft, while spinning mountain goat wool. This design is taken directly from an old spindle whorl from the Emmons collection in the Smithsonian National Museum of Natural History (#221179-E).

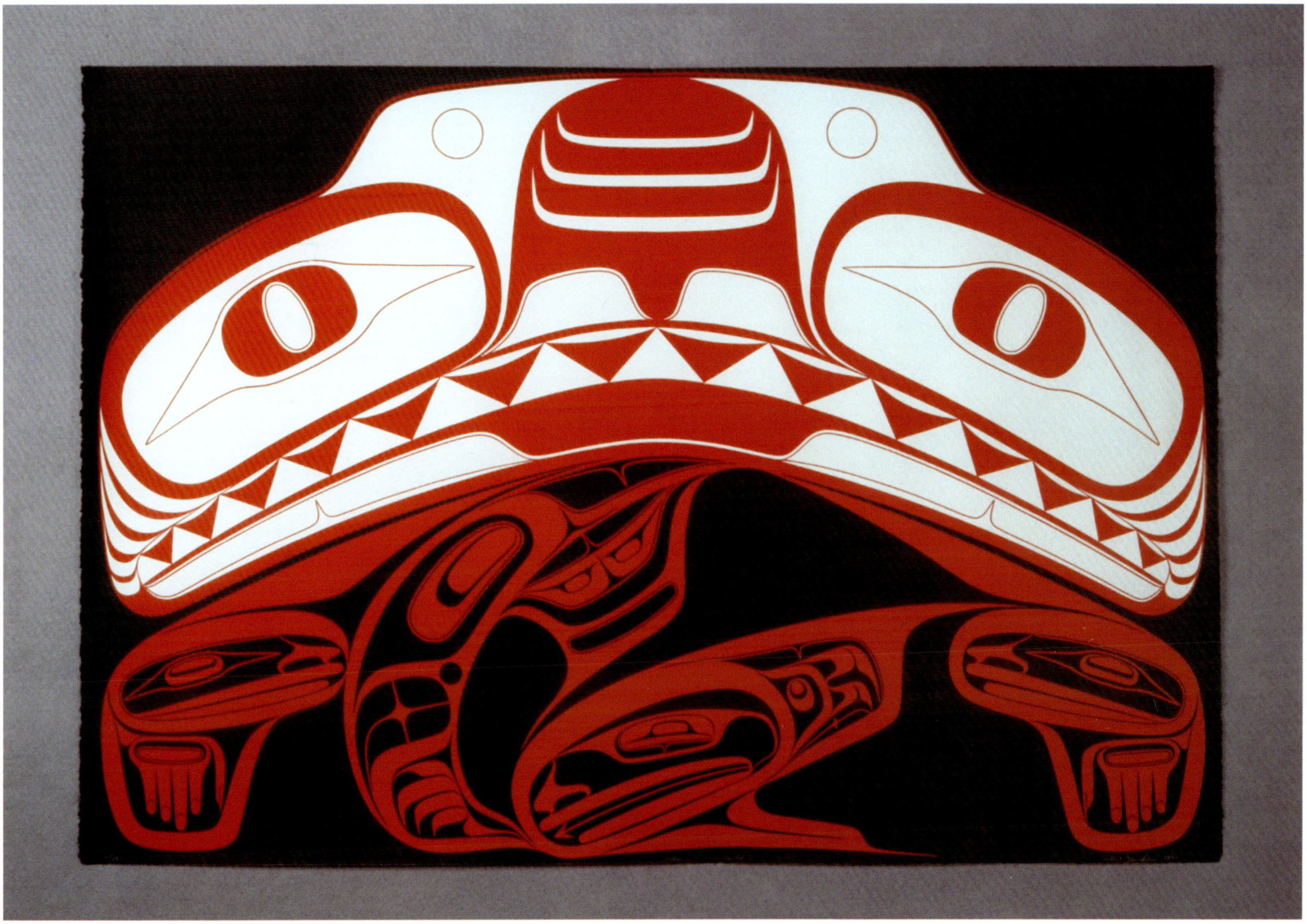

Robert Davidson (Haida). *Sisters of the Underworld*, 1998. Silkscreen print. 29.5 × 41.5 in. Gift of Douglas Jackson, Burke Museum #2002–20/4.

Inspired by nineteenth-century "ultraprimary" bentwood bowls and boxes, here Robert Davidson has placed red primary formlines of the shark's body directly on black ultraprimary formlines. The dogfish is a crest of the Haida Yahgu'laanas Raven clan. This is the clan of Davidson's father, Claude, and his grandmother, Florence Edenshaw Davidson.

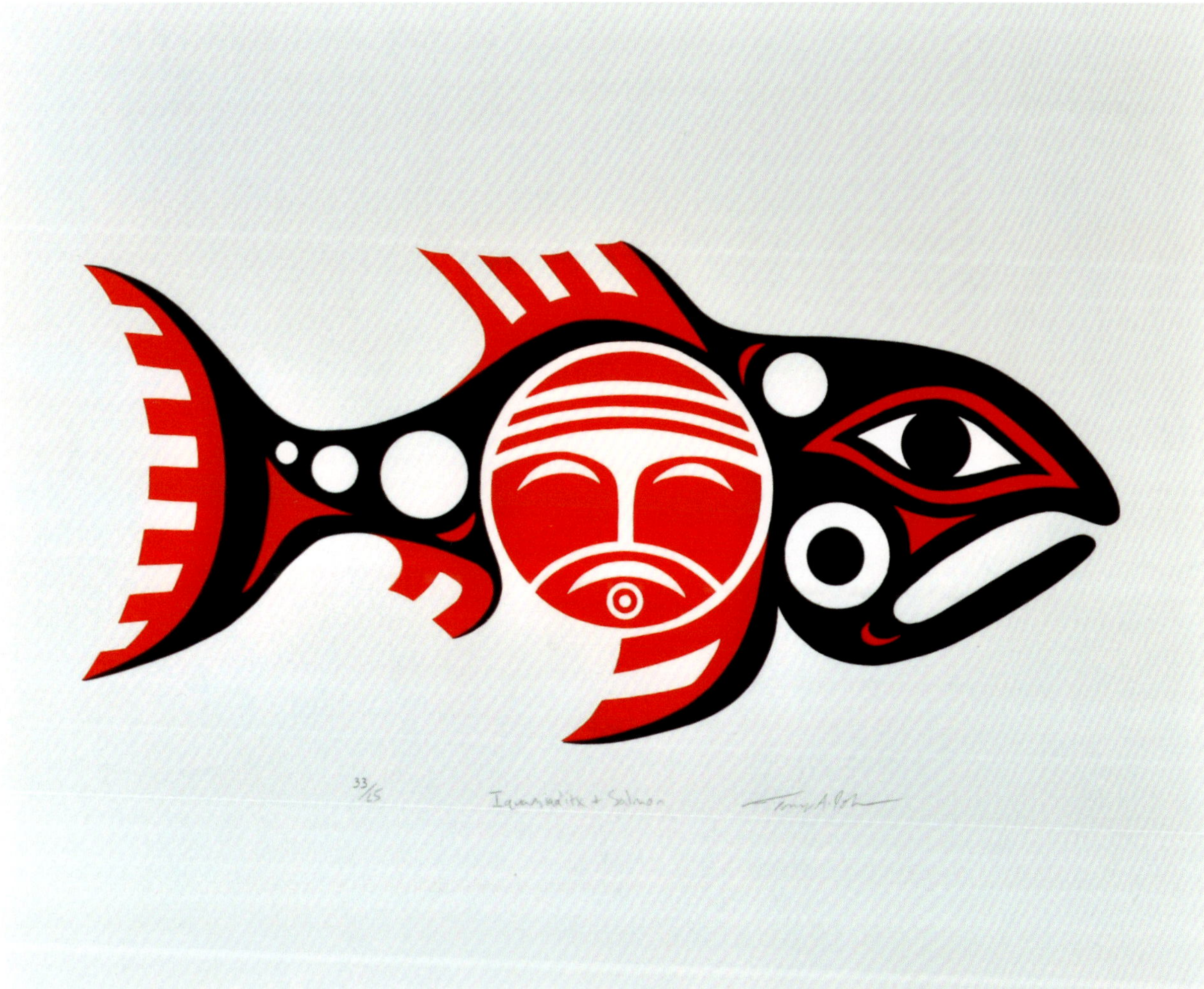

Tony A. Johnson (Chinook—Wahkaikum). *Íquamiaáitx and Salmon*, 1991. Silkscreen print. 11 × 13.5 in. Gift of Simon Ottenberg, Burke Museum #2000–148/8.

Íquamiaáitx is a Chinookan power figure that is gained by questing or through the family. It is one of several figures that lend knowledge to fishing. In this print he appears with a Chinook salmon. This design has been adopted as the logo of the Chinook tribe.

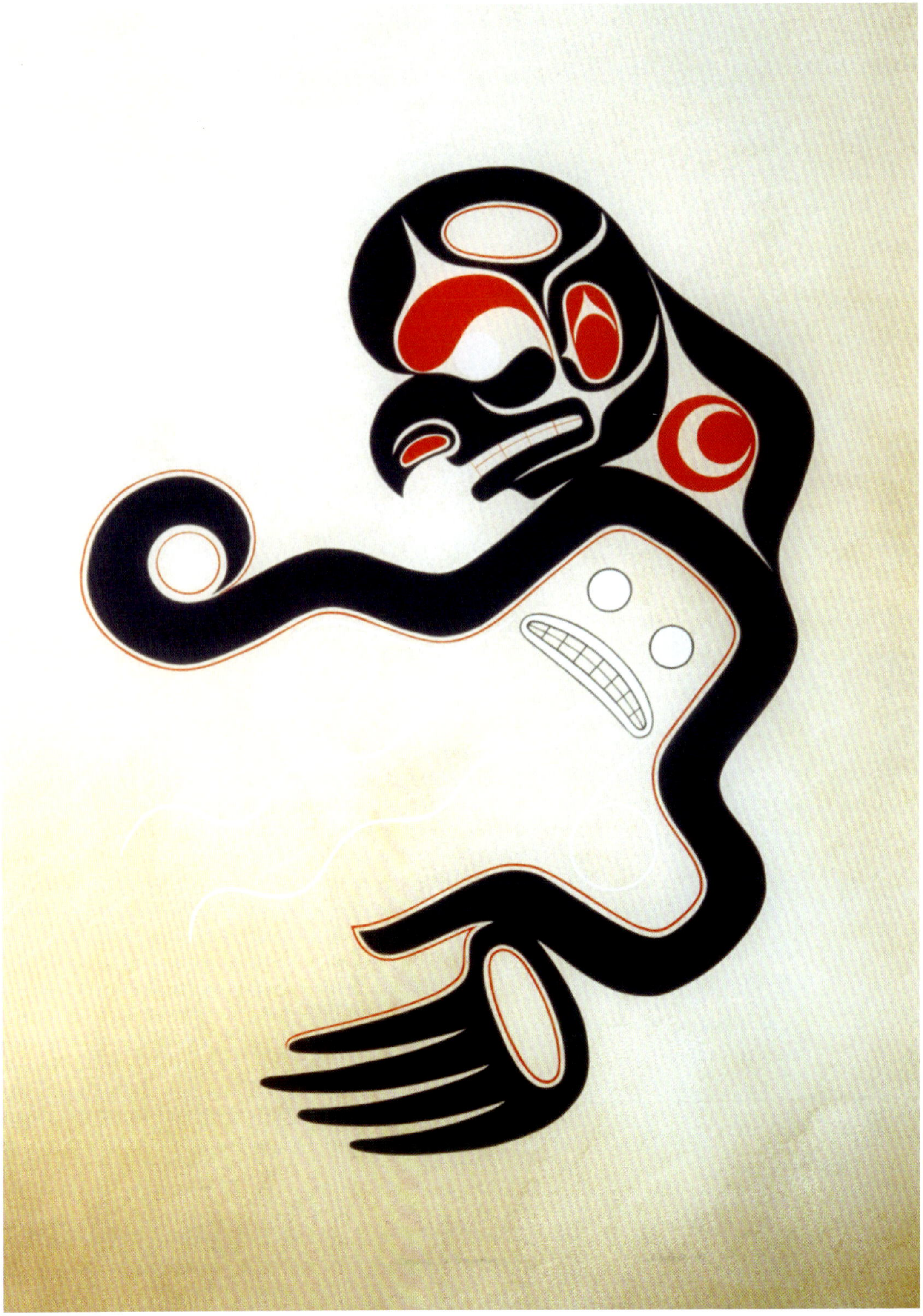

Joe David (Nuu-chah-nulth—Tla-o-qui-aht). *Octopus and Jellyfish*, 1991. Silkscreen print. 38 × 33 in. Gift of Douglas Jackson, Burke Museum #2002–20/10.

This design was first drawn on a place mat in the late 1970s and eventually painted onto a skin drum. An innovative photo-serigraph technique was used to make the final piece in which the optical effect of paint on hide was achieved through a photo-mechanical treatment of the printing plate. The serigraph design was applied on top of those prints.

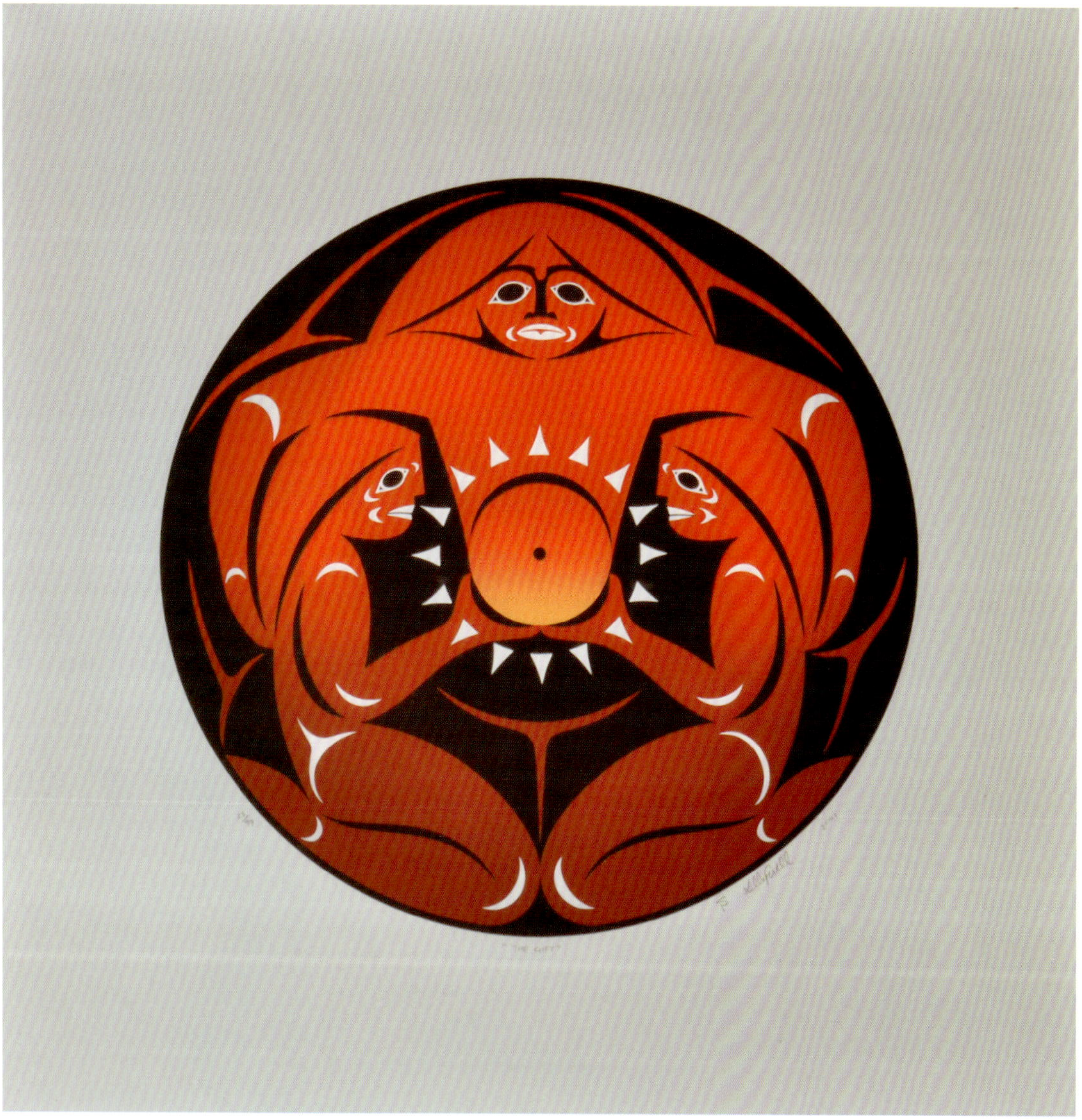

Kelly Cannell (Coast Salish—Musqueam). *The Gift*, 2001. Silkscreen print. 22 × 22 in. Gift of Arthur B. Steinman, Burke Museum #2004–2/379.

A mother's nurturing arms surround her children on this print made by Kelly Cannell, the daughter of the artist Susan Point, in collaboration with her mother. The hands of the children focus the viewer's attention on the shaft hole of the spindle whorl design, centered at the womb of the mother.

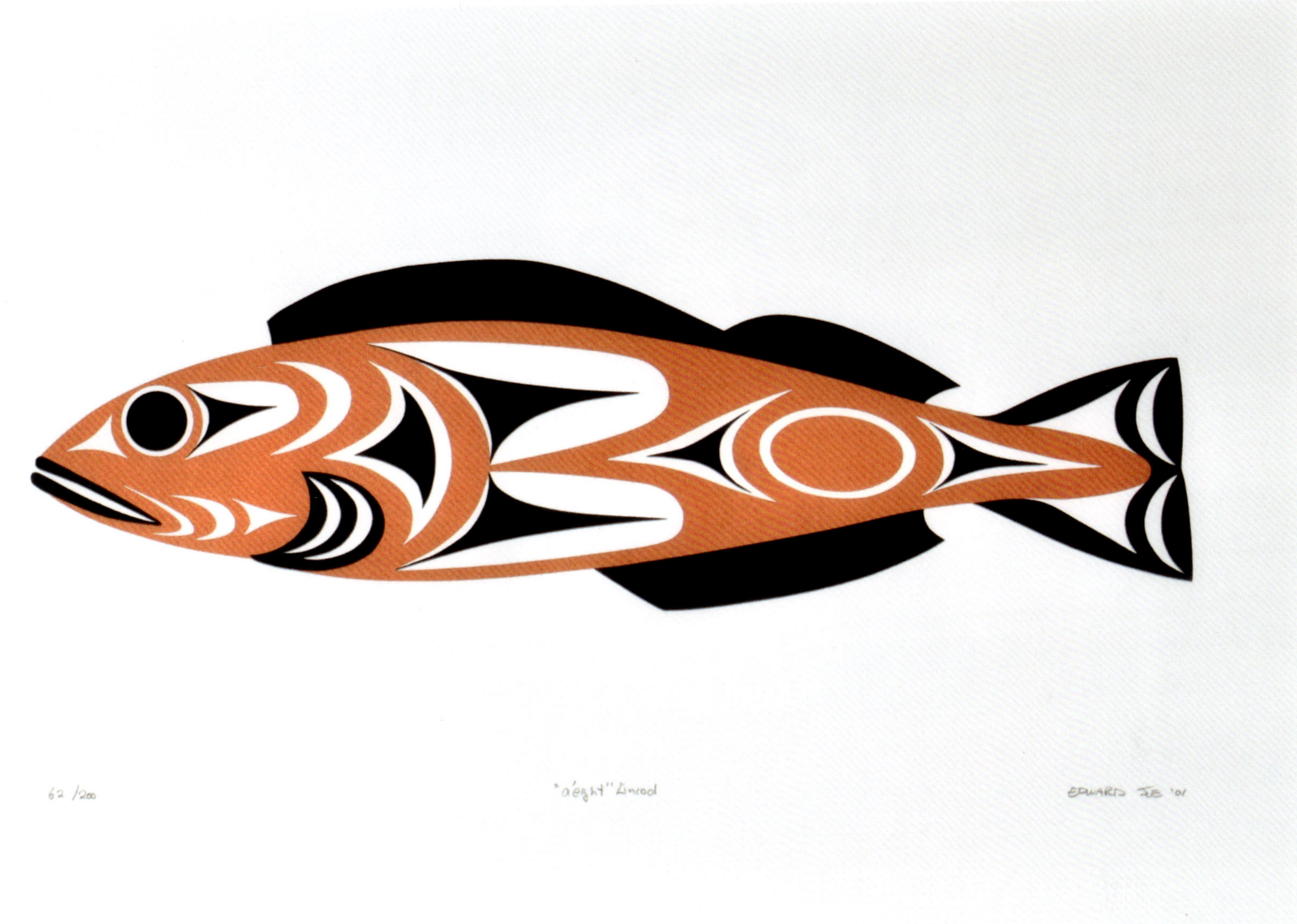

Edward Joe (Coast Salish—Cowichan). *A'eght, Lincod*, 2001. Silkscreen print. 13 × 20 in. Gift of Simon Ottenberg, Burke Museum #2005–47/46.

"The Lincod is the fish that is the most abundant when other food source fish are not available. In March they become aggressive and protective of their eggs. They are found in reefs." —Edward Joe

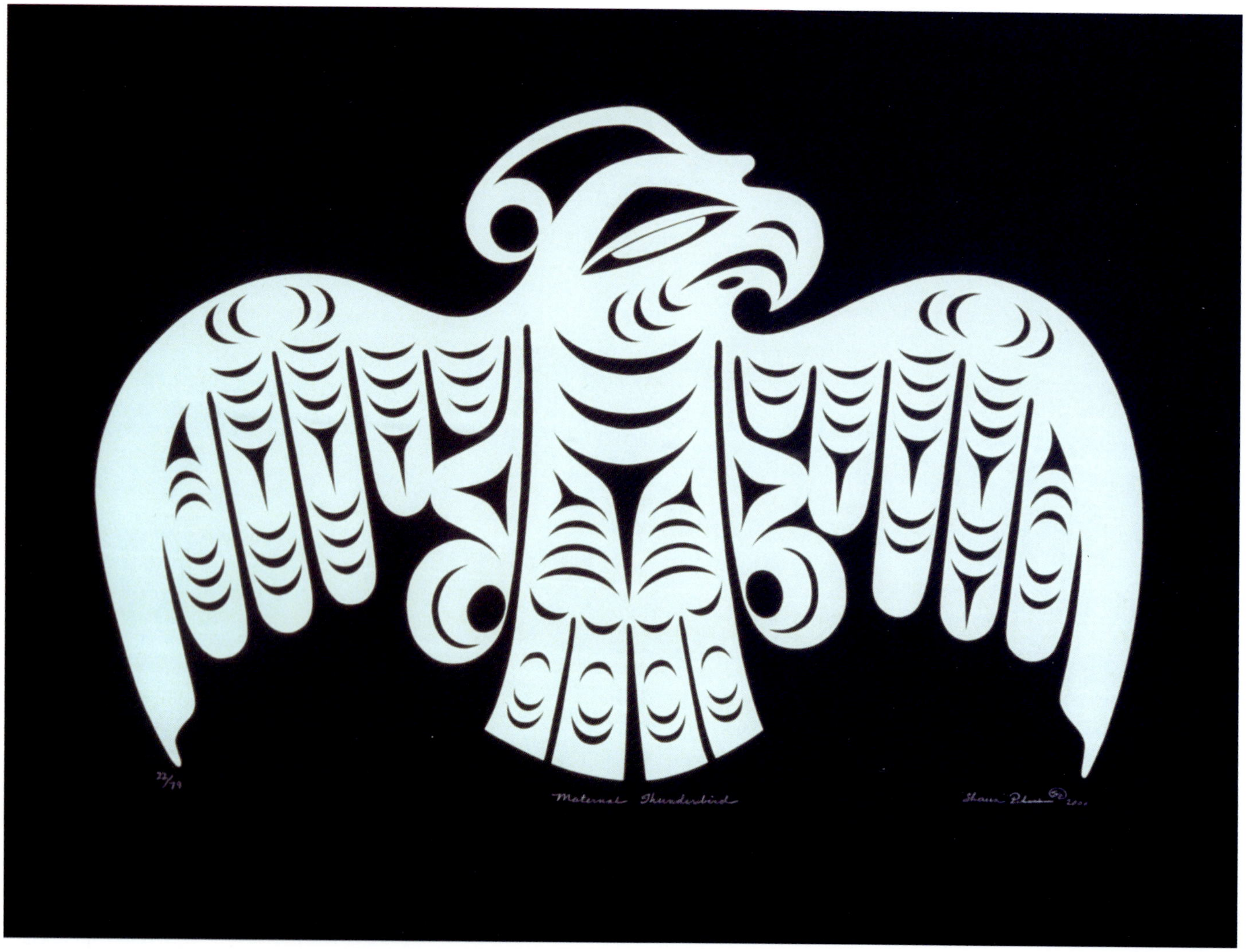

Shaun Peterson (Coast Salish—Puyallup, Tulalip). *Maternal Thunderbird*, 2000. Silkscreen print. 19.7 × 25.6 in. Gift of Simon Ottenberg, Burke Museum #2005–47/79.

This print honors the artist's maternal grandmother, Lauretta Jane Wright. In this image the symmetry of the Thunderbird's sheltering wings brings the viewer's eye back to the only non-symmetrical section of the design—the Thunderbird's head with its fierce beak and protective gaze. The Thunderbird glows in pure white against the dark sky of the background.

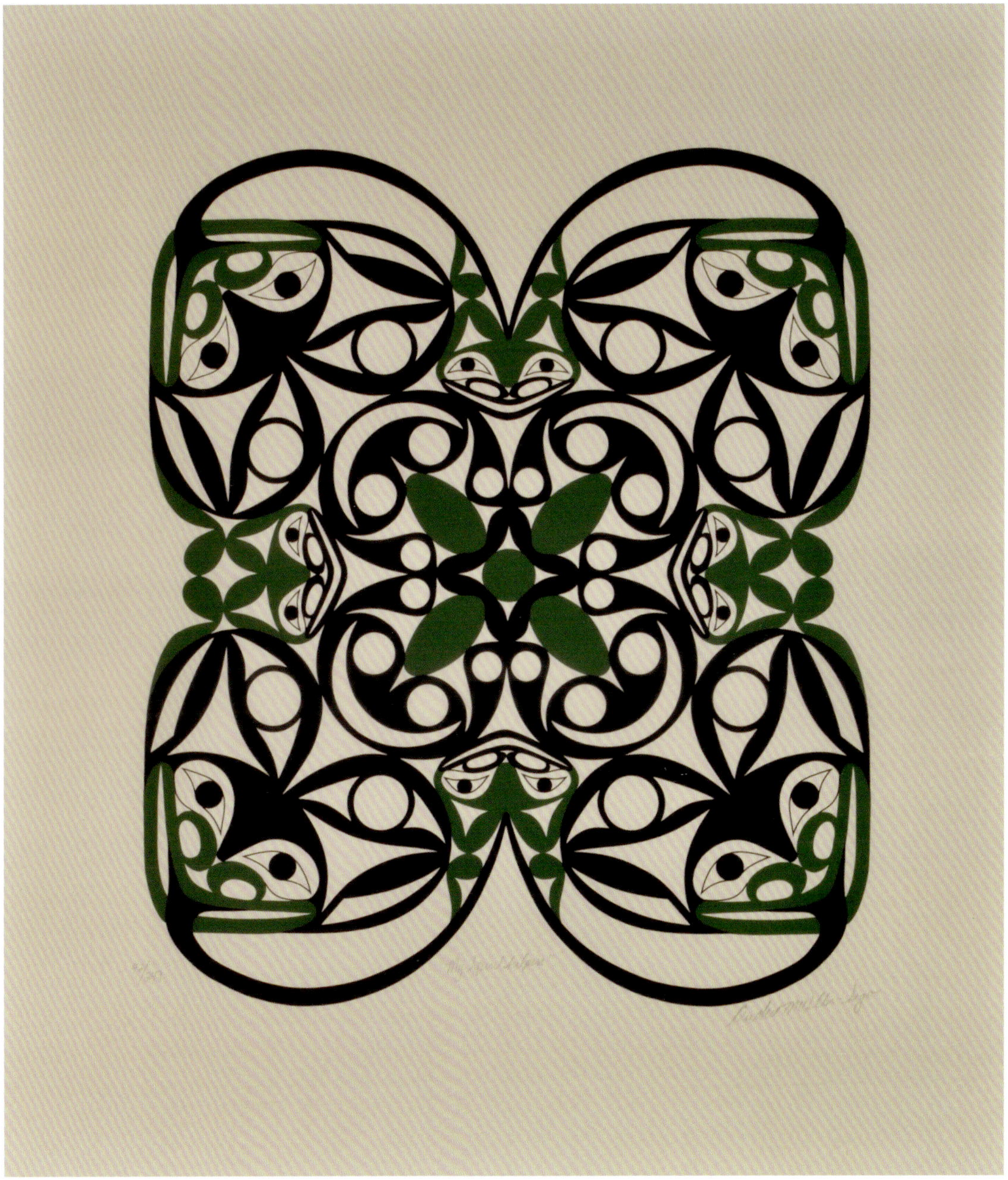

Andrea M. Wilbur-Sigo (Coast Salish—Squaxin Island). *My Spirit Helpers*, 2001. Silkscreen print. 25.75 × 21.25 in. Gift of Simon Ottenberg, Burke Museum #2005–47/119.

As with nineteenth-century Coast Salish art, depictions of spirit helpers are deliberately obscured to the viewer. Here the artist evokes frog-like beings intertwined in a lacey butterfly-patterned structure.

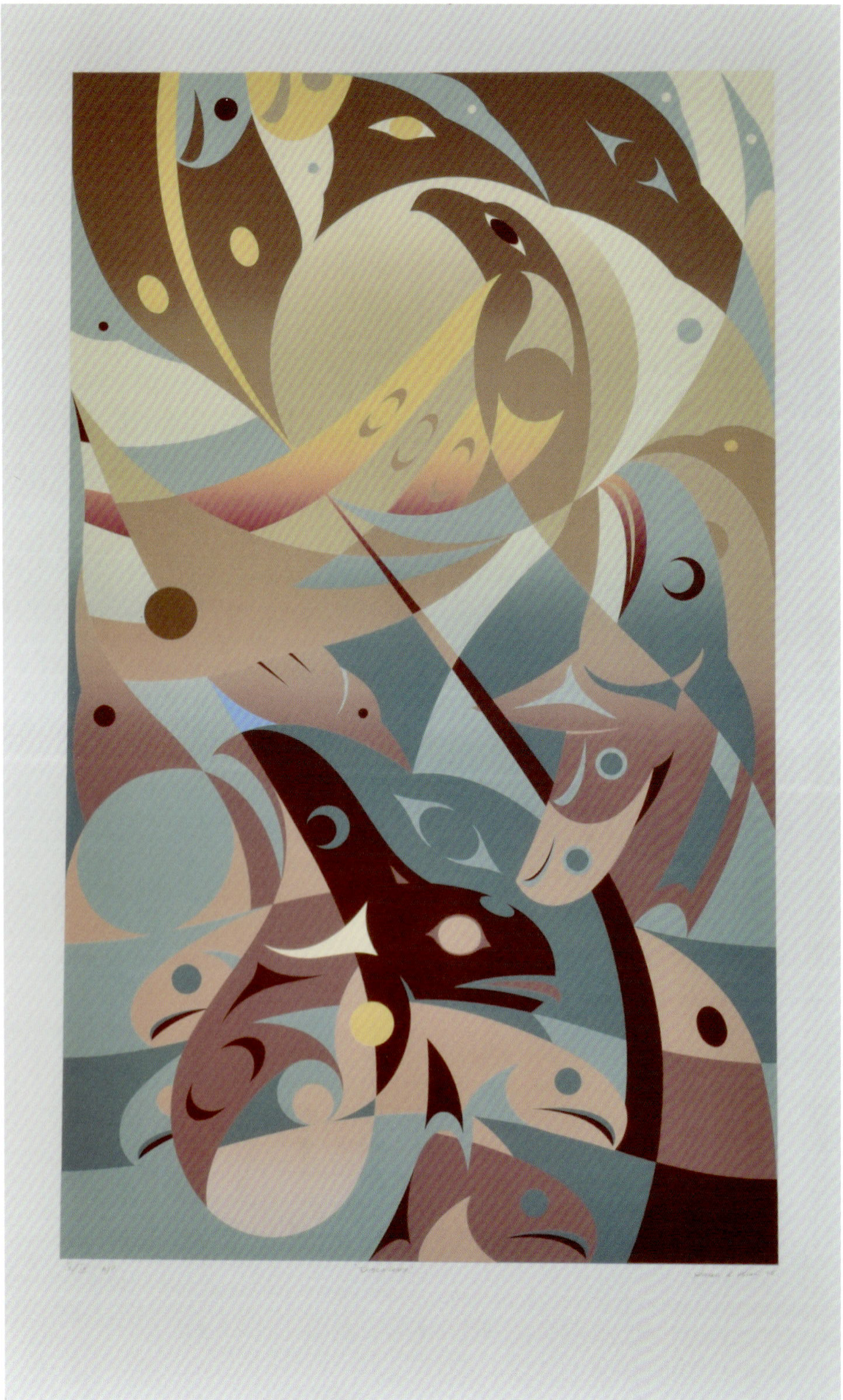

Susan Point (Coast Salish—Musqueam). *Discovery*, 2005. Silkscreen print. 33 × 20 in. Gift of Susan Point, Burke Museum #2007–12/2.

Always experimenting with new colors and forms, Susan Point swirls the profiles of birds, fish, and whales in subtle and overlapping shades of brown, blue, and gold to achieve a sense of motion and fluidity.

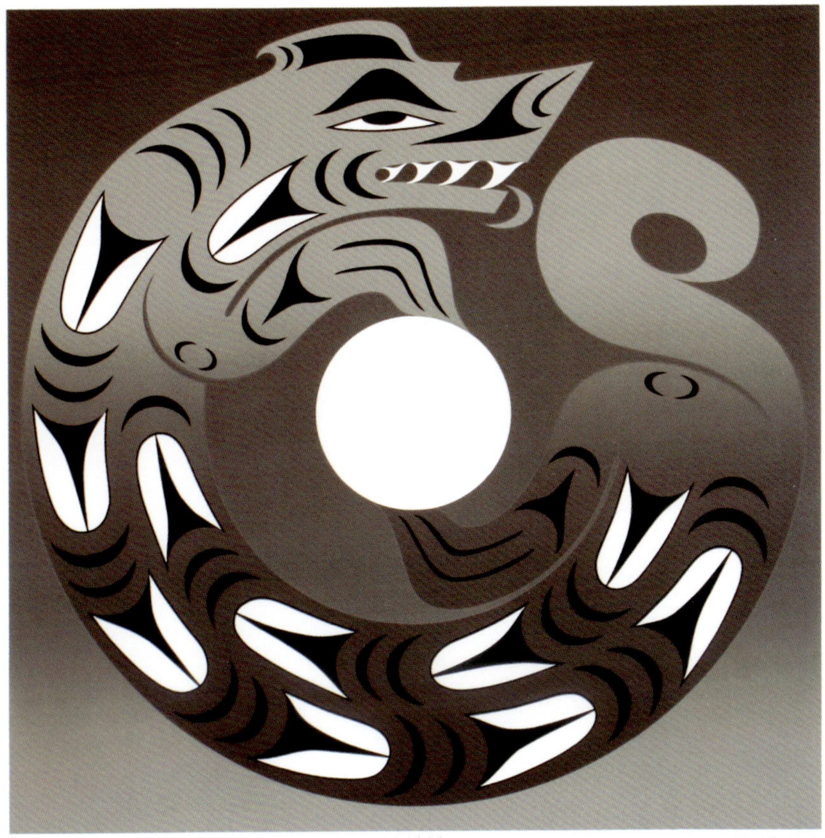

Shaun Peterson (Coast Salish—Puyallup, Tulalip). *Embracing the Moon*, 2006. Silkscreen print. 27.5 × 21.5 in. Gift of Lauretta Jane Wright, Burke Museum #2006–172/1.

The elongated body of a wolf stretches around and grasps the moon in the manner of nineteenth-century spindle whorl designs. A subtle gradient of grays from light to dark in the background is balanced with the opposite gradation in the body of the wolf. This tells the story of the agreement between Wolf (the keeper of justice) and the moon (*dúkwibəl*, the transformer/changer who was half human and half from the sky world). When the moon returned to the sky world, he made an agreement with Wolf to look out for the people, and so Wolf sings to the moon when the moon is full in keeping that promise.

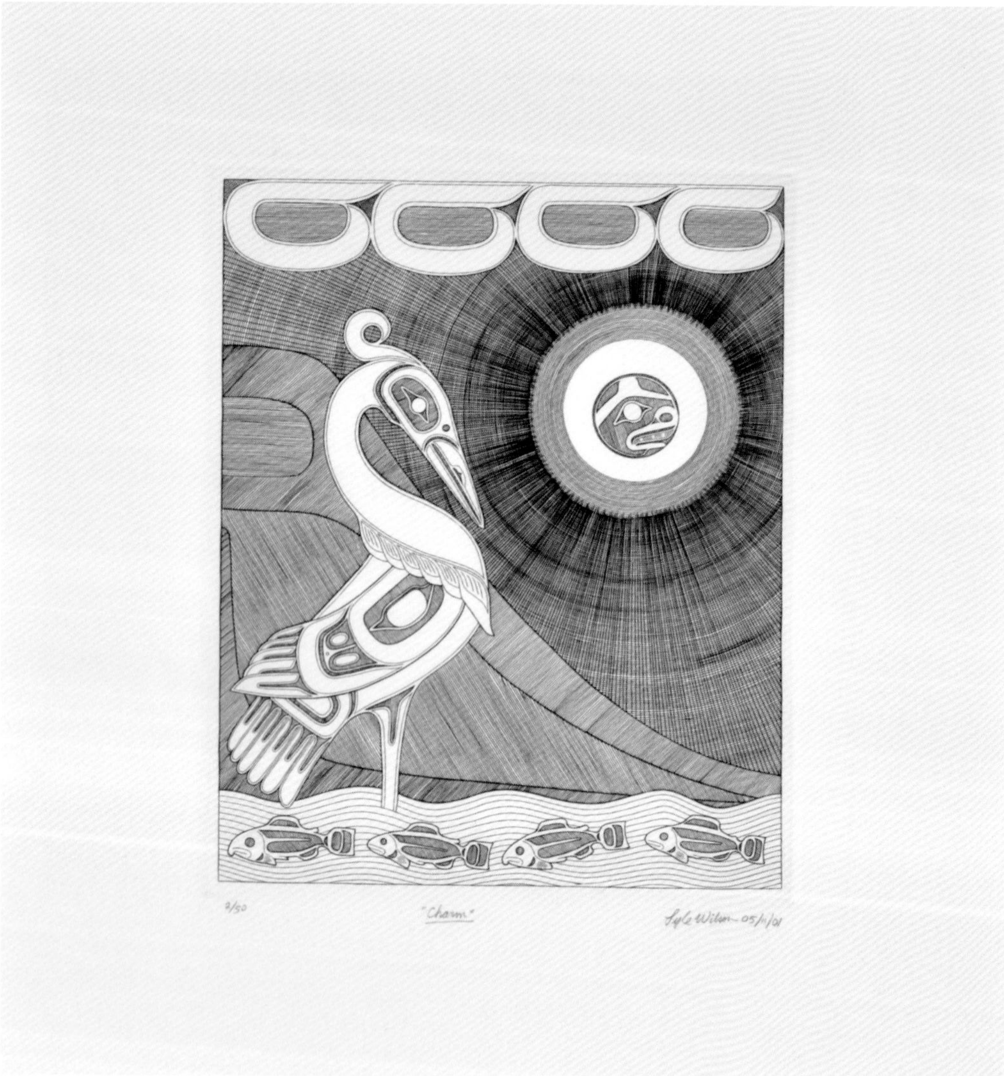

Lyle Wilson (Haisla). *Charm*, 2001. Engraved intaglio print. 20.1 × 17.7 in. Gift of Arthur B. Steinman, Burke Museum #2004–2/289.

"As a young child, my father and uncle took me down to a river and placed some devil's club in the river: it would bring them luck by charming the fish. This print is my equivalent of that charm. I have included four salmon . . . to raise the consciousness to our incredibly beautiful environment. . . . The salmon symbolizes such disappearances and the heron as a 'fisherman' became a metaphor for all of us—watching and waiting." —Lyle Wilson

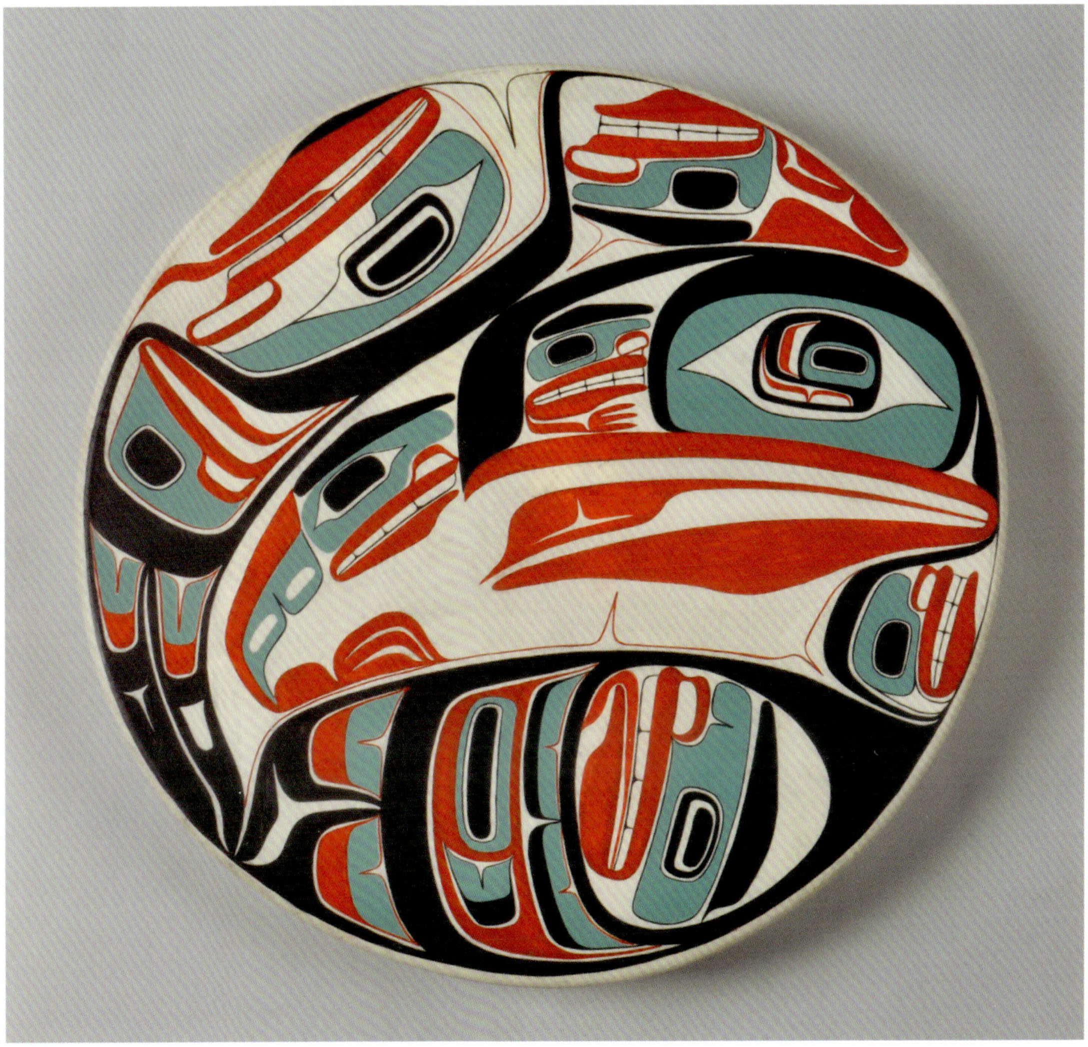

Reg Davidson (Haida). *Raven Drum*, 1999. Wood, hide, sinew, paint. D. 19.75 in. Gift of Arthur B. Steinman, Burke Museum #2004–2/141.

Small, round skin drums were used during the nineteenth century primarily on the southern coast by Coast Salish religious dancers. On the northern coast they were used primarily by shamans in their curing work. Perhaps through their use to accompany the singing at gambling games *(lehal)*, the use of round skin drums has spread during the twentieth century to become the most frequently used drum at potlatches and other social occasions.

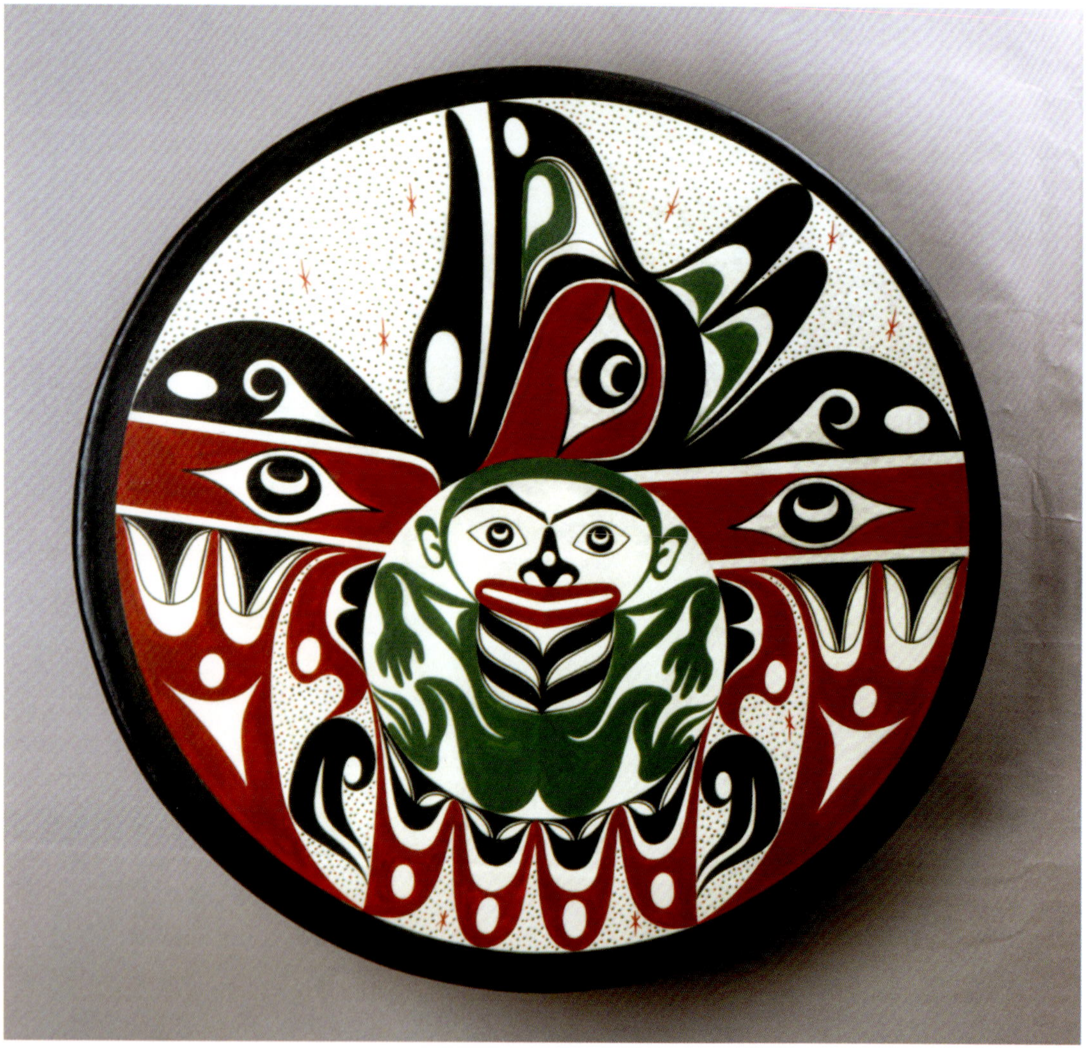

Art Thompson (Nuu-chah-nulth—Dit-i-daht). *Birth of Kaht Ku'uss Drum*, 1998. Wood, hide, sinew, paint. D. 24 in. Gift of Arthur B. Steinman, Burke Museum #2004–2/147.

"Kaht Ku'uss" means people. Since the first contact with Europeans in the late eighteenth century, this has been generally used to mean "First Nations peoples." In this drum Thompson's fluid painting unites the various creatures suggested here. In the wings of the central creature, Thompson has repeated the eye form set in a band of red, similar to the straight painted band that crosses the face on so many Nuu-chah-nulth masks. This particular shade of green was a signature of Thompson's, and he applies it here to the human spirit with only a small echo of green in the beak and feathers. This drum design was made into a serigraph in 2000.

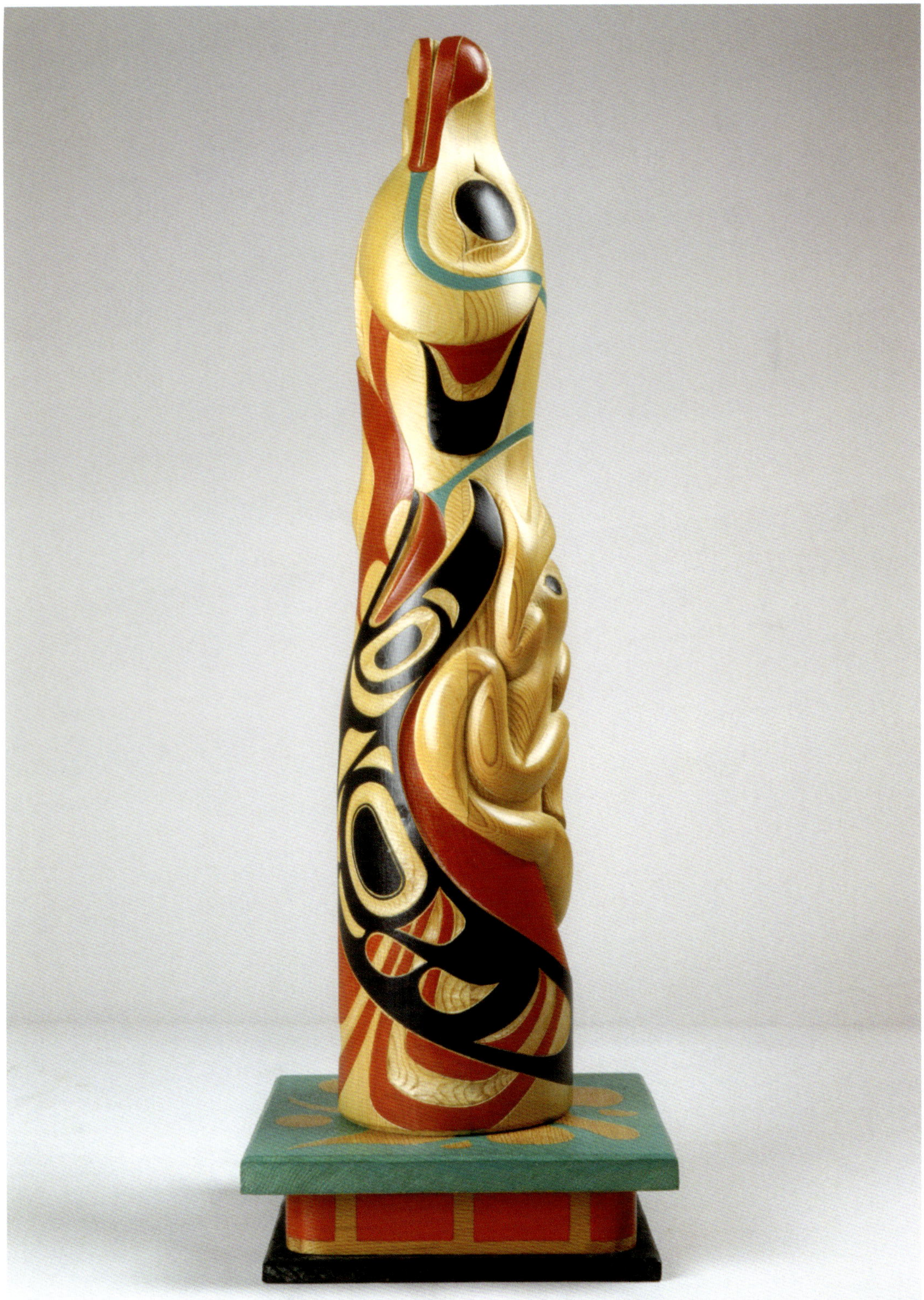

Ken Mowatt (Gitksan). *Horn and Rattle*, ca. 2000. Red cedar, paint. 20.9 × 7.9 in. Gift of Arthur B. Steinman, Burke Museum #2004–2/324.

The double-reed horn is a type traditionally played to give voice to supernatural spirit beings during dance or shamanic performances. The artist has embellished this new instrument with an innovative and interlocking low-relief sculpture representing a wolf at the mouthpiece end, entwined with a raven, a frog, and a woman. The horn sits on a square base that doubles as a rattle.

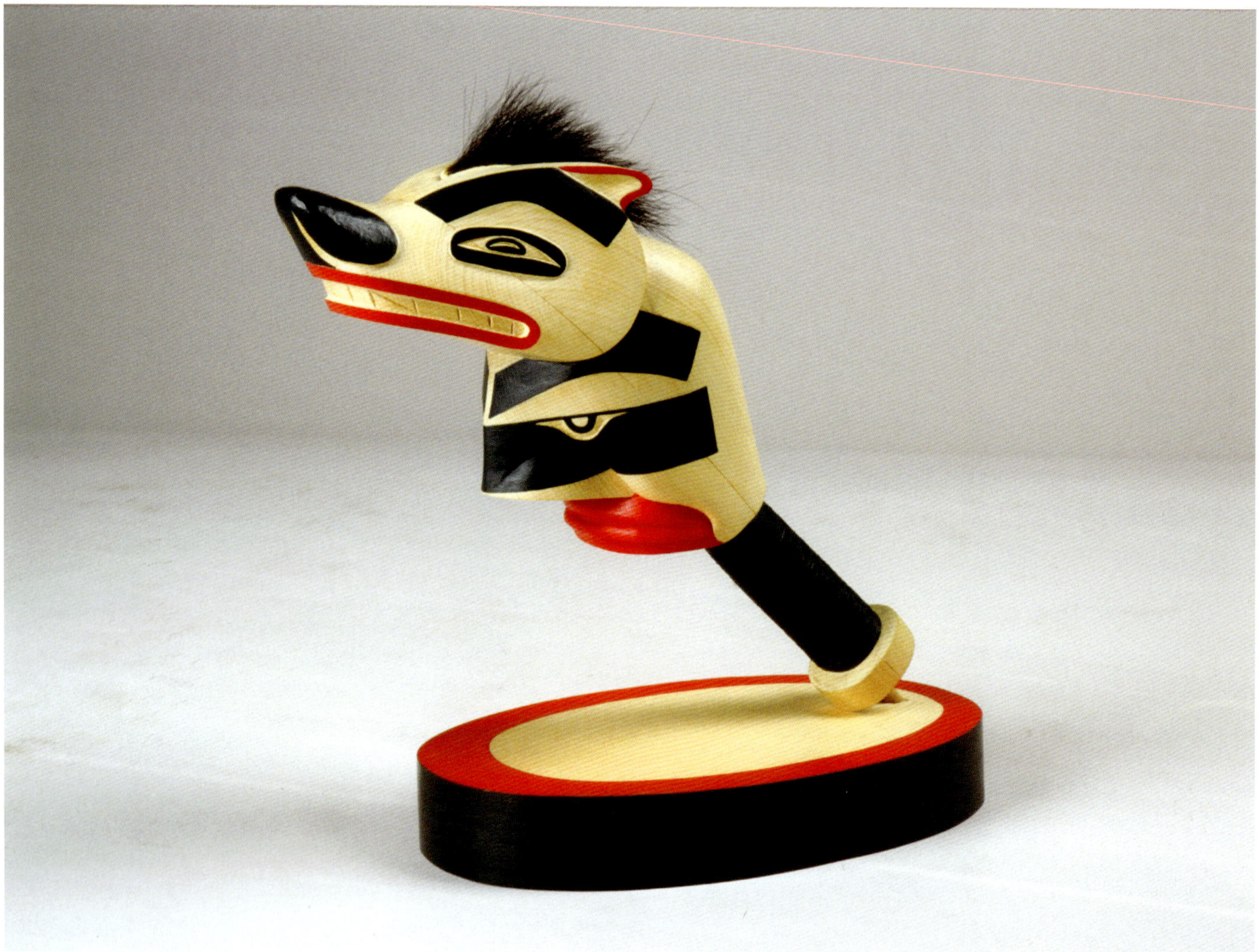

George C. David (Nuu-chah-nulth—Tla-o-qui-aht). *Wolf Dancer Rattle*, 1999. Wood, paint. 10.8 × 3.2 in. Gift of Arthur B. Steinman, Burke Museum #2004–2/298.

The Tlookwana is the most important winter ceremonial of the Nuu-chah-nulth. Initiate dancers are taken away by wolves, taught by them, and later recaptured by their families. After their recapture, they perform the dances given to them during their training. This rattle depicts a dancer wearing a traditional wolf headdress of the type worn during the Tlookwana.

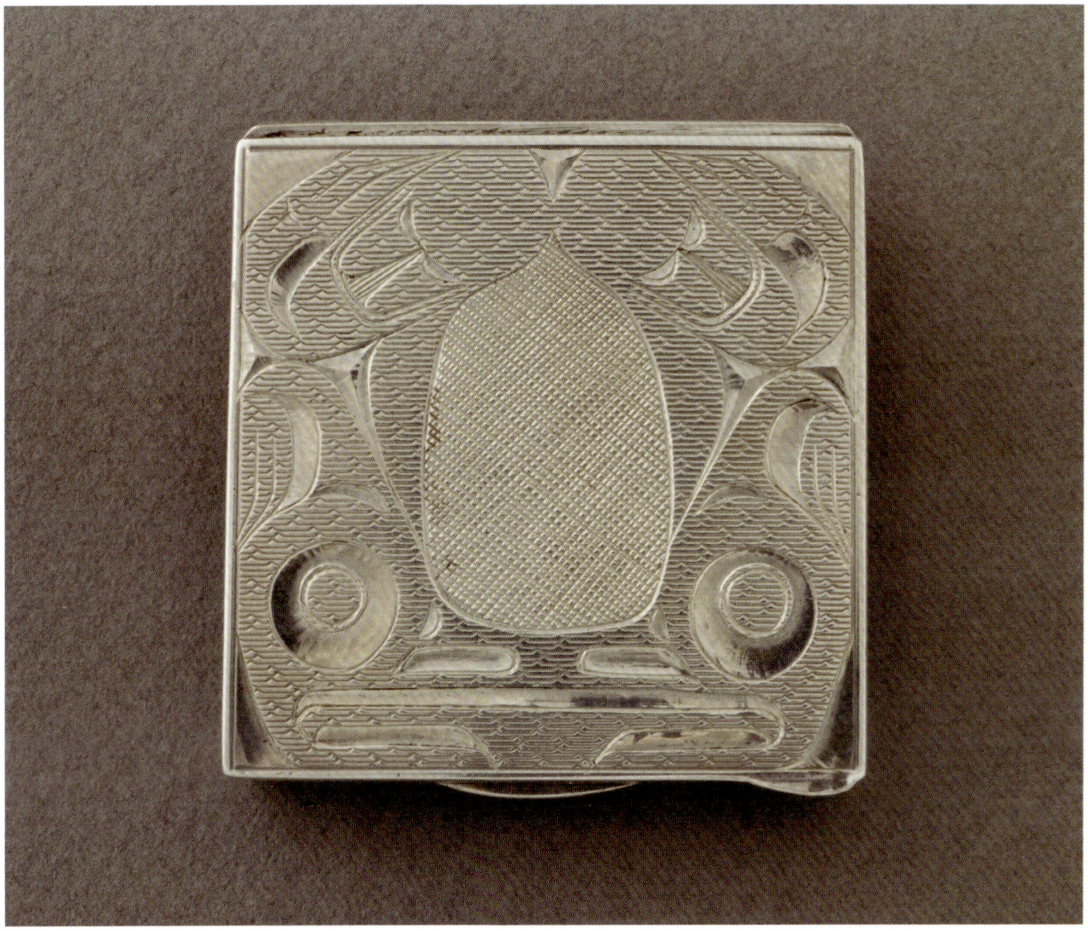

Derek Wilson (Kitlope). *Bear and Frog Compact*, late 1990s. Engraved antique silver compact. 1.8 × 1.9 in. Burke Museum #2007–18/1.

Derek Wilson's *Bear and Frog Compact* is an imaginative redesigning of an antique silver compact. The delicate patterns on the surface of the art deco–style compact are conserved by the artist, becoming markings in a bear's coat and evoking the spotted pigment of a frog's skin. Other surface areas were reworked into the expected cross-hatched background of Northwest Coast engraving.

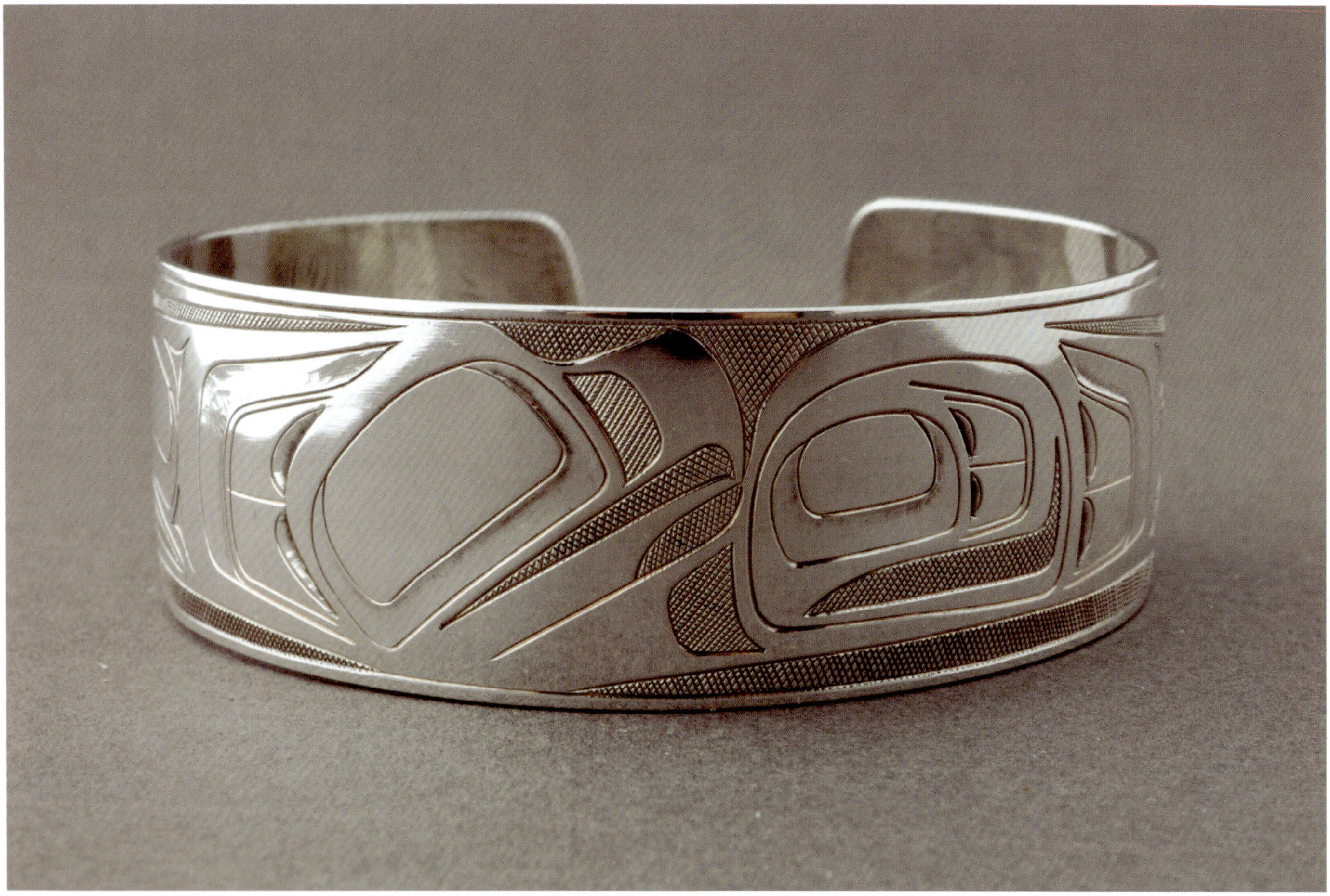

Francis Williams (Haida). *Eagle Bracelet*, 1986. Engraved silver. 2.5 × .88 in. Mark Kernaghan Collection, given in honor of Sandra and William J. Dunn Jr., Burke Museum #2007–4/1.

Engraved silver broaches and bracelets were first worn by Northwest Coast Native women to display their inherited crests during the late nineteenth century, when they were no longer able to display their crests by wearing ceremonial regalia or tattoos. Today, such displays of cultural identity are legal, but bracelets continue to be important ceremonial and everyday wear.

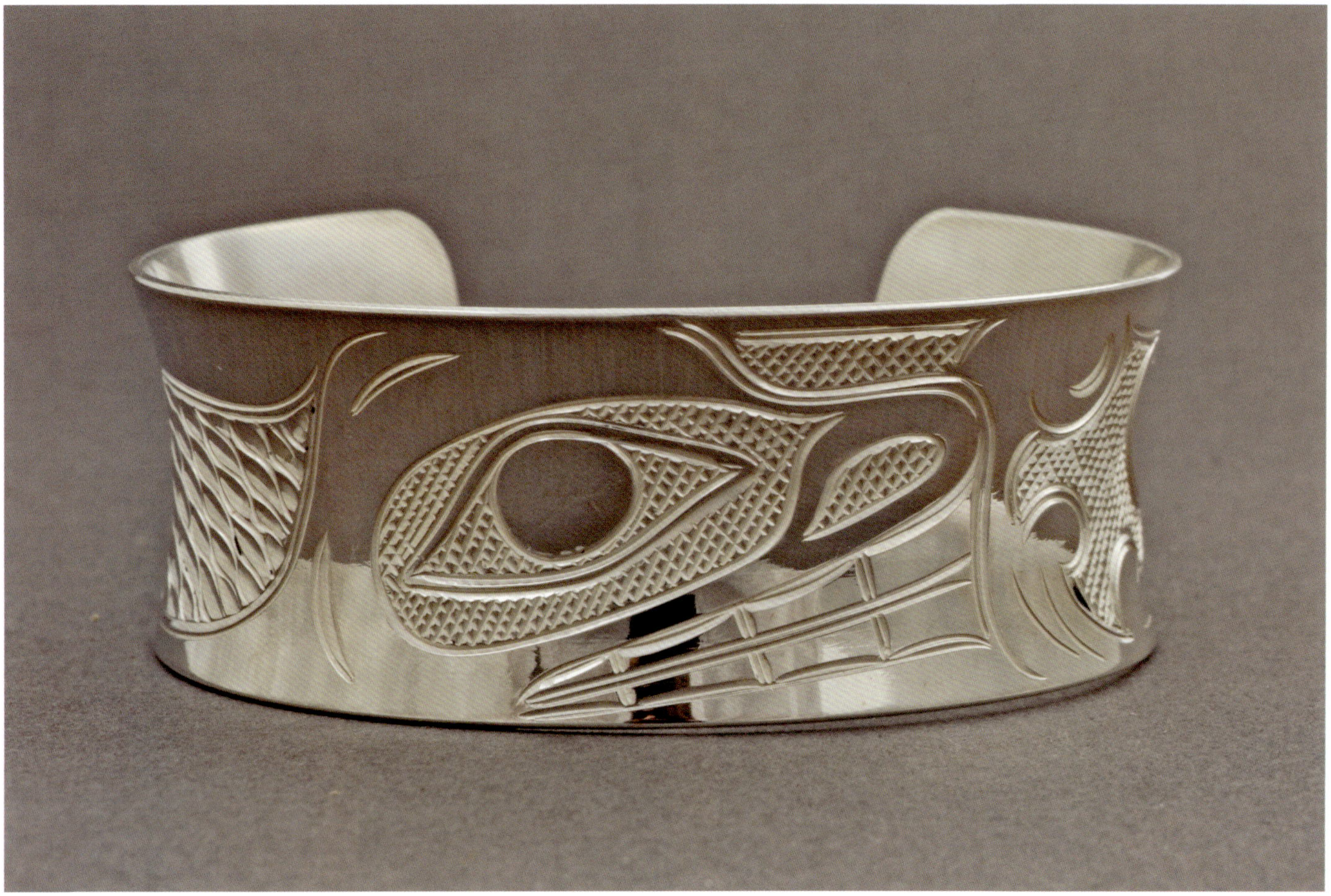

Nicholas Galanin (Tlingit/Aleut). Bracelet. Engraved silver. 2.5 × 1 in. Burke Museum #2008–87/1.

Nicholas Galanin is more often known for his work in alternative media, asking politically charged questions regarding appropriation, authenticity, identity construction, or other issues responding to a market still plagued by conservative expectations of style and form (see fig. I.7). This bracelet is part of his ongoing explorations in jewelry. Often the form of Galanin's bracelets themselves depart from the customary cuff-form with one crest figure. He separates designs over a number of bracelets, meant to be worn separately or stacked together. Or, as in this sea lion bracelet, an unusual shape dominates where the concave, rather than convex, surface lifts away from wrist, accentuating the wave cresting ahead of the sea lion's head.

Works Cited

Alsop, Joseph. 1982. *The Rare Art Traditions: The History of Art Collecting and Its Linked Phenomena Wherever These Have Appeared.* New York: Harper & Row.

American Museum of Natural History. 2003. *Totem to Turquoise: Unpublished Video Transcripts.* New York.

Appadurai, Arjun. 1988. *The Social Life of Things: Commodities in Cultural Perspective.* Cambridge: Cambridge University Press.

Askren (Dangeli), Mique'l. 2006. "From Negative to Postive: B.A. Haldane, Nineteenth Century Tsimshian Photographer." M.A. thesis, University of British Columbia.

———. 2007. "Bringing Our History into Focus: Re-Developing the Work of B.A. Haldane, 19th Century Tsimshian Photographer." *BlackFlash: Lens, Site, Scene* 24 (3): 41–47.

Barbeau, Marius. 1916–1954. Unpublished Notebooks, Notes, and Correspondence. Ottawa: Canadian Centre for Folk Culture Studies, Canadian Museum of Civilization.

Beals, Herbert K., trans. and ed. 1989. *Juan Pérez on the Northwest Coast: Six Documents of His Expedition in 1774.* Portland: Oregon Historical Society Press.

Benedict, Ruth. 1989 [1934]. *Patterns of Culture.* Boston: Houghton Mifflin Company.

Benjamin, Walter. 1968. "Unpacking My Library: A Talk about Book Collecting." In *Illuminations.* Edited by Hannah Arendt, 59–68. Translated by Harry Zohn. New York: Schocken Books.

Blackman, Margaret B.. 1982. *During My Time: Florence Edenshaw Davidson, a Haida Woman.* Seattle: University of Washington Press.

———. 1985. "Contemporary Northwest Coast Art for Ceremonial Use." *American Indian Art Magazine* 10 (3): 24–37.

———. 1992. "Feastware: Haida Art Goes Couture." *American Indian Art Magazine* 17 (4): 56–65.

Blackman, Margaret B., and Edwin S. Hall Jr. 1981. "Contemporary Northwest Coast Art: Tradition and Innovation in Serigraphy." *American Indian Art Magazine.* 6 (3): 54–61.

———. 1982a. "The Afterimage and Image After: Visual Documents and the Renaissance in Northwest Coast Art." *American Indian Art Magazine* 7 (2): 30–39.

———. 1982b. "The Fuzzy Formline: A Dialogue on Boundaries in Contemporary Northwest Coast Art." Paper presented at the Conference on Native American Art History, March 22–24, Ames, Iowa.

———. 1986a. (with Lynne S. Fullerton) "Calculating Killerwhales: A Computer Based Study of Northwest Coast Serigraphs." Unpublished paper presented at the Alaska Anthropological Association Meetings, Fairbanks.

———. 1986b. "Snakes and Clowns: Art Thompson and the West Coast Heritage." *American Indian Art Magazine* 11(2): 30–45.

———. 1988. "Alaska Native Art in the Twentieth Century." In *Crossroads of Continents: Cultures of Siberia and Alaska.* Edited by William Fitzhugh and Aron Crowell, 326–40. Washington, D.C.: Smithsonian Institution Press.

Blackman, Margaret B., Edwin S. Hall Jr., and Lynne S. Fullerton. 1986. "Calculating Killer Whales: A Computer Based Study of Northwest Coast Serigraphs." Unpublished paper.

Boas, Franz, and George Hunt. 1897. *The Social Organization and the Secret Societies of the Kwakiutl Indians.* Washington, D.C.: Government Printing Office.

Brown, Steven C.. 1987. "From Taquan to Klukwan: Tracing the Work of an Early Tlingit Master Artist." In *Faces, Voices, and Dreams: A Celebration of the Centennial of the Sheldon Jackson Museum.* Edited by Peter Corey, 156–75. Juneau: Division of Alaska State Museums and Friends of the Alaska State Museum.

———. 1997. "Formlines Changing Form: Northwest Coast

Art As an Evolving Tradition." *American Indian Art Magazine* 22 (2): 62–73, 81, 83.

———. 1998. *Native Visions: Evolution in Northwest Coast Art from the Eighteenth through the Twentieth Century.* Seattle: Seattle Art Museum and University of Washington Press.

———. 2005. "The Coast Salish Two-Dimensional Art Style: An Examination." In *Contemporary Coast Salish Art.*" Edited by Rebecca Blanchard and Nancy Davenport, 7–20. Seattle: University of Washington Press and Stonington Gallery.

Bunn-Marcuse, Kathryn. 2007. "Precious Metals: Silver and Gold Bracelets from the Northwest Coast." PhD dissertation. University of Washington.

———. 2010. "In(tension)al Enchantment: Cedar Clothing by Haida Weaver, Lisa Telford." *FiberArts* (February): 52–53.

———. In press. "Form First, Function Follows: The Use of Formal Analysis in Northest Coast Art History." In *The Idea of Northwest Coast Native Art: An Anthology.* Edited by Charlotte Townsend-Gault, Jennifer Kramer, and Ron Hamilton. Vancouver: University of British Columbia Press.

Burke Museum of Natural History and Culture. 2005. "Two New House Posts by Nathan and Stephen Jackson." Online at www.washington.edu/burkemuseum/bhc/projects_houseposts.html. Accessed November 15, 2008.

Calkins, Harry J. 1977. "Art Legacy of the Coast Salish." *Puget Soundings* (April): 26–27.

Canadian Indian Marketing Services. 1977. *Northwest Coast Indian Artists Guild: 1977 Graphics Collection.* Ottawa: Canadian Indian Marketing Services.

———. 1978. *Northwest Coast Indian Artists Guild: 1978 Graphics Collection.* Ottawa: Canadian Indian Marketing Services.

Castille, George Pierre, ed. 1985. *The Indians of Puget Sound: The Notebooks of Myron Eells.* Seattle: University of Washington Press.

Chalker, Kari, Lois S. Dubin, and Peter M. Whiteley. 2004. *Totems to Turquoise: Native North American Jewelry Arts of the Northwest and Southwest.* New York: Harry N. Abrams and American Museum of Natural History.

Collison, William H. 1981 [1915]. *In the Wake of the War Canoe.* Victoria, B.C.: Sono Nis Press.

Curtis, Edward S. 1915. *The North American Indian, Being a Series of Volumes Picturing and Describing the Indians of the United States and Alaska.* Edited by Frederick Webb Hodge. New York: Johnson Reprint Corp.

Dangeli, Mique'l Askren. In press. "Looking to Our Past to Inspire Our Future: Strengthening Native Communities through Historical Photograph Research." In *Visual Sovereignty: Indigenous Photography.* Edited by Hulleah J. Tsinhanjinnie and Veronica Passalaqua. Seattle: University of Washington Press.

Dauenhauer, Nora Marks, and Richard Dauenhauer. 1987. *Haa Shuká, Our Ancestors: Tlingit Oral Narratives.* Seattle: University of Washington Press, in association with Sealaska Heritage Foundation, Juneau.

De Laguna, Frederica. 1972. *Under Mount Saint Elias: The History and Culture of the Yakutat Tlingit.* Washington, D.C.: Smithsonian Institution Press.

———, and George T. Emmons. 1991. *The Tlingit Indians.* Anthropological Papers of the American Museum of Natural History. Volume 70. Seattle: University of Washington Press.

Duff, Wilson, Bill Holm, and Bill Reid. 1967. *Arts of the Raven.* Vancouver: Vancouver Art Gallery.

Dundas, Irene. 2007. "Identifying Cultural Affiliations of Saanya Kwaan and Taant'a Kwaan At.óow." Paper presented at Sharing Our Knowledge: A Conference of Tsimshian, Haida, and Tlingit Tribes and Clans, March 23, Sitka, Alaska.

Elsner, John, and Roger Cardinel. 1994. *The Cultures of Collecting.* Cambridge: Harvard University Press.

Fleurieu, Charles Pierre Claret de, trans. 1801. *A Voyage Round the World, Performed During the Years 1790, 1791, and 1792 by Etienne Marchand.* London: T. N. Longman and O. Reese.

Glass, Aaron. 2008. "Crests on Cotton: 'Souvenir' T-Shirts and the Materiality of Remembrance among the Kwakwaka'wakw of British Colombia." *Museum Anthropology* 31 (1): 1–18.

Griffin, George Butler, Adolph Sutro, and Donald C. Cutter. 1969. *The California Coast: A Bilingual Edition of Documents from the Sutro Collection.* Norman: University of Oklahoma Press.

Hall, Edwin S., Jr., Margaret B. Blackman, and Vincent Rickard. 1981. *Northwest Coast Indian Graphics: An Introduction to Silkscreen Prints.* Seattle: University of Washington Press.

Harriman Alaska Expedition. 1910. *Harriman Alaska Series: Reports of the Harriman Alaska Expedition.* Volumes 1–14. Washington, D.C.: Smithsonian Institution.

Henrikson, Steve. 1992. "Yeil Koowu: The Reemergence of Ravenstail Weaving on the Northern Northwest Coast." *American Indian Art Magazine* 18 (1) (Winter): 58–67.

Holm, Bill. 1965. *Northwest Coast Indian Art: An Analysis of Form.* Seattle: University of Washington Press.

———. 1972. "Heraldic Carving Styles of the Northwest Coast." In *American Indian Art: Form and Tradition.* Minneapolis: Minneapolis Institute of Arts.

———. 1974. "The Art of Willie Seaweed: A Kwakiutl Master." In *The Human Mirror: Material and Spatial Images of Man.* Edited by Miles Richardson, 59–90. Baton Rouge: Louisiana University Press.

———. 1981. "Will the Real Charles Edenshaw Please Stand Up?" In *The World Is As Sharp As a Knife: An Anthology in Honour of Wilson Duff.* Edited by Donald Abbott, 175–200. Victoria: British Columbia Provincial Museum.

———. 1982. "A Wooling Mantle Neatly Wrought." *American Indian Art Magazine* (8) 1: 34–47.

———. 1983a. "Form in Northwest Coast Indian Art." In *Indian Art Traditions of the Northwest Coast.* Edited by Roy L. Carlson, 33–46. Burnaby: Simon Fraser University.

———. 1983b. *Smoky-Top: The Art and Times of Willie Seaweed.* Seattle: University of Washington Press.

———. 1987. *Spirit and Ancestor: A Century of Northwest Coast Indian Art at the Burke Museum.* Seattle: Burke Museum and University of Washington Press.

———. 1988. "Art and Culture Exchange at the Tlingit-Eskimo Border." In *Crossroads of Continents: Cultures of Siberia and Alaska.* Edited by William W Fitzhugh and Aron Crowell, 281–93. Washington, D.C.: Smithsonian Institution Press.

———. 1990. "Art." In *Handbook of North American Indians.* Volume 7. Edited by Wayne Suttles, 602–32. Washington, D.C. Smithsonian Institution.

Holm, Bill, and George I. Quimby. 1980. *Edward S. Curtis in the Land of the War Canoes: A Pioneer Cinematographer in the Pacific Northwest.* Seattle: University of Washington Press.

Hoover, Anna. "fashion STATEMENT: Native Artists Against Pebble Mine." Master's practicum report. University of Washington, Division of Art History, 2011.

Hoyt-Goldsmith, Diane. 1997. *Potlatch: A Tsimshian Celebration.* New York: Holiday House.

Jonaitis, Aldona. 2008. "A Generation of Innovators in Southeast Alaska." *American Indian Art Magazine* 33 (4): 56–67.

Jones, Marianne. 2006. "Haida Art and Haida Gwaii." In *Raven Travelling: Two Centuries of Haida Art.* Edited by Daina Augaitis, 28–39. Vancouver: Vancouver Art Gallery.

Kan, Sergei. 1989. *Symbolic Immortality: The Tlingit Potlatch of the Nineteenth Century.* Washington, D.C.: Smithsonian Institution Press.

King, Eleanor M., and Bryce P. Little. 1986. "George Byron Gordon and the Early Development of the University Museum." In *Raven's Journey: The World of Alaska's Native People.* Edited by Susan A. Kaplan and Kristin J. Barsness, 16–53. Philadelphia: University Museum, University of Pennsylvania.

Kramer, Jennifer. 2012. *Kesu': The Art and Life of Doug Cranmer.* Vancouver: Douglas & McIntyre Press.

Litwin, Thomas S., ed. 2005. *Harriman Alaska Expedition Retraced: A Century of Change 1899–2001.* New Brunswick, N.J.: Rutgers University Press.

MacDonald, George F. 1996. *Haida Art.* Seattle: University of Washington Press.

Maquet, Jacques. 1971. *Introduction to Aesthetic Anthropology.* Reading, Mass.: Addison-Wesley Inc.

McFadden, David R., and Ellen Napiura Taubman. 2005.

Changing Hands: Art without Reservation 2, Contemporary Native North American Art from the West, Northwest, and Pacific. New York: Museum of Arts and Design.

McLennan, Bill, and Karen Duffek. 2000. *The Transforming Image: Painted Arts of Northwest Coast First Nations*. Vancouver: University of British Columbia Press.

Miller, Jay. 1997. *Tsimshian Culture: A Light through the Ages*. Lincoln: University of Nebraska Press.

Moore, Emily. 2010. "Propatriation: Possibilities for Art After NAGPRA." *Museum Anthropology* 33 (2): 125–36.

Muensterberger, Werner. 1994. *Collecting: An Unruly Passion: Psychological Perspectives*. Princeton, N.J.: Princeton University Press.

Murray, Peter. 1985. *The Devil and Mr. Duncan*. Victoria, B.C.: Sono Nis Press.

Neel, David. 1995. *The Great Canoes: Reviving a Northwest Coast Tradition*. Seattle: University of Washington Press.

Niblack, Albert P. 1888. *The Coast Indians of Southern Alaska and Northern British Columbia*. Washington, D.C.: U.S. National Museum.

Reid, Martine J. 2010. *Time Warp*. Vancouver: Bill Reid Foundation.

Rhyne, Charles. 2009. "The Challenge of International Standards: Nineteenth Century Native American Totem Poles as a Case Study." In *KulturGUTerhalten*, 209–18. Berlin: Staatliche Museen zu Berlin.

Samuel, Cheryl. 1982. *The Chilkat Dancing Blanket*. Seattle: Pacific Search Press.

———. 1987. *The Raven's Tail*. Vancouver: University of British Columbia Press.

Sealaska Heritage Foundation. 2005. "Totem Pole Project." Online at www.sealaskaheritage.org/programs/programs_totem_pole_project.htm. Accessed November 15, 2008.

Seattle Art Museum. 1995. *The Spirit Within: Northwest Coast Native Art from the John H. Hauberg Collection*. New York: Rizzoli.

Sloan, Kay. 2005. "For the Benefit of Others: The 1899 Harriman Expedition to Alaska." In *The Harriman Expedition Retraced: A Century of Change 1899–2001*. Edited by Thomas S. Litwin, 11–19. New Brunswick, N.J.: Rutgers University Press.

Steltzer, Ulli. 1984. *A Haida Potlatch*. Seattle: University of Washington Press.

Swan, James Gilchrist. 1886. *Tattoo Marks of the Haida Indians of Queen Charlotte Islands, B.C. and the Prince of Wales Archipelago, Alaska*. Fourth Annual Report of the Bureau of Ethnology to the Secretary of the Smithsonian Institute, 1882–83.

Swanton, John. 1905a. *Contributions to the Ethnology of the Haida*. Leiden: E. J. Brill.

———. 1905b. *Haida Texts and Myths, Skidegate Dialect*. New York: Bureau of American Ethnology.

———. 1908. *Haida Texts: Masset Dialect*. Leiden: E. J. Brill.

———. 1909. *Tlingit Myths and Texts*. Washington, D.C.: Government Printing Office.

Thornton, Timothy F. 2008. *Being and Place among the Tlingit*. Seattle: University of Washington Press, in association with Sealaska Heritage Foundation, Juneau.

Wagner, Henry R., and W. A. Newcombe. 1938. *The Journal of Jacinto Camaano. B.C. Historical Quarterly* 2 (part 1 and 2), 3 (part 1), 4 (part 2) (July and October): 189–222 (part 1), 265–310 (part 2).

Wardwell, Allen. 1996. *Tangible Visions: Northwest Coast Indian Shamanism and Its Art*. New York: Monacelli Press with the Corvus Press.

Weiner, Annette B. 1985. "Inalienable Wealth." *American Ethnologist* 12 (2): 210–27.

Worl, Rosita. 2005. "Standing with Spirits, Waiting." In *The Harriman Expedition Retraced: A Century of Change 1899–2001*. Edited by Thomas S. Litwin, 31–39. New Brunswick, N.J.: Rutgers University Press.

Wright, Robin K. 1991. *A Time of Gathering: Native Heritage in Washington State*. Seattle: Burke Museum and University of Washington Press.

———. 1996. *Pacific Northwest Native American Art in Museums and Private Collections: The Bill Holm and Robin K. Wright Slide Collections*. Seattle: Burke Museum.

———. 1998. "Two Haida Artists from Yan: Will John Gwaytihl and Simeon Stilthda Please Step Apart?" *American Indian Art Magazine* 23 (3): 42–57, 106–7.

———. 2001. *Northern Haida Master Carvers*. Seattle: University of Washington Press.

———. 2009. "Zacherias and the Chicago Settee: Connecting the Masterpiece to the Master." *American Indian Art Magazine* 35 (1): 68–75.

Index

Note: page numbers followed by "f" refer to illustrations and captions; those with "n" indicate endnotes.

Contributors

MARGARET B. BLACKMAN is Professor Emerita of Anthropology at the College at Brockport, State University of New York. A cultural anthropologist, she has conducted research on the Northwest Coast and in Arctic Alaska. She is the author of two life histories of Native American women (*During My Time: Florence Edenshaw Davidson, A Haida Woman* (1992) and *Sadie Brower Neakok, an Iñupiaq Woman* (1989), both published by the University of Washington Press, and an ethnographic memoir, *Upside Down: Seasons among the Nunamiut* (Univeristy of Nebraska Press, 2004).

KATHRYN BUNN-MARCUSE is assistant director of the Bill Holm Center for the Study of Northwest Coast Art at the Burke Museum. She is a visiting lecturer in art history and American Indian studies at the University of Washington, where her courses focus on indigenous art in North America and Polynesia. Her dissertation, "Precious Metals: Silver and Gold Bracelets from the Northwest Coast," explored the many functions of jewelry. Her publications have examined films of the Kwakwa̱ka̱'wakw, Northwest Coast silver jewelry and tattooing, the tourist trade in Alaska, and dress on the Northwest Coast.

JOE DAVID is of Nuu-chah-nulth heritage. He was born in the Clayoquot village of Opitsat on the West Coast of Vancouver Island. He grew up in Seattle and attended art school in Texas. His monumental welcome figures can be seen at the Museum of Anthropology at the University of British Columbia and in the Vancouver International Airport. In 2005 his work appeared in *Changing Hands: Art without Reservation 2* at the Museum of Art and Design in New York. He has been instrumental in the resurgence of Nuu-chah-nulth art and ceremony. His art reflects a deep commitment to spirituality and cultural heritage.

BILL HOLM is Professor Emeritus of Art History and Curator Emeritus of Northwest Coast Indian Art at the Burke Museum. He is recognized internationally as one of the most knowledgeable experts in the field of Northwest Coast Native art history. His important book *Northwest Coast Indian Art, An Analysis of Form* (1965) is one of the best-selling books published by the University of Washington Press. This book is credited with having drawn a remarkable number of artists into their own practice of Northwest Coast art. Holm's classes at the University of Washington broadened the understanding and appreciation of that art in several generations of students.

EMILY MOORE wrote her dissertation on the New Deal totem parks of Southeast Alaska. In 2007 she was a visiting researcher at the Bill Holm Center, where she had the opportunity to study the Burke's collection of Chilkat tunics and the Jackson Kaats' posts firsthand. Her essay that addresses other "propatriated" totem poles by the Jacksons appeared in the Fall 2010 issue of *Museum Anthropology.*

QWALSIUS-SHAUN PETERSON was born in Puyallup, Washington, in 1975 and is an enrolled member of the Puyallup tribe. He has worked in many Northwest Coast design traditions but has focused on his Coast Salish heritage. He has done a number of public and private installations in such established forms as poles, panels, drums, and prints. In recent years he has explored new techniques and new materials, creating a unique blend of traditional form and modern media. In the spirit of his ancestors, he forges a path to create new traditions for another generation to build on in the ongoing cycle of the Salish creative process.

LISA TELFORD is a Gawa Git'ans Git'anee Haida weaver, born in Ketchikan, Alaska. She comes from a long line of weavers, which includes her grandmother, mother, aunt, cousins, and daughter. Her award-winning work is done in both contemporary and traditional methods of weaving, including twining and plaiting. The methods encompass baskets, traditional hats, and cedar bark clothing. Her baskets can be seen in the collections of the Oregon Historical Society, the Hallie Ford Museum of Art, the Smithsonian National Museum of the American Indian, the Heard Museum, the Museum of Art and Design, the Portland Art Museum, and the Burke Museum.

ROBIN K. WRIGHT is a professor of art history at the University of Washington, curator of Native American art, and director of the Bill Holm Center for the Study of Northwest Coast Art at the Burke Museum. Her award-winning publications include *Northern Haida Master Carvers*, which won the 2002 Washington State Book Award, and *A Time of Gathering*, which won the 1992 Washington State Governor's Writers Award. She is currently researching a set of Haida house models from the village of Skidegate, Haida Gwaii, that were made for the World's Columbian Exposition in Chicago in 1893.

EVELYN VANDERHOOP is a Haida artist from the Gaw Git'ans Git'anee family of Massett, Haida Gwaii, British Columbia. She comes from a family of artists. Her grandmother, Selina Peratrovich, was a culture bearer as a Haida basket weaver. Her mother, Delores Churchill, continues to weave textiles and teach basketry as her mother did. Vanderhoop is a professional watercolor artist as well as a weaver. She is one of only a few weavers who have accepted the challenge of weaving the complex and exquisite chief's robe, the Naaxiin. She has gone on to win awards and numerous commissions for her *naaxiin* and Ravenstail weaving. She currently teaches Northwest Coast First Nations textile weaving.